To AYERS ROCK *and Beyond*

BILL HARNEY

IAN DRAKEFORD PUBLISHING

First published this edition 1988 by
Ian Drakeford Publishing Pty. Ltd.
26 London Drive, Bayswater, Victoria, Australia.

National Library of Australia
Cataloguing-in-Publication entry

Harney, W. E. (William Edward), 1895–1962.
To Ayers Rock and beyond

ISBN 1 86280 003 0.

1. Ayers Rock Region (N.T.) — Description and travel.
I. Title.

919.429′10461

First published 1963 by Rigby Publishers, Adelaide
First limp edition published 1984.

Produced by Island Graphics, Australia
Printed in Australia by the Book Printer

CONTENTS

PART II

THE RAGGLE-TAGGLE

ILLUSTRATIONS

MAPS

NOTE ON AYERS ROCK

AYERS ROCK is a large solid sandstone dome covering an area of 1,200 acres and rising 1,143 feet above the surrounding plateau. Its ever-changing colours during the daytime have become a thing of beauty to the tourists as it was a symbol of faith to the Loritdja tribespeople who lived and hunted around that area in days gone by.

The Loritdja tribal name for Ayers Rock is 'Uluru', and 'Topidj' for the smaller hill adjoining.

The word 'Uluru' comes from the Loritdja word 'Luru' (forehead or fluted), the same term as that given to the fluted parallel grooves cut on to all aboriginal wooden artifacts of importance in hunting and camp-life. Those parallel gutters on the crest and sides of Ayers Rock, caused by the weathering of the vertical sandstone strata, must have given rise to the name. As the 'luru' grooves were always cut in secrecy by the tribesmen as a part of a sacred ritual concerning the settlement of disputes, they undoubtedly caused the mountain to be called Uluru, which in this sense signified something sacred in their way of life, a fact confirmed by my informants who all agreed that the Rock of Uluru was the repository of sacred knowledge of the pre-existence of a soul, and so of everlasting life.

W. E. H.

PREFACE

And all men kill the thing they love,
By all let this be heard. (Wilde)

FOR seven months each tourist season from 1957 to 1962 I lived under the shadow of a great rock in the centre of Australia. My job was Ranger for the Northern Territory Reserves Board. The locality was called the Ayers Rock–Mount Olga National Park.

During that time I met many tourists and nomad aborigines coming and going into and from the area. This is the story of my observations during that period. On foot, in motors, or from the backs of camels I gathered this material in the course of countless talks with the Loritdja aborigines of that part. I was also helped by the intense arguments among tourists who held a great variety of opinions.

This book actually requires no preface because it is itself but an introduction to a subject that, to me, seems endless. I must, however, thank the Commonwealth Literary Fund who gave me a literary grant to help me with this book. To them and the Loritdja aborigines who provided much of the material I give a 'Thank-you' for their assistance.

W. E. (BILL) HARNEY

Ayers Rock, N.T.

Prologue

SOMEWHERE, sometime, a small idea arises that gives birth to unforeseen events.

I was out visiting my friends the Webbs at Jay Creek, which is a government settlement thirty miles westward from Alice Springs. John was the Superintendent who looked after the needs of the aboriginal people, and with him in the work was his wife Dawn who looked after the women and children who were always up at her small medical centre over 'sickness-business'.

The homestead was built of concrete bricks that had been made on the site and the whole place breathed an air of hospitality. As is usual with all these places, the hills through which the Jay Creek ran during the rain-time, were crowded with mythology. When the old people were not chanting about these things they were up around the Lutheran place of worship singing the hymns of that denomination. The hymns they sang were in the Aranda tongue and as they harmonized the chants in the cool night's air the hills around re-echoed to the songs. One thing I noticed was that all the men took off their head-covering as they sang the hymns but left it on when the tribal chants were on. I never asked them the reason because it was their business.

Yet during my visits there I loved to sit on the long spacious verandah where we would chatter away about other northern days which reminded us of rain and billabongs full of lily-blooms and wild-fowl. What a contrast between these two lands, the centre with its high mountains and ever-changing colours, the northland with its jade-coloured seas.

It was on such a night that a utility van pulled up outside the main gate and in walked Harry Giese, the Director of Welfare in the Northern Territory of Australia. He was on one of his routine inspection trips over the Centre and as we had the usual drink of tea the conversation got around to the Native Reserves which at that time were in the public eye. The main part of the talk was on the newly-transferred portion of the south-western aboriginal reserve to the Ayers Rock–Mount Olga National Park, an area of 400 square miles to be preserved as a place where tourists could go to see the scenic wonders which were slowly drawing the travellers from the cities into these hitherto unknown areas.

During the conversation I was asked, Would I care to go out to be the first Ranger of the area? Being out of work at the time I naturally jumped at the opportunity of going out to a place I had never visited, but had heard so much about both from white travellers and from the Loritdja aborigines who once lived in that locality.

Next day Harry was away on his inspections and a few weeks later I was busy in the town of Alice Springs getting the necessary gear together for the job. As there was no dwelling for the new Ranger at Ayers Rock I was issued with a ten-by-twelve tent and fly which would be my living quarters and office. With these things went the usual pots and pans for cooking, a bed to sleep on and, in keeping with the job, a list of instructions as to what I had to do as regards control of the area. I must issue permits to people entering the National Park; native cave art must be protected and nothing removed from the area. The list of instructions was a long one but the job was new and I was glad to be away.

Len Tuit, of 'Tuits Tours', ran a tourists' service to the Rock at that time. He, more than any other man, was responsible for tourism in the Northern Territory. His first season out to Ayers Rock over five years before my time totalled twelve people. Those twelve must have returned with good reports for others came on their trail. Writers and landscape painters moved in with the tourists. The residents of the Alice were wary at first, but as more tourists came they realized that here was a new form of trade.

The Welfare approached Len regarding transport for myself; to this he readily agreed and in that year of 1957, just prior to the Easter holidays, I was over at the Mount Gillen Chalet with all my dunnage and stores awaiting the tourist season to begin.

That morning of our departure from Alice Springs was a great day for the tourists and myself. What a lot of chattering went on as we were loaded into the passenger coach for the journey. Boxes, swags, foodstuffs, water, and all the hundred and one things that go to make a trip successful. Len is full of banter with some of the travellers who were always asking questions. They have paid for the trip and want to get their money's worth. 'Right-O,' from Len as he starts the engine running and we are away.

Len has some business to attend to in the township so we turned up Railway Terrace. Passing by the main gates of the railway yard I cast a glance at the 'Ngoilya' stone which symbolizes that creature of mythological times who was denied a feed after he had pulled down a kangaroo for the hunters. The legend records that on that spot at 'Djoritja' (Alice Springs township) the ritual dog 'Tmerga' who had come from 'litrika' (sundown-way) waited with his small puppy that still rests beside him—waited for his female mate who was at 'Ngoilya augala' (a patch of black stones once seen near the Caltex Oil Depot). Sad then was that guardian dog, for legend records how the hunters cooked and ate a kangaroo at the oven of the 'burnt-stone-place' and had refused him and his a feed. Thus does he become angry when strangers are around and refuses to be subdued by their rubbing.

But legend remains with the dog. We must away around the corner into Parsons Street and on till we pull up at a store where Len loads some parcels which he will later on deliver to cattle stations on our way out. Our long journey of three hundred miles is about to begin. Our destination is Ayers Rock.

PART I

THE MOTLEY

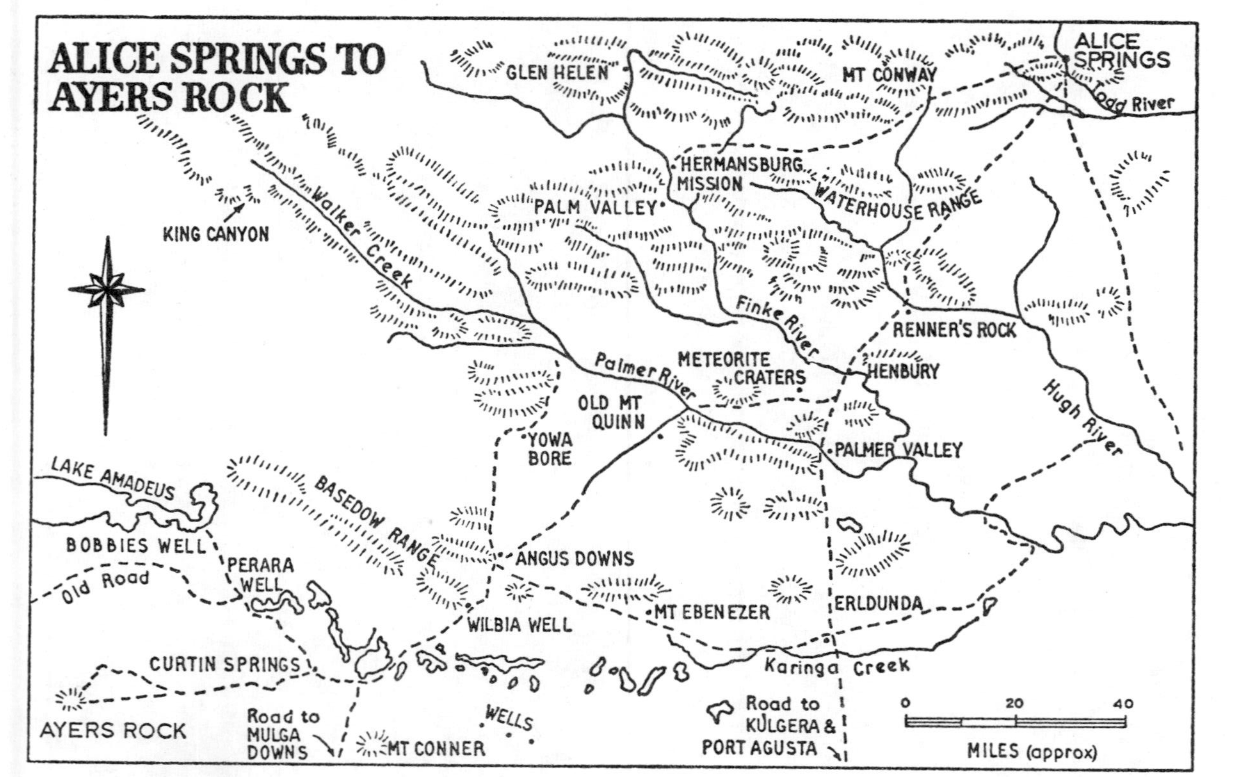
ALICE SPRINGS TO AYERS ROCK
ALICE SPRINGS
Todd River
GLEN HELEN
MT CONWAY
HERMANSBURG MISSION
WATERHOUSE RANGE
PALM VALLEY
KING CANYON
Walker Creek
Finke River
RENNER'S ROCK
METEORITE CRATERS
HENBURY
Palmer River
OLD MT QUINN
Hugh River
YOWA BORE
PALMER VALLEY
LAKE AMADEUS
BASEDOW RANGE
BOBBIES WELL
ANGUS DOWNS
PERARA WELL
Old Road
ERLDUNDA
MT EBENEZER
WILBIA WELL
CURTIN SPRINGS
Karinga Creek
Road to MULGA DOWNS
WELLS
Road to KULGERA & PORT AGUSTA
AYERS ROCK
MT CONNER
0
20
40
MILES (approx)

Chapter One

Alice Springs

THE township of Alice Springs rests between the parallel folds of the Macdonnell Ranges like coloured gems in the wooden carrying bowl of a giant aboriginal hunter. Resting as it does on a 1,900-foot plateau, it can become extremely cold during the winter months and hot in the summer, caused, so I have been told, by atmospheric conditions in a low rainfall away from the sea shores.

The township straddles both sides of the Todd River, which is a broad band of sand studded with river gums and which becomes a swirl of brown, foam-flecked water when storms at its head send down the river in flood.

Rains and floods alike bring life to the Centre. The red dusty earth is transformed as though an emerald-green bedspread had been thrown over it overnight. The quiet of the dry-time departs with the strident cries of the cicadas as they renew their cycle of life in the tree-tops and along the banks of the rivers. Not only does insect life sing its song of praise, but everywhere is movement as the aboriginal kiddies dig out the succulent grubs from the earth, as children of all colours splash in the water-pools which have just been made by the flood-waters. How good, then, to sit upon that seat beneath a shady cedar tree beside the foot-bridge over the river to watch the children at play in the shallow pools.

Often I would be joined by some old aboriginal who would talk of the old days with its history and ancient mythology concerning the land around us, and talking we would watch the motors and people passing to and from the shopping centre on the right-hand bank of the Todd River.

Nowhere in Australia can one see such a diversity of people go by as at that spot. Here one sees the old inhabitants of this land drift by with bags over their shoulders, children on their hips, with an odd assortment of dogs following at their heels. All are chattering away as they make their way to the trees of the river-bed where they will rest in the shade of the old gum trees during the heat of the day.

Aranda, Loritdja, and Kaitish tribespeople in every style of get-up from the primitive hair-do to the latest crew-cut. To me, the people of the Centre make the Alice. Here one finds families who have grown up in this strange land. A dozen languages can be heard as one walks down the main street where cattlemen, white and black, drift by against a background of river-gums and distant hills. Two miles up the Todd River from the footbridge is the old telegraph station which is well worth a visit because it records the beginning of things in this land of strange contrasts. Here one can see the old foundation-stones of the fort-like buildings with, above them, the loop-holes for the rifles should the place be attacked by the aboriginal huntsmen from the hills near by.

Alice Springs township itself is a mass of coloured houses against a background of trees, ravines, and hills that reveal new vistas of places where one may rest to dream about the past and future of the land.

A few miles west along the Jay Creek–Hermansberg road is 'Flynn's grave', a place well worth a visit because of its memories and its strange setting. Here is a monument to a great man; it marks the spot over which John Flynn's ashes were cast from an aeroplane flying over Mount Gillen, which towers behind.

The rounded boulder that marks the spot came from the 'Devil's marbles', 260 miles north along the Stuart Highway. Aboriginal mythology records the spherical boulders of that area are the eggs of the Rainbow Serpent of life who laid down that area in the dawn of time. Christian endeavour mixed with pagan myth against a background of Mount Gillen always associated in aboriginal legend with the people of the Kangaroo totem. Such is the contrast in this land where history and mythology is blended as a memorial to one of the truly great.

A few miles north of Flynn's grave is Morris soak where the aboriginal painter Albert Namitjira lived in a black's camp painting landscapes which glorified his country. His home was a shady gum tree—a spot, during his lifetime, which was a must for the tourists of those days. Many times have I been out to his camp to have a yarn, for he was always a tribesman in spite of his ability and prestige as an artist.

Tourists came to his camp at all hours during the daytime, and often in the evening. How many, I wondered, came out to see him with the respect which was his due? Few I honestly believe. Most of them came out of idle curiosity or to take his photo. To see the way they pushed the polite Albert about when they wished to take his photo was a revelation in manners. To most of them he was regarded as a freak, to be pictured and forgotten. What patience Albert had. What patronage those tourists gave to him. All were out to buy his pictures, but at the lowest price. His life's work in painting gave the Centre the boom it needed for tourism, but I am pretty sure that many of the white people who now sing his praises were those who reviled him during his lifetime. I myself have heard missionaries refer to him as a 'cancerous growth in their side', and others commented bitterly that it was 'a bad day for the aborigines when Albert and his Aranda school started to paint'.

The trouble, of course, was money, which was glibly quoted from the Bible as the 'root of all evil'.

Poor Albert—think well of him as you look upon the coloured mountains of the Centre. He was born in the bush, perhaps beneath one of the ghost gum trees he loved to paint. Rex Batterby gave him a start along the right road, then on he went to outsell his master, making thousands of pounds which, under strict tribal law, he doled out to his kin. It was the law of kinship which kept Albert poor and finally sent him to court for supplying liquor to his kind. Many white people who were jealous of his success claimed his paintings sold only because he was an aboriginal who used his race to peddle his art. Albert did not worry about what they said; he just painted away to turn out the hundreds of landscapes which now take pride of place in homes over the face of this earth.

A few years after I went out to Ayers Rock, Albert passed away. I was sorry to hear that he had died, for he was one of Australia's sons. He died in poverty, if one counts money as such, but he was rich in memories and friends who understood his worth.

Well do I remember the uproar from the South when Albert was denied the right to build a house in Alice Springs. A thousand excuses were invented to show that such a thing was wrong. At this time Albert's pictures sold well, bringing him in thousands of pounds yearly; but all that time the Aranda master Albert lived beneath the shady trees which to him and his family were home. I often asked him about the business but at my question he only smiled and replied that he was O.K. under the tree, but if his friends in the South liked to worry about him he was not one to interfere with their pleasure.

Such was his philosophy. He was above enmity. When I heard of his death a few years later I wrote a verse in memory of a friend:

Sleep on, Ungata, sleep. The spirits of your tribe.
Weep by Kulrungga's steep and stony peak;
The Finke's white gums and teatrees sigh and sway
As church-bells toll to bless the weak and meek.

The weak and meek . . . 'Twas you who blazed the trail,
A giant 'midst the ashes of your land;
Painting a dream where ritual song-men died
As tribal waters choked with drifting sand.

'Twas you who showed us all the land you loved,
Loved above critics' learned jibe and scorn;
Amidst the dust your colours ever flowed,
The hues of evening and the glowing morn.

The domes of Katatjuta and the blue
Of early morn by Sonder's sacred peak;
The red of Karinyarri and the white
Ghost-gums that gleam beside the sandy creek.

You shared with us the pleasure of your art,
And freely gave your kin the wealth you earned;
Amidst the ashes of your clan you toiled,
Painting by fire-light as the mulgas burned.

Sleep well, my friend . . . The spirits of your tribe
Grieve on with those who understood your worth;
The bellbird calls at dawn to tell your clan
That peace is yours at last . . . O! Mother-earth!

The Alice Springs with its people who come and go, each with their problems and their philosophies; the aboriginal people tramping down the streets or taking life easy beneath the shady gum trees of the Todd River—watching them I often wonder would they ever make the grade into our way of life. Are they the people of open spaces such as one finds amidst the Tinkers of Ireland, the Gipsies of other lands, and the strange nomadic tribes of Asia—people who fiercely resist enclosed places? Or have they come from an ancient cave-dwelling branch of the human race who now live in the houses of towns and cities? Time alone will tell.

The people who call themselves aborigines in the South are citizens in the Northern Territory. They all live in houses, but even with them the kinship ties are strong and it is this rigid law that can wreck the harmony between the coloured people and the whites. Everywhere is peace around the area till the kinfolk arrive—Granny with her canine pets, uncle with a camel which is a part of his transport system for getting around the desert.

I know a mate of mine who was tolerant in racial matters until his wife became a nervous wreck through the uncontrolled yelping of dogs during the night. He was a peaceful, jovial man who was soon devising methods to rid the area of the wailing mongrels that made the night hideous. The final straw was when a neighbour's camel stepped over the dividing fence to munch at the succulent bush in his garden, followed by a medley of yowling dogs which descended from everywhere on to the beast just as it was feeding beneath his clothes hoist. The result was chaos as the startled camel poked its head through the cross-arms of the clothes line before galloping round and around like a merry-go-round. The disturbance ended when the animal brought down the hoist and dragged it away over the fence and bush to a chorus of gunshots, barking dogs, and humans telling one another off in no uncertain fashion.

Such incidents disturb friendship and lower the value of property near by. People who are pro-aboriginal change face overnight and become the subjects of criticism from those who live away from the battle-line.

Racial problems and prejudices exist everywhere among people of different creeds and colours. The Alice has her share.

Here in the Alice one often comes across some of the Aranda artists peddling their paintings. Not far away some old-time tribesmen selling 'synthetic' Churingas which have been recently quarried near Karanyarri, engraved by the tribal Elders around the missions or cattle station homesteads, given an antique look with a coating of red ochre and bullock-fat, and after much polishing to get the correct patina sold with much heartbreak and mythology as a relic of a dying race who wish their sacred things to be preserved.

The old and the new. The aborigines have entered into the tourist trade. On the walls of many houses in Australia and overseas aboriginal landscape paintings are shown with pride. Now and then an old Churinga will be brought to the light of day. The story will then be told of the sorrowing Elder who recognized the present white owner as a sort of tribal brother.

The aborigines change as does the Alice. The cave art of yesterday is a lost craft, its meaning forgotten. The original Churingas lie deep within the sacred places of the tribal lands. The abstract cave art of the aborigines has been replaced by the Aranda school of realism.

Here along Todd Street one can see the old and the new. Around us in that morn as we waited for Len Tuit to complete his business so that we could be once more on our way I visualized it all. Everywhere is reality. In every hill and range a legend. A land of contrast as its name suggests. Alice Springs.

Chapter Two

The Alice and Beyond

WHAT visions of running water and sylvan glades does the name of Alice Springs conjure up in our minds; the newly arrived person looks through the river-gums on to the sandy bed of the Todd River to wonder what it is all about. Yet to the water-hunting explorer, Mills, who first passed up the Todd River in the centre of Australia, and came upon that small spring where the telegraph station was afterwards built, it brought up visions of rest and peacefulness.

To that man does the name of Alice Springs owe its origin, for he called the river the 'Todd' and the site of what we, today, call the 'Bungalow' was named by him 'Alice Springs' after the wife of Charles Todd who was responsible for the building of that overland telegraph line across Australia.

The Alice, as it is locally called, was once a peaceful bush town of desert-oak slabs, stone and mud-mortar walls with thatched roofs, the lot surrounded by giant peppercorn trees and gardens. In 1957 it was beginning to blossom out; now as I write its town roads and houses are forcing back the bushland into the high mountains around. North, south, and east-side the town expands and bulges out like a thirsty beast 'blows-out' at the watering places on the cattle runs.

As water is the life of the Centre, the people gather after work around the local 'Troughs' as the bushmen and cattlemen call the hotels. Grog is the settler of all disputes and the fountainhead of good cheer. At one time the 'Troughs' were quiet inns, where 'one could lay down on the bar floor with his grog beside him and not get chucked out', as a mate of mine bemoaned after he had been told off by a new policeman and was grumbling about the changed conditions of the country now with regulations laid down and enforced.

The same regulations that made Sam rear up from the floor forced the publicans to give the stone and mud walls a face-lift. Slowly the change came in until now the hotels are equal to the best that is in the cities.

But at the time of my first going out to Ayers Rock, the famous 'Drunk's-seat', beneath a shady bull-oak tree, was still going strong as the place where the 'down and outs' could sit awaiting the moneyed captains to arrive. What yarns were told there as the thirsty ones peered along the roads from their vantage point in Todd Street.

That morning as we waited for Len to get the cattle-station owner's stores, I could see a reveller from the night before prowling about, hoping for an opportunity to nip around the back to get a little of the hair from the dog that bit him. Vain hope indeed, for the law was on the morning prowl. Seeing the cop coming the questing one was off down a side lane where he could go in to smoke till the road was clear for him to seek once more.

Watching the early morning scout out after a drink I smiled to myself as I remembered how I had once been introduced into the mystery of pub-drinking on Sunday in one of the old bush hotels.

My mate, who was proud of the fact that he had the inside knowledge on Sunday drinking, whispered into my ear that I should wait for him on a fixed spot at a certain time one Sunday afternoon.

'Don't make it too conspicuous,' he added, 'we don't want to draw crabs on the publican.'

At the appointed time I was 'on the ball', and passing me in the approved manner of an anarchist going to a secret meeting Sam whispered, 'Follow me'.

Proceeding as ordered we went down a back lane and through a side gate which came out at a rubbish-cum-woodheap at the rear of the hotel premises to arrive finally at a door. Pausing before this Sam gave me a wink and knocked in a manner which was definitely some pre-arranged signal. About a minute later an answering knock came. The code word or knock for this was a gentle stamp on the floor, satisfied with this mine host unlocked the door. Then in we went into that holy of holies in drunkdom. This, I afterwards learnt, was a special privilege and in theory I could consider myself a captain amidst the drinking fraternity of the village.

The secret lodge I had been initiated into was known as the 'afternoon session'—a ritual not unlike getting into one of the secret and sacred lodges of whites and blacks. I never went again because I wasn't a good drinker and the closed-in space of the smoke-filled room gave me the 'dry-horrors'.

The boozer on his morning's prowl had just poked his head around the corner of a lane when Len returned to the coach, the engine revved and we were off down a bitumen road that stretches a thousand miles north to Darwin but ends at the Alice Springs aerodrome eight miles to the south.

Down Todd Street and the south road we travel. Modern history and legend is all around us: the Flynn Church to the memory of a great man; the memorial to those who came into the Centre years ago; then beyond that place, on our left, is the small stony hill of Anjalka which marks the spot where the false-eyed Caterpillar Totem-men of tradition rested awhile as they created this country in that time of dreams.

Passing it I remembered that a rough road up this low stone hill was the spot where I passed for a driving licence in 1931! How Anjalka must have winced at that insult.

From the place of the Caterpillar-men my eye roved to sun-tipped Mount Gillen with a green patch on its eastern flank that symbolized the 'wind-break' where the ritual men of mythology circumcized a youth at that place; and farther west, just below Mount Gillen, was that red patch on the mountain side which is the bloodstain from the ritual cutting.

Legend is everywhere in this area. Just beyond Mount Gillen on the way to Jay Creek I have often been shown the stone of 'Umbajalla' where a child was burnt to death while his parents were out hunting.

Everywhere, along the road we are travelling smoke comes trailing from the chimneys into the morning air, reminding us that in every home a housewife is busy preparing the morning meal before the menfolk go out to work and the children to school. What an array of colours is revealed by those painted walls and gardens to remind us travellers that the citizens of this town are full of civic pride.

It is really too early for humans to be about on the streets. Their place there is taken by their canine friends who are now assembling on the street corners to discuss the night's ramblings before they return to their respective homes to sleep through the day.

A tourist's life for us in the coach, and a dog's life for those who hole-up for the day in readiness for another night of courting, snarling, and fighting which will keep the human workers tossing in their sleep or trying to scheme out some means of ridding the earth of such canine pests. But futile are their dreams because the dogs are protected from their wrath by the love of children, some hidden atavistic comradeship in man, and the fierce complex that surges in the breast of childless women.

About a mile down the road we pass a cluster of buildings beside a church. This is the 'Mission block' and the home-place of the town aborigines who have come in from the Hermansberg Mission some seventy miles to the westward. Living in the area at that time was a great friend of mine called Pastor Albrecht. Aged now, but he was a vigorous man when he came out to help the desert aborigines who were 'doing it the hard way' in the late twenties of this century. Drought, disease, death, and neglect was their lot then, but he and others 'fought the good fight' to give them some security. Now he lives among his people, so I lifted my hat as I passed by the home of one who battled hard to help a minority in its darkest hour.

About half a mile farther on we pass, on our left, a cluster of cottages amidst a clump of grey-green feather-leafed trees that gives the locality the name of 'Athel Grove'.

What a book could be written about the folk who live within those few acres with its dwellings that are often called 'Rainbow-towns'—so-called because the houses were built during the war years to shelter the halfcast people who came under the Aboriginal Act, by which they were treated as 'Wards' until a few of their kind championed the granting of citizenship rights.

Now we are nearing the gateway into or out of Alice Springs according to whether one is going north or south. The road swings over to a built-up highway that lays between the River Todd and the archaeozoic granite gneiss cliff-faces of the Macdonnell Ranges, overlaid by 'Pertanurra' quartzites. These stones are recorded in aboriginal mythology as being the people of the 'Yereringa' caterpillar totem who came into the country in the dawn of time.

From the reality of the township and the science of the geologists (who have written extensively on this locality) our tale passes into legend and history. This Heavytree Gap, named by the explorers after Charles Heavytree Todd, was originally called 'Andareppa' by the Aranda aborigines, who also recorded that to the right, as we go through the opening, is the small cave of 'Andareppa' which gave the gap its name—a place sacred and secret as the repository of the ceremonial objects of their ritual. But man in his desire for progress broke down the cave as he made a cutting into the cliff face after stone for the railway line. Now all that was has gone before the roar of trains as they go north, or south, the thumping of motors along the bitumen, and the laughter of children as they pass through the gateway of the Centre on their way to the schools of Alice Springs.

Passing through the Gap, Len points out on our right a tumble-down stone building with a peppercorn tree in front, explaining that it was once a police station out of which rode those men of the law who protected the whites and brought peace into the country around. As I had been a patrol officer in the Native Affairs Branch in the past, and had read a book by one trooper, and had perused the reports of another, I could just imagine the way law was enforced to get the desired results. The old peppercorn tree, around which the aboriginal prisoners were chained until they went on their long 'foot-walk' march to the railhead hundreds of miles away and so to the jails of the south, was a dumb reminder of those lawful, awful, lawless days which represented whichever side of the fence one happened to be on.

Legend, geology, and history. Now a sign on the opposite side of the highway proclaims to all that here was a road which led to a caravan park on the opposite side of the Todd. Everything is in order around the Alice, the old days of 'tossing the swag, or horsepacks' under a shady tree for a camp have departed before a wave of new laws and parks to cater for our needs.

Opposite Johnny's Heavytree Caravan Park is an interesting place called 'Pitchi-ritchi'. It was originally owned by the late George Chapman who was the first to put down a sub-artesian bore on the Granites Goldfield. Remaining behind the field after the others went on, he got results, for out of his patience came the gold that built this place which he named the 'Pearly Gates'.

Now a mate of mine owns the place and it was he who gave it the present name. Leo believed in the spirit of mateship in the best bush style. Instead of the open fireplace and the billy-can for boiling water he installed a power point beneath a shady porch with a hot-water jug, some tea and sugar, with an invitation to all that they were welcome. They were welcome, too, until someone admired the hot-water jug and stole the lot. So much for those who give and those who take away.

Ahead of us is the 'Yeralba' range of the old black people, and just on the town side of a stony hill which is called Mount Blatherskite is a place of trees and gardens. Here is the Old Timer's Homes of Flynn's dream. The coloured houses in which the old men live are a pleasant sight to behold. John Flynn was a great man who had the interests of the bush-people at heart. His name is deeply engraved in the memories of Territorians in the Centre and has no need for the memorials that have been erected to him along the highways. Why this place was put so far away from Alice Springs is beyond the comprehension of many bushies who wish to be near a town during their old age, for hotels and the 'Seats of Knowledge' in the parks have always been the meeting places of aged people. The place is a credit to those who run it, but I know of a few of my old bush mates who entered its portals, became bored with its isolation, and ended rolling the swag, getting out into the bush once more to be in their familiar surroundings. Roamers will ever roam however; perhaps that is the main cause of the old people's discontent. As they roamed once, so do we speed past the sign that tells travellers what it is about, but about three hundred yards farther on a bush-road swings to the right before the sign of St Mary's Hostel. Of all the people who travel that way few know the place exists, yet in that group of buildings in a large paddock is the home of many coloured children who have been sent in from the bush to be educated in the main schools of Alice Springs. Many of my mates have children there and I know quite a few of its inmates who have passed through its doors to make a name for themselves in the district and the cities of the South.

Beyond St Mary's we come out of the hills into open country; before us is the ribbon of bitumen that ends at the aerodrome, but before we reach it we turn to the right and are on an earth road that goes under the high sounding title of the Adelaide Highway.

My memories of the places we pass by is interrupted by a babble of tourists' voices as everybody attempts to stand and peer ahead. I also peer and see one of our domestic cats returning from the nightly hunt with a bright-coloured mulga parrot in its jaws. Consternation now reigns as the passengers' sympathy sways betwixt the cat and the bird. One elderly lady is all for the bird and is holding forth on what she would do if she could get hold of the cat. A wail of despair, interrupting her loquacity, comes from all as a huge eagle swoops out of the sky in the approved manner of the fleet-winged 'Kunmurri' evil spirit in eastern Aranda mythology. One minute the cat is speeding back home with its kill, the next it is the kill of a massive bird which has grabbed it in its powerful claws. How the great wings spread out and thrashed the air as it picked up power to enable it to rise with its load. Suddenly it seemed to pause in the air; when this happened the mighty bird released its victim as does a grab-scoop on the end of an earth moving shovel and down on to the ground came the cat with the bird still clamped in its fixed jaws. Its hitting the earth coincided with a roaring wail from the tourists. Some of the women put hands over their eyes to shut out the sight and so missed the graceful banking of the bird as it came in once more to clutch the now dead cat, then away to a tall tree, with us in the coach taking sides. Amidst the chattering I heard the elderly lady who was against the cat in the beginning now holding forth on what she would do if she could get her hands on the bird.

Hearing her talk (which wavered from cat to bird loving), my thoughts went back to my Darwin days when my mates and I were awakened each morning by a rifle shot from a bird lover next door to where I lived. His love was so great for the cat that he had built a bird-bath in his garden to decoy the peaceful doves for his feline friend.

His plucking of the bird each morning was his early chore and watching him through the louvres I wondered where did his love of nature begin or end. Kindness and death was with him each morn and ever around his legs was his beloved cat awaiting the morning sacrifice.

A big bull-dust hole in the road with everybody up in the air and falling down with a crash on to their seats had them talking about roads and roadmakers. Thus did we travel till we came to a creek that had a signpost which told all that we were now crossing Templebar Creek.

Crossing the gum-tree lined sandy creek I recalled how an aborigine of this country had once told me the legend of how the 'Adjunba' (monitor-lizard) ritual men of the dream-time made this creek and the country around as they came from 'Andilindja' (painted) corroboree rock to wend their way through Simpson's Gap on their ritual wanderings north.

Legend and mystery was here in the ranges and creeks along our road. To the left of us is the Bat Cave with, not far away, the small increase stone that must always be cleaned of grass for fear a bush fire would touch the rubbing-stone of conception and prevent spirit-children from passing into their tribal mothers for re-birth.

But the Easter holiday people were not interested in pagan ritual although the very word Easter comes from a pagan goddess of light. Someone starts singing and to the swaying of the coach we are all yelling at the top of our voices in a grand festival mood.

We pass by the Waterhouse Range and a passenger in the coach who is reading a book points out a chapter that is about this very mountain we were passing by. The book is called *The Changing Face of Australia* by Lasceron, and in it I read about this natural marvel which is really a world unto itself. In the book is an aerial photo revealing that the top of the mountain is not unlike the mighty wooden carrying bowl used by aboriginal women during the hunt.

Beyond the Waterhouse is the James Range and within it our roadway winds down a ghost-gum lined stony defile that goes under the ominous title of 'Hell's Gates'. Through the Gates we go to cross the Hugh River up which McDouall Stuart moved with his exploring party on his trip from Adelaide to Chambers Bay and the northern waters of Australia.

A mile or so from the Hugh River we come upon the one-time residence of that well-known bushman Bob Buck, who was going strong at that time but has since passed away. What a strange place was Bob's residence when he was living there; built by bushmen from the things of the bush, it epitomized the old-time pioneering spirit out of which Bob seemed to emerge when he came out of the wobbly door of his hut to greet us. All around one could see camel, horse-pack, and riding saddles together with greenhide hobble straps, bits of horse-shoes, and the inevitable cast-iron camp-oven so beloved by bush cooks.

Nothing worried Bob. He did not give out those hackneyed excuses about the untidiness of his place; it was his home and that was all that mattered. His was a quiet dignity amidst his aboriginal people from whom he received respect, and homage from all the whites who had read about his exploits in Ion Idriess' book *Lasseter's Last Ride*.

A toot from Len and we all 'pile' into the coach. Then away once more to pass by Maloney Creek with its fossils of the Ordovician geological age, finally to come out of the sandhills where we stop at the Finke River to have the morning drink of tea.

Chapter Three

The Finke and Beyond

LEN's cry of 'Gents to the right and women to the left' causes a movement among the passengers who slowly disappear into the 'Ilbilba' tea trees or behind the gaunt river-gums that grow along the bank and bed of this one-time mighty river.

While the pot is boiling I take a stroll towards the Henbury cattle station homestead which is but a short way down the river. It is dry now, but becomes a roaring torrent when the heavy rains fall on the ranges to the North.

The Finke is today a poor image of its former self; rising somewhere near the Ormiston Gorge with its ritual red-ochre mines and its honey totem dreamings, it becomes lost in the sandhills of the Simpson Desert. I myself have crossed it at eleven different places along the four hundred miles over which it flows in a fair season. Everywhere it is hindered by sandhills; these form meandering flats which become a sea of shallow waters during a good season. Can I forget that time when I was in that area during a heavy wet, when, camping on a high ridge, I could see water everywhere between the buck-saltbush and dead coolibah trees that had been stricken by a prolonged drought. There before my eyes was a dying land that had been given a new life by a water transfusion from the Master Physician. On the gaunt branches of the dead trees and wading around the bases of the trunks in that senile land were wild-fowl by the thousands. Gazing upon that scene I could picture what this country was like when the Larrapinta, as the aborigines called it, flowed as an unbroken stream for over a thousand miles to the south where it entered the southern ocean to form the delta which is now called Spencer's Gulf.

The Finke, named thus by Stuart after a friend who had assisted him with finance for his journey, was then and still is the drainage channel of the Centre. The well-worn stones in its river bed are remnants of once high mountains and ranges that are now small ridges or bedrock deep beneath the layer of earth that now covers all. Yet those stones and small residual hills tells the questing geologist the story of this country. Here one stands upon ancient sea-beds and glacial sediments of a lower Permian geologic age. Viewing those sediments when sitting beneath a shady gum tree to get away from the heat of the sun, I find it difficult to believe that this was once a country of ice and roaring torrents.

Len called out that the billy had boiled and to 'Come and get it'. So drinking the tea and munching at some cake I listened to the idle chatter of a tourist who had just seen a ragged-looking aboriginal go by, and was complaining bitterly about the Government and its apathy to 'these wretched niggers'.

Her tirade was cut short when an aboriginal friend of mine rode up on a stock horse to give me greetings and pass the time of day. He was an aged man named Kudekudeka. He sat loosely in the saddle to inform me that his job on Henbury cattle station was to 'tail' some bullocks that had been mustered for the southern markets. His English was perfect as it should be with one who had been schooled at Hermansberg Mission and had been all his adult life with white people. This surprised my critical friend who had never seen an aboriginal in her life, and had grown up to believe they were 'wasters who wouldn't work and were always on the cadge'.

Kudekudeka asked me what I was doing. When I told him I was going to Ayers Rock as a Ranger he straightened up in his saddle and looking over us whites remarked proudly: 'That my proper country . . . I grew up there as a little boy and in that *inmma* (ritual) I was made a man.'

He paused awhile and as he did a strange look came into his rugged face. Then I saw his lips move . . . low at first, to become a little louder as he chanted for me the opening songs of that ritual which has made Uluru—the aborigines word for Ayers Rock—the sacred abode of 'Wonambi the all-knowing one'. I did not know his Loritdja tongue but I had seen the great 'Kerungra' ritual of the 'Mother-place' amidst the northern tribes. My going out to his birth and ritual place had made him 'sorry' for his country in the thought that I was going out to a mountain which was the 'memory-fix' of the Loritdja songmen for that ceremony about the great Earth-mother of the creative.

In his eagerness to chant his songs he had raised his voice and after he had finished a roar of laughter arose from the tourists who firmly believed it was some sort of a show put on for their benefit. One of the tourists who was interested in music spoke in a foreign language to his wife, and I never saw a man so surprised in his life when the old aboriginal answered him in German. Amid general laughter Kudekudeka explained how he had learned the tongue at the Lutheran Mission where many of the pastors talked it during their rest hours. 'We learn plenty languages,' Kudekudeka explained to the German, but I did notice that he spoke English in deference to the language of the country.

Kudekudeka then turned to me and touching my arm he said softly: 'When you get to my country you will know nothing. What about I come out there to tell you the story?'

Len's voice calling us into the coach and the honking of the horn demanded our attention, so hastily I told him I would like him to come with a friend to sing their songs for me. 'You write big-boss in Darwin,' he replied. 'I come.' Leaving him I hopped into the coach and we were off down the road on the next leg of our journey.

Four miles out, as we were passing the Henbury Station airstrip into which the Connellan planes come with mails and supplies, Len explained that a few miles to our right were craters that were made when a series of aerolites struck the earth to form what is known to science as the 'Henbury craters'.

I had been to the site before and was amazed at the large craters which had been blasted out under the impact, but few of the small meteorites remained as the place had been 'well done over' by the white bushmen and aborigines who sold them everywhere to collectors and museums.

An aboriginal who came from the area was with me when I visited the crater-site, so I naturally asked him if there was any legend in their tribe about this roaring fire in the sky and the explosion which followed. He stated that he himself knew of none but would inquire on his return to the station homestead. His inquiries discovered nothing, but he did state that the area was under some sort of a taboo that had been handed down from 'long time ago'.

Glaciers, fiery masses, and legends relating to Rainbow serpents making the rivers are here to stir one's imagination, but for us the reality of the open road. This branches beyond the airstrip; the one to the left is the Adelaide Highway which passes the Palmer Valley Cattle Station and Erldunda where another bush track goes off to the right through Mount Ebeneezer station and Angus Downs. But our coach turned to the right on what was called the 'short-cut Mount Quinn road'.

The 'short cut' was marked by a big sign that said it was a dry stage without water and human habitation for eighty miles. Heedless of the sign, Len swung the coach to the right and away we sped along the short-cut road. Up and down ridges we went to turn once more at a place called the 'Dead-bullock dam'. 'Not far now,' called out Len who could tell that everyone was feeling a bit peckish from the fact that they had ceased talking and were becoming a bit 'browned-off' by the bumps and twists of the road which went through a land that was constantly changing colour under the slanting rays of the sun.

A red-coloured hill appeared on our left hand. 'Mount Quinn,' from Len. 'Soon we'll be crossing the Palmer River and the next stop is the old Mount Quinn homestead where we'll pull up for lunch.' As he spoke we came upon the gum trees of the dry Palmer River, and about three miles farther on we pulled up at a dilapidated mass of slabs and stone that was once the homestead of the Mount Quinn Cattle Station.

I had visited this place when it was a going concern and the home of Bob Buck and his mate Alf Butler. The place brought up memories of Alf and his kindness to me when he lived beside the *tithera* (shell-parrot) aboriginal well a little to the right of the Henbury–Erldunda Road, the then head-station homestead of their Palmer River Cattle Station, which they sold afterwards to one of the larger companies of the Centre.

Bob and Alf had been mates for years, but the rift in their friendship began when a party went by to seek for Lassiter's gold. They wanted a bushman to go out with them and that man should have been Alf who knew the country, but Alf was busy at the time and he got Bob to go instead—the rest is literature and history.

Reading the story of how Bob went out I can picture him on a camel beside one of the tribesmen who knew the road where Lassiter was buried. Thus did they ride out to find and bury that man who dreamt of masses of gold and died as he sought the eldorado of his fantasy.

But Bob remained to become a legend in his own time and a must for the tourists. Now as I write this I picture him regaling his admirers with stories of his derring-do, gazing into the popping eyes of the womenfolk. Now and then he would cast a wink at some mate near by. He was the white songman of the Centre and will be remembered as such, but I think we should not forget the toiling Alfs who gave freely to all but had no trick by which they would be remembered.

Now all that remains of their last joint homestead is a well of brackish water and this deserted place with a goat-yard piled deep with manure. Where Alf and Bob had their frugal meals the tourists were eating their salad lunch, branded as 'rabbit-tucker' by the former owners. The table they were eating from would be classed as antique in a few more years, for it had been made from desert-oak timber adzed into rough hewn planks. The place where we boiled the billy for our mid-day tea was of stone and mud. To the tourists it brought up memories of a drink of tea, but for me it recalled days when the aboriginal girls cooked up grilled rib-bones over those very fires. Grilled them as they passed lewd remarks about the 'Ki-i' bones which were said to be a bush aphrodisiac for the run-down male elders, white or black.

After lunch we were off again over the next fifty miles to Angus Downs. A good deal of this country would be considered wasteland by the cattlemen, but to the tourist it is full of interest because of its tree and brush growth amidst the sandhills.

Here one will find the light greens of the desert mallee and the casuarina blending into the darker shades of the kurrajong and that wild peach which is known everywhere as the quandong. Great emu-tucker are the red fruit of this medium-sized tree, a fact well attested by its seeds that were spread over the countryside where they have been deposited in small mounds after passing through the birds.

At one stop, where we all piled out to photograph a monitor lizard which had struck a pose at the noise of the motor's engine, one of the women picked up a handful of these predigested quandong stones. Inquiring as to how they came in these small heaps she quickly dropped them on hearing Len's answer.

We all laughed at her embarrassment, for after the midday lunch we were easily pleased. Len himself was full of beans, and coming across a number of wild camel tracks he regaled us all with tales of these animals which ran in large herds during the winter rutting season. The cows were guarded by savage bulls that fought each intruding bull to the death and were not afraid to attack a human if they were on foot.

Strange how it is that trees and flowers, even the footprints of animals, bring on a spate of tales. Past a hill called the twenty-mile we entered a patch of sand which Len called the 'Mad-mile'. It was certainly a mad race across it. How the coach engine boiled as we swayed from side to side in low gear, and after we got clear Len regaled us with harrowing stories of people bogged in sand and going through all sorts of hardships waiting for a rescue.

The 'Mad-mile' was the testing place on the road. Men have bogged there and while walking for help have perished on the road through dehydration, yet back in the bogged motor was water enough to have kept them going for days. Panic is the curse of a stranded traveller. But I remember two elderly ladies who were bogged on this same 'Mad-mile'. Did they panic? Not they. Incredible as it seems they just erected a calico between two trees, boiled the pot and made, of all things, some tea in a tea-pot. When the rescuing motor came upon them two days later they found the area tidied up of rubbish, a table laid and the two old dears sitting up in the approved English tea-room manner, inviting their rescuers to a 'cuppa'.

Asked what would have happened if they had run out of water, they replied that they had plenty. 'We happen to be English,' they replied. 'Our ancestors used little water in times of stress and what they did so can we.' The desert makes people think; with water there is no second time.

The water canteens were well filled in Len's coach. So laughing, talking, and taking photographs of objects we passed by, we finally arrived at Angus Downs Cattle Station homestead to be besieged by a horde of aborigines who sped towards us in the hope of selling their wares.

Chapter Four

Angus Downs and West

As we were the first 'tourist-mob' to be going out to Ayers Rock that season the owner of Angus Downs, Arthur Little, and his wife Bessie, were out to welcome us in.

Arthur was the son of a well-known pioneer settler called Billy Little who took up this country in 1927, and it was he who gave it its present name. Billy was a sheep-man so the indigent aborigines who hunted over the country became his shepherds and shepherdesses responsible for his flocks.

Everywhere over the run one can still see today the old brush sheep-yards that protected his sheep overnight against the onslaughts of the raiding dingoes that looked upon his flock as fair game in the battle for survival. In those days there were no fences and the flock was watched day and night. Many a time have I watched the aboriginal women shepherding sheep amidst the mulga trees or over the hills. Watching them running around with a stick in their hands, and a small lamb under an arm I was always reminded of those scenes from Biblical days.

At the period of Len Tuit's first tourist party of the season Billy had gone to live in Alice Springs and had handed over the property to his sons. But each had gone their way, and now only Arthur remained to convert the place into a cattle-run.

The present homestead was four miles away from the original home of Wolra, which had been established there after the hardy Little senior had ridden by on a camel searching for water. He had heard from the aborigines that the Wolra native well was in the Basedow Range out from some red ochre deposits and just as he was about to give up searching he saw some finches coming from a small cleft in the earth beside a creek. Digging down he found the water that every aboriginal knew about, but would not reveal to the white men.

Thus was Wolra formed, and only when good water was tapped in a sub-artesian bore on the site of the present homestead was the main station place shifted to this locality.

Arthur's wife, Bessie, also came from pioneering stock who opened up this country. She was a Breaden who were the first people that rode into this area, it was they who opened the land and tended the original cattle herds of the Centre.

Should one go to Henbury Cattle Station homestead he would see a brass plate affixed to a bush post beside the gate that leads to the house. The names of those who came out in the early days are engraved upon it and the name of Breaden is there among them.

To get the feel of Angus Downs as it was a few years before the time of my first going to the Rock, one should read Arthur Groom's book *I Saw a Strange Land.* Although I and many other bushmen do not agree with him on the way he always walked away from the road, instead of on the back of his camel and thus get a better picture of the country he was passing through, nevertheless I do admire his powers of observation and his determination to get into strange places. He has now passed on, but his memory remains among the many people of this country who saw him pass by. As he received hospitality with the Little family so have I over the years.

The olden days were ones of peace, but since the advent of tourism the quiet times have departed and the rush is on. People who have paid sums of money to visit the Centre are just interested in the things about them. 'We have paid,' is their motto, and having paid they are out to get their money's worth. The only difficulty is that what is new and interesting to them is old and uninteresting to the people who live in the area. The continually repeated questions as to 'How long one has lived in the area', 'Do the children go to school?', 'Do you like living here?', become painful after one hundred times. Arthur and Bessie were just 'sitting-shots' for the seekers of knowledge. They stood it for a while but soon went 'under cover' by shutting the front door of the house when tourists arrived. Thus, the people who live along the 'tourist-lanes' get the names of being 'strange'.

The aborigines were quick to learn that to be ignorant of the English language was to be free of perplexing questions, so they always put on a vacant stare that naturally gave the tourists the impression they were stupid. Remaining thus, yet hearing all that was being said about them, they enjoyed a situation which was recounted over and over again after the tourists had departed.

To the tourists the aborigines were 'terrible'. To the aborigines the tourists were *karnbas* (crows) because of their combined cry of 'Two-bob, two-bob' as they moved towards a group of aborigines who were peddling their wares.

On that first trip of the year with Len, the aboriginal salesmen were not there in force, but the articles for sale were well made and worthwhile. The black people had not yet come up against the 'heavy-loadings' of tourists that came later and forced them to hack out anything so as to get a few shillings. It was the beginning of the 'dry-rot' that marked the end of native artifacts which were originally made to the accompaniment of traditional chants and therefore as perfect as the craftsmen could make them.

So much for progress, I thought, as I watched the passengers advance into the fray, giving now and then the familiar 'crow battlecry'. A high-pitched voice from one of the tourists had me looking that way and who should it be but the lady of the Finke River smoko camp who was always complaining about the ill treatment of 'niggers'. She was brandishing a well-made boomerang over her head and was haggling with an elderly aboriginal woman over the price of the article.

The black-mother had a small girl sitting straddle across her shoulders and was endeavouring to get a word into the argument. Apparently she has said something that has made the white bargainer's hackles rise, for I heard her voice rise to a bleat as she exclaimed, 'What rot, ten bob for this.'

'Five karnba . . . that right . . . we savee,' said a bushy-whiskered old man who happened to be passing and wished to air his knowledge.

As the boomerang was a well-turned job with neatly fluted lines and worth one pound because of the labour put into it, I felt like going over and buying the thing myself, but business is business everywhere so I just sat back to listen.

If ever there was such a thing as bargain abasement here it was at its worst. The bargainer knew it was a good boomerang by the obvious way she clutched it in her hand, and attempted to push some money into the black-mother's hand. How long the show would have gone on I do not know; the only thing that decided the matter was the little girl weeping bitterly as she spoke into her mother's ear. In a flash the mother snatched the money from the tourist's hand and only afterwards did Bessie tell me that the tourist won because the little girl wanted some lollies and fruit that the money would buy, and under the tribal law of kinship the child was always the master and must not be denied.

Looking back upon that scene of people, white and black, buying and selling, the black people fixing a price and the white ones trying to beat them down, I wondered why people could be so grasping. The tourist waved her prize above her head in an elated manner, but I noticed that the ends of the boomerang were—unknown to her—inverted as a sign of defeat. With no other object to sell, the mother and child moved out of the bargaining battle. As she did I noticed a smile spread over her rugged face when one of the elderly women tourists thrust something into her hand then hurried away as though she was afraid of being seen. I did not see the amount she gave, but her action somehow redeemed the meanness of the other, and it made me happy to think that many whites were not of the bargain abasement mob.

As the new owner of the boomerang was coming back to the coach she spied an old aboriginal and went over to him inquiring if the weapon was a 'Come-back-one'. Taken by surprise and thinking she was trying to trap him he shook his head in the affirmative sign; as he did she handed him the weapon and asked him to throw.

Surprised at the onslaught he immediately asked in his language the usual question as to what it was all about, and had the woman paid for the article so that he would not be blamed by his clan if he broke a blackman's weapon, given a tribal assurance that it was sold and he could do with it as he wished he gave a short run and away the boomerang sped into the air. Amazed at the throw, I watched the boomerang glide through the air like a bird. In a wide sweep it went till, crashing into a dry bloodwood tree in its path, it fell in shattered pieces on to the earth. Now what a roar of laughing came from the hitherto quiet black people; even us white people joined in the merriment as the haggling one went over to pick up the pieces of her worthless purchase.

The aborigines, who knew no English before, were now shouting at the top of their voices and pointing to the owner of the broken weapon. 'You lose . . . you lose,' they shouted. 'Must be devil-devil from sky give trouble over buy-business.' Even the old thrower of the weapon was doubled up in glee and from the way he enjoyed the joke I was certain that his aim was but to destroy a thing that had caused so much ill-feeling and greed.

Len's honking horn had us back to the coach and to Arthur and Bessie's farewells we were off once more. We passed by a low mountain on our right that was called by the aborigines Wilbia, but by the white people the Basedow Range. The small Wilbia spring gives its name to the area. I was not to know till later on (when I walked around Ayers Rock with my aboriginal friends), that this place and the Rainbow Serpent above Maggie Springs of the Rock were remembered by an incident which shows that the 'All-knowing-one' of the Loritdja tribesmen remembers his people and shares in their sorrows.

The area of Wilbia is but a part of that Basedow Range and receives its sacredness from a small ridge which holds the secret and sacred rubbing-stone within a circle of cleared earth. This taboo spot is always kept clean of grass and rubbish and is kept smeared over with emu fat and blood so that it will maintain its ritual power.

Though but a small stone it is nevertheless sacred in ritual and always avoided by the aboriginal hunters and horsemen who ride down the bush track that passed the place.

The Wilbia stone is that to which all *arukata* (initiates who are being made ready for the secret life) are led to be passed into manhood. At that place the *Irakapa* (head-dress of white feathers with hair-bun) is cut off by the initiate's guardian (brother-in-law). Afterwards he is rubbed with food by his mother-in-law, her brothers, and her sisters, a ceremony that places him in line of kinship so that he is afterwards taboo to her and thus receives her daughters as wife or wives.

Thus it can be discerned that not only is the Wilbia stone a doorway to manhood but it is also a place of betrothal made when the tribal elders and others witness the ritual.

Wilbia is an example of how uninteresting places to the eyes can hold sacred meanings to the aborigines. The grand and awe-inspiring spots, such as Ayers Rock, Mount Olga, and King's Canyon are also invested with sacred significance too, but the Wilbia stone holds precedence to them all, for it is to that area the initiates go to pass into a sacred way of life.

The Wilbia stone also carried within it the secret of subincision of men and the deflowering of girls; those who do the act are the same kin as those who rubbed the initiates, male to youth and female to girl in the same kinship act of betrothal. Thus do we gaze from our coach at commonplace Wilbia where a tribal David conquered a Goliath in sacred ritual.

Past the Basedow Range we came to a dry salt lake that was known to the Loritdja as *puntus* because of the white salt-encrusted surface. These *puntus* were once lakes caused by the slow meandering of a tributary of our old friend the Finke. The air-map shows its course from the north-west to the south-east. In places it is salty, in others, as at Lake Karinga, it is covered with salt-bush. Today it is but a dead watercourse, but during a heavy wet, like the one in the early twenties, it ran water over its entire length to reunite once more with its parent stream.

A little to our left, as we travelled along the edge of the *puntu* is the mountain of Conner. It is the cinderella of the three great monoliths, Conner, Ayers Rock, and the Olgas, that run from east to west along this two-thousand foot plateau which we now travelled along. In the afternoon it was enchanting to behold as it sat squat on the desert sands rising to a height of eleven hundred feet above the bush road and the *puntus* around. Bushmen who have climbed on to its summit from the southern side have told me that mulga trees of giant size flourish up there in a little world of their own.

Looking upon that azure-coloured mount in that afternoon's light I could well imagine why the aborigines called it Adtilla to commemorate that here the great left-handed hero Linggi, of the yellow-lizard totem, threw his *karlee* of light from the east. As it rose into the heavens—like the sun which now follows its path—so did Linggi speed beneath it then, with feet apart, he leapt astride over the place and his action formed the mountain below.

The white encrustations on the surface of the *puntus* gave to the aboriginal creative and imaginative minds the numerous legends which belong to that area. The mirage in the morning and during the day, together with the heavy dawn frosts in the winter months, were said to be the work of tribal spirits who governed all this phenomena. Chief of these were the dancing mirage-people of the early morning who lifted the country over their heads to lower it once more as the sun rose higher in the heavens.

Legend also recorded how the white frosts were brought in by the *ninya* (cold) men who were reported to dwell in the dark deep caverns beneath the numerous *puntu*, and creeping out during those months when the sun-woman was on her northerly wanderings, they caused the cold winds and the ice.

In this strange land are small seepages of slightly brackish water—remnants of once powerful springs that gave life to a country that now lies white with saline mud, or a mantle of white rock which undoubtedly formed when the travertine limestone was slowly evaporated from these thermal flows.

At one of these springs, or wells, a few years before my going to Ayers Rock, lived Paddy de Conlay who had leased the country around. He was one of those tough and wiry types, who as 'doggers' or 'dingo-scalpers' helped open this land.

But of interest to us now is the fact that not far from his bush-built homestead, which is now in ruins, occurred a tribal murder that has become history.

I heard the tale, as it was told to me by one of the tribesmen, as we sat one Christmas Day at Angus Downs when I looked after the station homestead while Bessie, Arthur, and the children were having a holiday in Adelaide.

We were sitting beneath an athol tree's shade, and the wind sighing through the leaves seemed to give a background to the tribal story. The aboriginal told me the tale in grim detail of the missing aboriginal and the capture of the prisoners at Middleton Ponds beside the Palmer River. He told me about the digging up of the body of the murdered man. How the policeman nonchalantly shook the skull and, hearing a rattle inside it, found the man had been killed by a rifle bullet in the head. From tribal business it now became murder, so he chained up the culprits to a large tree, but that night they escaped and were fleeing to the westward.

The road our coach had travelled from Mount Quinn homestead followed somewhere along the path of the escapees with the avenging limb of the law on their trail. They by-passed the scene of the crime at Mount Conner to be off through the night on the long road to Ayers Rock over sixty miles farther on to the west.

He told me how the tired escapees tried to elude their relentless black trackers during the day by covering their feet with cloth and crawling beneath spinifex there to await the night; how the law tried to burn the spinifex country and so flush them out. But the Wonambi spirit of Ayers Rock protected them so well that the fire would not burn. But human endurance cannot stand up against fleet camels that can go long distances without water, and the final story was written in the shelters of Uluru under the watchful eyes of the tribal spirits.

Every time I went around Ayers Rock during the time I was Ranger there I looked up at a cliff face called the Mulu (nose) and pictured that final scene.

The trembling aborigines were jammed into a rocky crevice of the 'Nose', listening to the white-man's law climbing up towards them. The policeman, peering into the darkness of the crevice, could see nothing and would have gone away but for his tracker who claimed he could smell the sweat from the unwashed bodies of the wanted men. The aborigine who told the tale to me at Angus Downs went on to describe how the four men hiding in the crevice could hear the talking. Then faintly they heard footsteps creeping in, and in desperation, one of the escapees on the outside who was too stout to creep further into the narrow cleft of the mountain, leapt out with a stone in his hand in an effort to create surprise and thus get away.

Now spoke the rifle of the white-man's law and the doomed man toppled on to the floor of the crevice. Then a strange thing happened. The dying man, with a superhuman effort, crawled out of the cave and neither threats nor promises could make him reveal where the others were hidden.

The Mulu with its severed nose looks with passive face over the Loritdja tribal lands and keeps its secret well. Yet what a story it could tell of man's devotion to his tribal kin, even unto death—what a strange scene, the cowering men within the crevice listening to their dying comrade asking for water before he died and the last vision he had on this earth was the policeman's black-tracker pouring water into his parched throat. Thus died a brave man.

The police patrol retreated back to their camp beneath the mulga trees. There they rested for the night, but high above on the mountain face the Mulu saw frightened men creeping out from the shelter of his nose to blend into the welcoming darkness and so live for one of them to tell me the tale that Christmas Day.

But now we Easter holiday-makers were speeding on with Len at the steering wheel. The road was long and we were all weary, but Len refreshed us by calling out as we passed by a small windmill with a concrete tank of water: 'This is Yerka, friends. Down to the right is the small spring that gave this place its name . . . a few more miles and we'll be on the last stage of the journey.'

Len's voice showed no sign of fatigue. Men like him and the coach-captains belonging to the touring companies have driven many miles to establish the present tourist trade. This country owes a lot to men like Len but I am afraid it too often forgets.

Now he called out to tell us that seven more miles and we would be at the cattle station homestead of Curtin Springs which is only sixty-eight miles from Ayers Rock.

On we went through some desert poplar trees that line the road to come out at a cluster of galvanized iron buildings around a large spinifix-covered shed under which was a kerosene-burning refrigerator and of all things one would not expect to see in the desert, a long bench where two men were hopping, playing a game of table-tennis.

Seeing this I knew we are with the Andrews family who pioneered this area.

Chapter Five

Memories

SITTING under the spinifex, or should I call it 'porcupine-grass' shed which had been built by the Andrews as a shelter from the heat of the summer, and listening to Ossie and the others talking away about the cattle-runs and the 'dry' I could not but feel an affinity with these people who were the children and grandchildren of old Abe Andrews who came into the Centre some years ago. He came out with his camels, donkeys and all the paraphernalia that goes along with a man who is going to pioneer the land.

His old camp at Andalyu, near the road which leads from Angus to Tempe Downs, can still be seen. He and his wife lived there for many years until his son Merv Andrews came westward to find and dig out this native well of Djulu, the Loritdja aboriginal word for a hole in the earth or a well. Once this fresh water was found Abe and his clan moved in to the westward and, taking up this country during the war years, they named the place after the then Prime Minister Curtin.

Sitting there while Len filled up with water in case the surface water at Ayers Rock was low, my mind went back to the days when I was a lad and places like this were considered a luxury. Seeing the usual junk-heap (a must in these outback places) I strolled over to have a look-see, and there among the inevitable mass of old horse-shoes, pieces of iron, and saddle-trees were an old iron kettle and a rusted 'bull-wheel' that had once turned slowly at the head of a well to help water the stock of other days. Seeing it I thought of those days when . . .

The camel trod o'er the dusty 'walk',
And the bull-wheel creaked as the drovers talk
Of grass and camps, of stores and pubs,
Of cattle 'rushing' through the scrub;
Of cooks and 'blacks', the yarns they spin
As the bull-wheel creaked and the herds came in.

The yarns they weaved of days gone by,
These oral-tales of they who lie
Asleep as the herds go trailing by,
In graves beneath a desert sky;
Their songs are the night-winds in the breeze,
By cattle-camps and the 'bronco-trees'.

The windmill pumps as the drovers stand
On a 'turkey-nest' in the blood-red land;
They curse as a road-train thunders by
In a cloud of dust and a honking cry,
They roar through land in the grip of drought
With a 'load of fats' for the markets; 'South'.

The old goes out and the bull-wheels rust
By the unused well now choked with dust;
And the drover's plant now rots away
'Midst camel-packs and a disused dray;
And we have changed as the roads sweep by,
But our thoughts are out where memories lie
Amidst the sand of a painted land where the herds sweep by.

Strange is it not that when a person gets on in years he is always thinking back with a memory that is acute about incidents relating to long ago, yet forget the things of yesterday.

Looking at the Andrews' place I thought of those early days on the cattle-runs when we had no radio or any of those things that delight the youth of today. Then, when the day's work was over, we entertained ourselves with those sports which were a part of our daily lives.

At every mustering yard camp one would find the old jumping hand-stones formerly used by other stockmen. They were a part of the camp just as grinding-stones were the fixtures of an aboriginal camping site. With these the stockmen would be doing the 'Three long jumps', hop step and jump, broad jump, and without them the running long jump. How we strained as we leapt, and then afterwards talked about great jumpers of other days. I myself was not too good on the jumps, but in trying to excel others I got a ricked-knee that still reminds me of the afternoon sports in the cattle camps.

After the strenuous job of jumping would come trick-games such as picking up a short stick or match that was stuck upright in the ground while balancing oneself on the knees and elbows. Another trick was to see who could push the stick or stone farthest along the ground while balancing on the arm as a pivot and lever to get the player on to his feet again. After the trick games would come the strong-arm stuff. Two stockmen sat on the ground facing each other, each with the soles of his feet against the other's. Between them would be a short stick which they bent over to hold in both hands. When they were ready a signal would be given and each would strain to pull the other's rump off the ground and thus get the victory.

After sports would come the evening meal, generally a stew or sea-pie in the cast-iron camp-oven, and after that 'blow-out' we would sit around the camp-fire to sing songs or recite our favourite poems.

Each one, in turn, would have to put on his act, and failing this there would be a scruffing with much laughter as the non-actor was tossed into the nearby billabong or trough. Mostly everyone sang or recited. I am pretty sure that this bush school of oral teaching was the starting point with many a bush-poet and magsman, such as I, who kept up the yarning into later days. People talk a lot about empty heads making the most sound but I myself have learned from experience that the continual re-telling of a story polishes it up; in the telling one adds more until the small tale becomes a short story in the same manner as the ancient unknown 'song-men', black and white, have handed down those wonderful epics from other days. For just as the camp-side games gave to the cattlemen the exercise they needed after sitting in the saddle all day, so did the yarn spinning around the camp-fire give them the mental recreation which kept their minds alert.

During my early cattle days all mustering was done into drafting yards, and there the calves would be separated from their mothers into a branding-pen. Our head and leg-ropes were all plaited greenhide with an iron ring for the loop. The iron ring was cursed by the stockmen as something that gave lumpy-jaw to the cattle, but they did not alter the method until the drafting-yards was superseded by the 'tailing-yard' with bronco-panels and twisted greenhide ropes with a leather 'hoonda' for the ring.

As I sat and had the usual drink of tea at Curtin Springs I thought of those early days when the 'Outback' was governed by a strict rule of caste. A boss was the head-man and was called 'Mister' till he ordered otherwise, generally by elder people he knew; but to brats like me he was the 'Big I am'. The cattle-station homestead was the 'government house' of the manager. A tinkling bell generally called him to dinner, and should he wish it, a 'punkka' would keep him cool. The jackaroos lived in the 'Quarters', sometimes they ate with the boss, but mostly by themselves. Next in prestige—downwards of course—was the 'Men'—stockmen, blacksmiths, yard-builders, etc.—who ate their tucker in the 'kitchen'; the blacks of course, were just nothing, so they ate on the wood-heap. As a stockman I ate with the 'kitchen-class'. Out bush the scran was hard but when we came to the homestead we would be regaled with such luxuries as milk, butter, and vegetables. A real treat.

As the caste system ruled on the cattle stations so did the bush-hotels carry on the same idea. The manager and his ilk dined in a place called the 'coffee-room' and woe to any of the lower-downs who made a mistake by going into that Holy of Holies after a feed. Most certainly he would be ordered out by the pub-joint owner but should he get through the net he would be forever branded as a 'crawler' by his mates and as such would be excluded from the 'hate-sessions' about the 'top-dogs'.

Our main event during those times was 'Races Dance-night' at the bush-town's hotel. It was there that everybody got together for a good time.

The music in the galvanized-iron dance-halls was provided by concertina and mouth-organ. All the 'ringer' (stockmen) were in their Sunday-best at the start of the dancing, but the heat from hopping around had their coats off so as to have a good go.

'Races dance-time' was a time for the news. All were equal on that day when it came to having a good time in the dance-hall. Government-house men and women, 'slavies' and 'slushies' (the first so-called because they got little pay for hard work; the latter term meant a kitchen-hand, because during early shearing days the men 'slushies' were the ones who kept the fat up to the 'slush-lamps' as the toilers gambled through the night, and doing so they received a percentage cut from those who were lucky enough to win) all met on the dancing floor in a 'free for all'.

The pattern of living was as strict as that in an aboriginal tribe, each one fitted in and none intruded on the other's caste. Looking back now I somehow cannot believe that such squattocracy existed then, but strangely enough it still exists today for I know many cattle proprietors who dress for dinner and none of the lower-downs who have been invited would dare to take a seat until the Big-fellow gives them the sign.

But just before the First World War a change came as large overseas vested interests began buying up the properties that had been held over the years by individual families. As they came in, so out went the old retainers who drifted into the bush towns where they built shacks along the permanent waterhole or around a bore, to try and eke out a living on the old-age pension.

Their humpies became the centre of attraction for the stockman, who often threw off his packs under a shady tree near by, and tossing a 'Load of scran and beef' to his old pensioner mate he would settle in for the 'wet' or the slack season when the stockmen and station hands were no longer required. Thus did that area become a sort of bush theatre-stage where stories were told and re-told, so much so that they passed into the literature which is our heritage to this day.

What tales I heard then of great doings by mighty bush lovers. What laughs did I enjoy from those Rabelaisian tales and ballads.

But slowly a change came over the land. Those old-aged pensioners passed away as canned music came in, and the maudlin stuff of that time grew from bad to worse when someone discovered that gramophone needles could be played over and over if they were sharpened on an oil-stone.

Then with a roar and a blast of honking in the wake of the First World War came motors and bang went the horse-drawn coaches with their 'mail changes' which were replaced by petrol bowsers. As they went out so passed away the roadside stores, eating places and bush shanties which were pushed out of existence by speed. People were now in too big a hurry to stop and have a talk.

Horse and camel teams went the way of the rest. The old-time carriers tried to carry on but king-motor was here to stay, and only the outback places such as Wyndham in West Australia, Timbercreek on the Victoria River in the Northern Territory, Borroloola in the Gulf country, and around Alice Springs did they battle for a little while.

With them went those fascinating bush stores with their billy-cans, hobble-chains, stock-whips, and saddles hanging from the overhead beams close to the sides of bacon, gins' dresses, and all the gadgets which came into the life of the drover and cattleman. Gone too were those learned discussions on the relative quality of saddles—pack and riding, water-canteens, kangaroo-hide, and quart-pots.

By this time the movie, radio, and gramophone had taken over with new songs ranging from crooners and drug-store cowboys playing guitars surrounded by synthetic scenery—singing about their beloved broncos, six-shooters, and loved ones as they rode over the range. Australiana went out as the horse-opera came in. 'Fun in the stock-yard' became 'rodeo'. Stockyards were 'corrals', 'strides' became 'jeans'. The days of reality had departed; romance was in the air. The tough 'prads' of the cattlemen were now corn-fed 'broncs' carrying a cowboy dressed for the part across a scene made up of *papier mâché* and artificial trees. No more did cattlemen sing the old-time ballads while they rode around the resting cattle on night watch. The poems of Lawson, Banjo Patterson, Ogilvie, and Gordon slumbered in the ashes of the old-time cattle camps. They had departed with the horse and bullock teams and those old-time station cooks who ruled the roost with an iron will by virtue of their being able to cook the best bread in the country. Gone too with the cooks was their secret yeast bottle which they always carted around with their aprons and sharp carving-knives. Their glory had departed because anyone who could read labels on the tins of dried yeast powder could turn out bread equal to them.

With yeast powder came refrigerators that spelled 'out' to dried vegetables and the old Kolgardie cooler. All-weather roads gave a new lease of life to motor transport which took over from the horse-drawn wagon, and with these piled up on the junk-heap it moved out to displace the drovers. The first attack came silently as the motor trucks carted out food and vegetables to men bringing in the herds of cattle. The day of the 'bagman' (men on horses seeking work) fizzled out as the motor purveyors of foodstuffs became hawkers of picture-crank cowboys seeking work. With them came cowboy suits and chaps with brass and silver stars on bridles and around ten-gallon hats. In this scene the old-time drover faded away; the heavy motor prime-movers with trailers behind thundered through the night carrying stock to the railhead and markets, doing as many miles in twenty-four hours as the drover would do in eight weeks.

With motors doing most of the droving (or should we say transportation of cattle) the cattle stations themselves were changed over to a new form of motor mustering. This meant the fencing off of permanent waterholes so that the animals could drink only at a trough which was put in a railed yard protecting the waters. The wide gate of the fenced-in enclosure was left open, but when the cattle of that part were to be mustered, the gate was shut and the only entry into the place was through a contraption called a 'bayonet' which was built with logs having sharpened ends in the same manner as a fish-trap.

Once the cattle went inside the 'trap-yard' they could not get out. Next morning the stockmen would motor down from their camp and it was a simple matter to draft the animals they required into an adjacent yard, brand them on the bronco-panel where the motor displaced the bronco-horse, cut out any bullocks they needed for the home paddock which was a sort of holding place awaiting the motor transport for the railhead. No galloping and hard work now.

This procedure meant fewer horses needed on the cattle-run. Out of sympathy for their old-time friends the cattlemen turned the horses out to grass where they became, in time, the herds of wild horses that ravage the lands of their one-time masters. Everywhere over the land the wild herds roam. Horses, camels, and donkeys abound, and among them with racing Jeep and Land Rover are a new type of 'Brumby-shooter' shooting them down. The camels being creatures of the desert keep out into the dry lands and so escape the bullets of their former masters.

Len's call of 'All aboard' aroused me from my reveries and soon we were on the last sixty-eight-mile leg of our journey to Ayers Rock which we reached about sun-down.

Now, writing this five years later, I think of Curtin Springs and the changes that have come upon it. The place is now owned by my good friends Peter and Dawn Severin and the old spinifex-covered shed with the iron buildings around it has been pulled down.

The new place is at another well about four hundred yards north of the old. Around the homestead now are groves of athol trees—the tamerisks of Asia; everywhere is new life and only the other day a tourist came by my Ranger's cottage with greetings from Ossie and

Merv Andrews. They have departed from the old days too, for when my visitor saw them they were transporting 'fat cattle' from a cattle station to a railway siding so that they could be trucked to the markets of the south. Their motor roars through the night as the herds sway back and forth to the bumps in the road. Everything is in the process of change, but I must go back once more with the story of my first days at Ayers Rock at the tourist camp of my mate Len Tuit.

Chapter Six

First Days at the Rock

NEVER can I forget that first day I saw Ayers Rock. We had just come through a fairly big clump of mulga trees within which was a forty-gallon drum that had toppled off one of Len's trucks carting water from Curtin Springs during the dry-time of the previous year. Len had just been telling the tourists a yarn of how it was put there for the convenience of motor people who broke down on the road, and that story had everybody nattering away about the hospitality of the bush-folk.

About a mile farther on Len called out, 'There she is!' and looking in the direction he pointed I could just discern a rounded hump above the sandhills. 'Thirty more miles to go yet,' he continued. 'This is where we hit the curves of the road so hold on tight.'

The road curved all right. Now I saw the mountain on the right, then on the left and at other times dead behind. 'Sandhills,' from Len. 'Nobody has yet found a way to get over them so we will have to wait for made roads or wind around them.'

The great dome of rock rose up out of the ground like some great prehistoric leviathan surfacing from a weed-covered sea. Small wonder that first explorer Gosse wrote in his journal of 1763: 'When I was only two miles distant and the hill for the first time coming into view, what was my astonishment to find it was an immense pebble rising abruptly from the plain. . . . This rock is certainly the most wonderful natural feature I have ever seen.'

The sun was sinking fast as we sped on. It was a race between the sun setting and our getting there on time. Around we swished on the curves, and as we did I could not but admire the driver who seemed to know the exact moment to pull on the driving wheel. Here was judgement, and although we were 'hitting it up' I noticed that no one was afraid.

Finally we came out of a small range of sandhills to see the mountain on our right. On we sped through a mulga scrub; then just before we topped the rise of the last sandhill the mountain seemed to speed with us as though it would block our path. Then over the last sandhill we travelled and there she was.

I had read about this Rock and had seen many pictures of it, but never did I expect to behold a thing that was greater than what I had expected it to be. That was my first impression and it was the judgement of all the people who came out during my stay in the area. The Rock was somehow overpowering, not only to white people but to many of the aborigines who saw it for the first time. They somehow could not take their eyes away from its cliff faces or its tall peaks.

But the Rock which I saw from the sandhills was nothing to the sense of awe I felt as we sped down the road towards its southern wall. For nine hundred feet its cliff face rises steep above the trees at its base, and in the evening light, as we moved towards it, I somehow got the impression that it was toppling over towards me.

'Maggie Springs to the right,' called out Len. 'Up there under that high peak is where a policeman shot the native.'

The grim looking wall face somehow aroused my Celtic imagination. An eerie feeling came over me as I pictured a night I had in Ireland with my friend Paddy Tunny wandering around the shore of Lough Deal while he regaled me with tales of the 'Little-folk' and the brave Cuchulain who tied himself to a tree so that he could keep fighting to the death. The 'Mummu' (little-folk) of these mountains which a Loritdja aboriginal had told me about, and the leprechauns of Ireland—the aboriginal and the brave Celt—both died to uphold the law.

A jolt on the road brought my memories away from my friends of Manor Cunningham out from Letterkenny. I turned my head to look behind me at the west wall of the mountain which had now taken on a blood-red hue from the reflection of the setting sun. Ayers Rock! What a heritage we had.

About a mile to the west Len turned off the Ayers Rock–Mount Olga Road and not long afterwards we were at a galvanized-iron building which was called Tuit's Camp. This was the first trip of the year, and what a dusting of pots and pans and gathering of wood there was to make a feed. The tourists pitched in and not long afterwards we had the little beach-tents up in the exact spots they had been rigged in the year before.

Then wonder of wonders, as we sat around an aboriginal completely naked walked up with a kangaroo slung over his shoulder. He was from the west and, talking in a very difficult English, he gave us to understand that he and his clan had travelled in from there with camels. They were camped just over the sandhill and as he was returning from the hunt he had heard the motor and naturally came over to investigate.

Len Tuit knew him and called him by the name of Paddy, explaining to us that he was one of his workers from the previous year. Next morning Paddy was over to take up his duties again, but before he commenced his work he gave the tourists a demonstration of aboriginal culinary art by cooking another kangaroo he had just caught. As he went through the procedure of fire-making and cooking I took his photo against the Rock's background, the first of many I was to take.

That morning Len took the people around the base of the Rock, and naturally I was one of the party. Coming in the evening before the mountain appeared massive, but walking around it that first day I was amazed at its proportions. It seemed hard to understand its dimensions because there were no objects around to compare against it. But seeing someone walking up the 'climb' brought understanding of the size. They looked like tiny 'rock-mites' on the crest of the spur.

To gape up and take it all in was just impossible. I looked up a blood-red cliff face at a place called the 'water-fall'—without water of course—and was trying to assess its height when Len explained. To get some idea of the height he asked us mentally to put against the cliff the Sydney harbour bridge from the water to the top of the arch. At this part of his description a gentle rebuke came from a Melbourne lass, but ignoring her Len continued. Now on to this put the I.C.I. building that is in Nicholson Street, Melbourne. A proud look now comes on the Melbourne woman's face so Len goes on. The two together would not reach the top of the cliff face. At such a belittling of the two features of the main cities, both women looked hurt as though Len had put them both into a sack and had tossed them over a cliff as was the practice in the good old Roman days.

Nevertheless his description gave me and others the height. Standing at the base of that sheer cliff face I somehow felt as the poet Byron did when he 'could not deem himself a slave'.

Yet as I went around that first day I was ashamed at the terrible names that had been given to such lovely places. 'Surely,' I thought to myself, 'the aborigines of this land must have given to these places names in keeping with their way of life? How thoughtlessly do we white people destroy. Not only the customs and hunting patterns of the people, but their mythological beliefs are trampled underfoot in our endeavour to save them from a very mythical thing called 'Hell-fire'. What names I heard that day, made up, not by asking the very people who once lived in the area, but from an imagination in keeping with our own ideas.

'Napoleon's Hat' or 'the Bell', the 'Sound-shell', the 'Stairs', 'Kangaroo-tail', 'Wine-glass'—somebody with a thirsty imagination must have suggested that—then came the 'Organ-cave', 'Brain', 'Joe's hole'. There were hosts of others including a well-worn hole in a flat stone that came from one of their legends, and this was known as the 'Port-hole'.

That first day I went around the Rock with Len made me determined to ferret out the complete story of this great stone. So a few days later, when Len Tuit had returned with his party and I was alone with the desert aborigines, I was naturally asking them about the mythology of the area. Imagine my surprise when they informed me that they were as new to this land as myself. 'Our country that way,' they answered, pointing to the west. 'We Windralga people from sun-down way.' To them it was strange (and therefore taboo) until an aboriginal, from the clans who lived about this mountain, initiated them into the country. They were aborigines from the western bushlands and could speak the same Loritdja tongue as the Ayers Rock people, but, 'No initiation from one in authority, then know nothing'.

These men were first-class trackers, and knew from experience that nothing is secret to the eye of a hunter. Each footprint is known; regardless of the person's age some peculiarity of the footprint remains constant, an identification card that can be used against an intruder should they do something wrong. Thus did I, too, come to understand that the mountain of Ayers Rock was a symbol of a ritual. As such it would be the repository of their sacred and secret cults and ritual objects that relate to their ceremonies.

That day we tramped around the Rock and that same evening a utility van with some aborigines aboard pulled up before my camp. As I was going out to meet them who should get out to greet me but my old mate Albert Namitjira. He was dusty as he got out of the motor, and after taking a few of the kinks out of his back we shook hands. Then he asked me where should he camp. Being my first customer since I had become the Ranger of Ayers Rock I pointed out a clump of shady mulga trees about a hundred yards away. As I pointed I could not suppress a smile that I, a white intruder, was giving permission to a tribesman where to camp.

But my musings were cut short as he pulled a newly-killed emu from his utility and standing beside the door on which was painted the sign telling his name and occupation, he asked me would I come over later and have a feed.

I have seen my late lamented friend many times when we crossed each other's path—in cities when he went to see the Queen at Canberra, on banks of creeks where I watched him paint. We sat together in the gutters of Alice Springs when he was worrying over 'drink-business', and he and I have flown up to Darwin about his trial. He as the defendant, I to give evidence on his behalf—a futile effort because the native law of kinship is useless against our moral code. But never had I a better vision of that great man than when he stood with the emu on his shoulder before Ayers Rock and invited me to share his fare.

Did I go? Well I was there at the cooking of the giant bird, and marvelled at the culinary art of a desert man—how he dug the hole in the earth then built a good fire in the cavity; how the fat was removed and wrapped in green leaves. But why go on with these things; sufficient to know that the meal was well cooked with a real bush flavour from the lemon-scented 'irairia' kangaroo-grass which grows under the cliff faces of the mountain. This, with the gravillia leaves into which the old chef put the fat to prevent it from spoiling during the cooking made a first-class meal.

As we ate, Albert told me about his family and what great artists they were, never about himself; as he spoke he would nonchalantly wipe his greasy hands on his mop of hair as though it were a table napkin, and seeing him at it I thought of him dressed to kill at a big feast when he met the Queen. There it was a cold collation of chicken and salad with all the trimmings that go on at those parties, now he was on to something toothsome and big in the fashion of his forebears.

No doubt Albert was a big man with an emphasis on the *big*; coming as he did from a race of people whose custom was to obliterate the memory of a deceased one, he became known because he was an artist of repute. He had no stepping-stones to help him as with many white people who always trundle their ancestors around with them to seek favours.

Next day Albert went westward, where? Well it was his business and I knew better than to ask. But his visit to the Rock had great repercussions among the Loritdja Elders. I heard snippets now and then, but one thing I do know: the great Aranda painter never visited the Rock again. It was not his tribal country.

The Ranger gives formal permission, but over all is the tribesmen who have the last say as to which aboriginal will come and go in their territory.

On Len Tuit's return he brought out with him Mrs Tuit, and if ever a woman deserved credit it was she. Driving the coach, cooking meals, and getting up in the morning before the crows to have Len and his workers out on the job was just a part of her daily chores. Now she took over the welfare of the camp; with her on the job, Len and the chaps he had working for him, worked hard at getting permanent water so that fixed camps could be built. Water! All our thoughts were on this main essential. Len was seeking a suitable site for a bore but as none had been put down in that part he had no guide to go by. We had the uncertain water supply from Maggie Spring on the southern face of Ayers Rock, but when it failed, as it did those first few months of my arrival, five-ton trucks with forty-gallon drums aboard had to go to Curtin Springs for the staple fluid. As Curtin Springs was nearly seventy miles away this meant rationing the water, and water in short supply meant discontented tourists.

The final straw that forced Len to seek water was when Maggie Springs went dry. In the past water could be found by digging a well in the sand but the nomads with their camels were hard at work seeking the water when we arrived to put down the well, and by the looks on their faces we could tell they had drawn a blank.

The camels were resting on the top of the bank as we came up, and they looked at us with that strange philosophical look which is a part of their make-up. To them the days were cool and the nights cold; as creatures of the desert they subsisted on the succulent herbage and brush around. The aborigines too were desert men. They had water in their canteens and being mobile they could always go to other watering places. Len also had tanks and drums of water around the camp, enough to tide us over for some time. The drying water was nevertheless a sign that unless permanent water was obtained around the Rock the tourist resorts could never increase.

'Pity we couldn't get some of those shrewd guys of the moving pictures that always find water in the desert,' said Len. 'They never miss.'

Never miss! So much flap-doodle against reality. Looking down on the aborigines resting on the dry sand after their futile work I could not but smile at one of them who had featured in one of these scenes. To Muturu this was the real thing. 'Before just nothing,' he laughingly told me as I quizzed him about the scene—the setting up of the camera for the best shot that would reveal the bush at its worst; the building up of the 'set' (a hole in the ground for the native well, a four-gallon tin full of water within it to be the supply). Next came a paper covering over the tin and this was covered with a light layer of earth. Then the Director called out 'Camera,' and the scene begins. The primitive aborigine seeking water by the signs on the ground, the hero and heroine staggering behind, the scooping out of that life-saving fluid as all bless the rain-gods, and the wonderful bushcraft of the aborigines.

'Not like that picture now'? I called out gaily; as I did so the ex-actor, bit-player looked up and answered, 'Longa picture always get water, here nothing.'

Getting up on to his feet he went over to his camels and soon they were away to new hunting grounds. Watching them Len remarked, 'Well, lads, this isn't the pictures but we're going to have a go at getting the water.'

A few days later some rain came in from the west to fill Maggie Springs, but we had been given the warning.

In a few days Len went over to Angus Downs on his way to Alice Springs. There he saw Arthur Little about a boring plant which Arthur told him he could use for the job. On the next trip out with tourists he told me that Arthur was coming out with the plant, and he was getting Merv Andrews of Curtin Springs to do the job.

Chapter Seven

Road out to the Rock

ROLLING out my swag on to the ground beside Len's camp and laying back for a night's sleep after returning from trying to get water at Maggie Springs, I could see the Milky Way overhead (always associated with the black-man's mythology, as a river or road) and gazing at it my thoughts travelled back to the bush highway over which we had been travelling.

For two-hundred and seventy miles it snaked over the land, now off to a cattle station, then around some sandhill to pass by a well or windmill, its path twisting and turning to keep to the good places. As it did I thought of how the tribesmen believed that the great Serpent of their ritual was he who made the rivers and their way of life.

The Finke River was one of these serpent highways. Anthropologists tell us that thousands of years ago northern tribes migrated from the north-east into the Finke oases system. Increasing in numbers they slowly spread out into the Macdonnell Ranges to form the tribes of the Centre.

As the rivers were the way of life then, so they remain today. The trading paths of the tribesmen went from native well to rock-hole over the land. Explorers drank from these places and white cattlemen put their cattle-station homesteads beside them. They are still there today, but try and find out who was the first white person to 'break the track' and one is up against a passive wall not unlike that which is encountered when asking aborigines questions about their sacred and secret rituals.

When looking for information about the Ayers Rock road I met this strange wall. From the Alice to Henbury the road was one to carry out supplies from the railhead after the old Finke River road was 'out' with the coming of motors and the passing away of the camel trains, just as the Oodnadatta–Henbury road was a carry-over from the old buggy and wagon days. In the same way were other roads cut out with the introduction of speed.

For just as the aborigines used the Finke River as a water supply-path during their migrations ages ago, so did the travellers and teamsters use it before the days of extensive boring over the land.

The junction of the Tempe Downs road to Angus Downs was the beginning of the Ayers Rock track.

What tribulation did those early road-makers have in cutting these tracks: dust and sweat was theirs in abundance; walking ahead and then retracing their footsteps when they found the going too heavy; cutting of trees to get through some heavy scrub; travelling for water, then conserving it as something greater than life itself.

I can picture old Abe Andrews and his daughter Gladys moving out with camel wagon prospecting and hacking out a track from that Mount Quinn, back in the days of Bob Buck and Alf Butler—the same Mount Quinn which is called by the aborigines Kalair-Djunda or 'Emu Thigh', a term commonly used amidst the Loritdja people and always denoting plenty of food in the vicinity.

Travelling over that road today I still marvel at their fortitude and courage up until as recently as 1946. It was heavy going through a dry land, yet they hacked away finally to connect another bush road, cut through by Merv Andrews and his nephew Ray from Angus Downs to Curtin Springs in 1944.

Slowly and surely are roads made, by trial and error through deep sand patches and heavy mulga scrub. Out of their efforts in the past the roads were built so that tourists could visit the land.

Yet long before the road-makers, explorers, anthropologists, and surveyors moved through the country with camels, buggy, and dray. Arthur Groom mentions in his book, which was written in 1948, that he saw motor tracks in the bush on the road to Ayers Rock. Kurt Johannsen had a motor truck far beyond Ayers Rock when he went with the Mark Foy party that searched for Lasseter's gold in the early thirties.

Michael Terry went out that way in 1933. Frank Quinn a little later, but they went the longer way around the Lake Amadeus.

The first man to take a truck in a fairly direct line was Sidney Stanes of Erldunda Cattle Station who took out a party to Ayers Rock in 1944.

A few years later Len Tuit was travelling out from the Finke siding with tourist parties. At that time the total number to visit Ayers Rock for the year was twelve. My last year as a Ranger in the area the number was over four thousand.

At first the roads followed the wheel tracks of Sid Stanes' motor. The going was terrible till the Department of Works at Alice Springs sent out a grader to level the surface. This was in 1953, and the man who performed that difficult task was Mark Gheel. What a job he did with that heavy machine. To try and straighten out the curves the Department gave him a Land Rover to test the sandhills, but try as he did he never broke down the hills which remained till 1960 when the same Department of Works sent out surveyors to straighten the road—a difficult task in that dry land, for the new-made roads became wind-swept in the dry year of 1961, and when I left the area the old Stanes road was still the highway into the Rock.

So are the roads of a country made out of the sweat of many people, known and unknown. The grader levels out the highway and after a time the travellers complain about the dust that gets into their cars. Everyone speeds and this makes new corrugations that cause more complaints. The rains come on and they bog in the mud. Everyone complains about the twists in the road, but should they come upon a fallen tree or branch across the way they try to get around the object and often put up a wail should they get bogged in the sand while doing so.

These incredible 'Clever-fellows', as the aborigines call those who will not stick to the rules of the road, were always seeking assistance from me or other fellow travellers after being bogged down hopelessly away from the hard well-beaten road. Their excuse was always the same: 'They thought the ground was hard.' In desperation I penned a verse for all new arrivals to read as they were issued a permit in the Reserve's board office. Some smiled as they commented about the doggerel but it did get results and I was happy.

> The clever-one so full of vim
> That graded roads are not for him;
> He tears down brush till bogged is he,
> Then claims the law 'Bush-courtesy';
> He sits and drives, we push and strain
> To get the Lordling free again,
> Then off he'll tear, he does not care,
> Obliging fools are everywhere.

The roads are made with sweat but many of them are lined with tragedy. Those sandhills west of the Finke have taken their toll of human life. A young man with a motor bike just out from Erldunda was caught in the heavy sand and perished. And two years after my job as Ranger death struck on the 'Mad-mile' over which we first travelled on our way to the 'incredible pebble'.

The day was December and hot, the sands ran like quick-lime when their utility stuck fast in the heavy going for many days. They could have stayed by their truck till help came, but the loneliness of the place had them walking for assistance which was twenty-seven miles away at Angus Downs. What happened to them was revealed by their footprints on the sand to the white men who came upon the dying dehydrated body of one beside the road. Charles Rye who found them told me how they walked over twenty miles on the road to Angus Downs then for some unknown reason turned on their tracks to come back to the truck. The water they had carried in a can with them was finished, but they did not live to drink their reserve water back in the motor.

The 'Mad-mile' carries memories for me too, for along it on my last year as a Ranger at Ayers Rock I walked with a mate called Doug to ask assistance for a broken-down coach full of passengers.

This short-cut, as it was called, was an unknown quantity at the opening of the 1961 tourist season. The coach, with its passengers was scheduled to go out along the longer Erldunda route but after smoko at the Finke the coach-captains Roy and Doug received advice from a traveller that he had come the short-cut and it was good going.

All went well till we were nearing the 'Mad-mile' twenty-eight miles from Angus Downs when two rear wheel tyres went flat and on pulling out the tool-box the drivers found the patching outfit was missing.

Each coach carried a portable wireless, but a bump in the road had apparently put it out of action so there we were, broken down and without the radio to call for assistance.

Only one thing to do: wait, but for how long? Twenty passengers were on board, six gallons of water and six two-dozen cartons of beer intended for the people along our route. We had a talk over the matter then decided that Doug and I would travel through the night to Angus Downs to try and get assistance.

Doug and I carried half a gallon of water and took things easy during that long cool night and about daylight we arrived at Angus Downs.

Yet as Doug and I walked through the night quite a lot of things were happening in the world outside our mulga and sandhills.

Dawn Severin of Curtin Springs, who had a fixed wireless schedule with the coach and the tourist people in Alice Springs, always kept contact with them so that all could have a drink of tea and cakes when they arrived at her place. Their time of arrival was about four in the afternoon but as we did not arrive she called over the air on the wireless.

The answering reply came, not from Alice Springs but from air-radio Sydney. She explained to them what was wrong and they in turn contacted air-radio Adelaide. From Adelaide the message went over a land line to Alice Springs. Back and forth went the messages for a distance of over fifteen thousand miles. The final message was to ask would she contact her husband Peter and get him to look for the lost coach-load of passengers.

Now Peter Severin took up the search, but he too went on the wrong Erldunda Road and only when he was returning did he decide to visit Angus Downs to arrive there about the same time as Doug and I.

With this news of the passengers' whereabouts Peter returned to Curtin Springs and arriving there was told that a relief bus was on the way out to the broken-down vehicle.

Hearing the full story later I was told that thirty-six people had relayed the messages over half of Australia, everyone worrying over us, yet all the time Doug and I were just plodding along the bush track and thinking we had been forgotten.

The passengers did not seem to care for all had a good time on the one hundred and forty odd cans of beer after the water gave out. A friend of mine who was with the coach told me that some of the non-drinking ones hung out till midnight, but when they got going the party was a real cracker show. Beer cans were everywhere and these could still be seen alongside the road when we returned at the end of the season, in spite of the drift-sand which was slowly burying them.

And talking of parties my greatest memory of that night was when we arrived at Angus Downs at the first peep of dawn. We called out to Jack Killeen, who was in charge at the time, but mistaking our parched voices for some nomadic aborigines who were continually pestering him, he told us in no uncertain terms to 'Go to hell'.

We then called our names and as we did he was out of bed in a flash to boil the billy and cook us a cracker meal.

The roaas of the bush and the hospitality one often finds along those highways! Tragedy and humour. Now my initiation to the Ayers Rock road was behind; a life for the years ahead was here at this National Park. *Park* did I write? Water was still to be found. Water! The night of Arthur Little bringing his boring plant to the Rock was full of interest. How we talked, and that night as I lay on my swag with the outline of the boring plant against the Rock, my thoughts turned to the supply we hoped to get. Thinking thus I fell into a deep sleep to be awakened by Len's morning call of 'Daylight, lads! We've got a long way to go so we better get moving'.

Chapter Eight

Water, Lodges, and Camps

We know you love to paddle in the water as you roam,
Your complex urges you to wash your feet;
But leave the smelly 'Mud-hooks' for the table water, home,
This drinking-water's ours and 'Plates-of-meat'
Encased in grubby 'Toe-jam' is not sweet.

THIS was my first burst into verse as a means of relieving my pent-up feelings when I found a woman tourist washing her feet in Maggie Springs, our only drinking-water for seventy miles. When I told her off she reckoned I wasn't a gentleman. What I thought of her went into the little piece of doggerel which I hung up outside my Ranger's tent so that others could read and heed.

Of all the trite sayings in this world the greatest is that one about 'water is life'. Every creature on this earth knows that one, even the fish that swim in it. The very first legend I heard at Ayers Rock was about the black stains on the face of the dome which symbolized life and birth because they were caused by running water in the rain-time.

To Len Tuit, who only dealt with practical things, water, and plenty of it, meant a fixed camp for an ever-expanding trade. Over past years the people of the Alice looked upon tourists as folk who came, gazed around for a short while, then went on their way without spending money, and as most people in this world are judged by the gifts they bring in they (in bush parlance) 'gave them away'. But progress must go on. The mountains around the Centre became places of interest. Touring companies began in a small way. Coaches pounded over the roads and camped under trees when they could not get suitable accommodation in the town. Out of it all came realization that here was wealth coming in nearly equal to that which was going out. Small shops selling foodstuffs, and all the gadgets which go into the tourist trade, sprung up behind petrol bowsers. Tourism was the order of the day. The cattle-station owners cursed the tourists because they shot at every animal they passed by, including blackfellows, pack-donkeys, camels, and blood stallions which they thought were wild horses. Even I came into the cursing when they bathed and polluted our main water supply.

So, on the adapted adage that 'Water is trade', Len was on the job looking for a sub-artesian bore and good water for his camp.

In this land where no other bore-hole had been put down it was just a matter of picking a suitable camp-site for the proposed 'Truit Lodge', or whatever it was going to be called.

The place selected was on the eastern side of the Rock about five miles east from his existing camp—the reason being that the tourists could see the sunrise on the mountain without moving away from the camp area.

To this place the boring plant was pulled by a motor truck, and if ever a person raved about the ingenuity of the bushmen building things from the materials around them, they had good reason to be proud of the boring-rig which was pulled into position over the site picked out by Len.

How did they pick out the place? Well they just marked out the area beside a large rabbit warren that showed grey earth, and that sufficed. Bush knowledge was the order of the day. Water-diviners and geologists all took a back seat when it was discovered that all were blind to what was beneath the earth. The geologist could tell once he was acquainted with the strata of a country. Diviners were loath to test themselves on virgin ground so they kept to areas where a plentiful supply of water had been found beneath the earth. But all of them, geologists, diviners and drillers, were on a fifty-fifty basis when it came to a new locality which was covered by a heavy top-soil.

'The drill-bit is the best diviner,' said Merv as he shovelled out a hole beneath the hanging bit in preparation for the job. 'Nobody is sure till the water is found, then they all know it was there.'

Now everything was set with the drill-rig over the site. I went over to give it a 'once-over'. What a contraption was here to open up a new land and industry!

Its base-stand was the chassis of an old motor truck that had seen much travelling over this country. To this was attached the tall derrick made up of part-adzed bush timber, with discarded wheels from old wells which were used for the bull-wheels. The 'walking-beam' was made from sturdy well-dressed desert-oak. The power plant to work the outfit was a Southern Cross diesel tied on one end of the chassis with bolts at first, but these had now broken loose and were replaced by the good old Cobb and Co. twitch.

Bush-craft and adaptability was in that old boring plant, and it had opened up much land during its life. Home-made from the things around, it is abandoned now because, in this nonchalant age, the things which should be in museums are cast on junk-heaps and are slowly pulled to pieces as iron is required for some other purpose or left to rot away.

When everything was in position the engine was started and with a clang the drill-bit struck into the earth after water. Yet strangely enough we had to cart water to get water, for the drill bit required moisture to keep the slush moving in the bottom of the hole. Every now and then the bit would be lifted and the sand-pump—a long four-inch pipe column with a valve on one end—would be lowered into the bore-hole to clean out the tailings. Up would come the sand-pump with its load, the valve would be dropped on to a peg in the ground and out would run the slush. More water would be added to the dry hole, the drill lowered and away the walking-beam would go, on to the job.

Watching them at their work and listening to the pounding drill I could not but think of how Moses smote the rock with his rod that water came out for the people. To read that passage from the Bible to a Centralian cattleman would bring on no argument, for the occurrence is an everyday event in their lives.

Merv Andrews, probing with a crowbar and breaking through the limestone wall of 'Djulu' well at Curtin Springs cattle station, and finding himself waist-deep in cool fresh water, could see no reason to doubt the Good Book, but he would be one of the first to deny that Moses' feat was a miracle.

The miracle was how the aborigines came upon these hidden desert waters, and how the rough mental maps were orally plotted by the song-men of the tribe, and then afterwards by the white bushmen who plodded wearily along the trails of the tribesmen.

Merve told me how his nephew Ray, who knew the Loritdja tongue, came, by ordinary conversation, to learn about the waters to the west of their place at Andalyu. The elders of the tribe and the whites just sat beneath a mulga tree. As was the usual practice of the aborigines they would now and then call the names of distant waters, pointing as they did in that direction. Hearing the word 'Djulu' they plotted it by compass on to a map. Thus did they determine the locality of the place with its mythological history.

Water! How it stirs the imagination of those who know from experience that on its supply and mineral content does a country prosper or become an arid wasteland.

Now here at Ayers Rock the walking-beam went pounding away at the new bore-hole. Man, who must have more and more water for his needs, must break away from the ancient pattern as laid down by the aboriginal creative heroes and search in new places for what he requires. What anxious moments each day as something occurred to cause misgiving! A boulder at the bottom had Merv sharpening his chisel-bit to enable it to bite into and remove the obstruction, grumbling all the while that the outfit has no 'star-bit' to enable him to keep the plant going.

How easy to write about sharpening the bit, yet to do it Merv had to turn to improvisation. First of all some charcoal was made from bloodwood trees felled, cut into lengths, partly burnt, then covered with a sheet of iron and earth to prevent them from burning into an ash. When ready the clean black charcoal was gathered into a drum and carried into a forge made from a cut-down forty-gallon drum. The fire was now lit, and with the engine going flat out to speed up the blower, the fire was soon off to a fine blaze. Then on went the charcoal which had to cover the drill-bit to be sharpened. Merv sprinkled a little water now and then to stop the flames from coming through into the open.

While the bit was being heated up Merv put up the 'dressing-post' into which the drill-bit would rest while the 'bit-face' was dressed. The dressing-post was a green bloodwood one sunk upright in the ground about four feet from another bit which acted as an anvil. A length of chain was used to enable the driller's offsider to turn the hot bit during the dressing process. The modern driller may smile at this and talk of electric spotting to dress the drill-bit, but those things were hundreds of miles away, the ground below hard, and the job urgent.

Each foot of rock passed through was tested by washing the pulverized tailings in an endeavour to find out something about the rock the bit was passing through. Everything was just blind stabbing. The depth and content of the water could be known only when the job was completed. When the practical driller was on the job the 'experts' came to explain where he was wrong and what he ought to do.

Diviners were on the prowl with intent looks on their faces, and the evidence of their art in their hands. All were right as regards the water below, but they never 'found' water where the drill-rig was, for somehow they never seemed to select the same 'divined-spot' as the diviners who had come before them.

At eighty-seven feet it was found the drill-bit was passing through layers of rock containing water in small supply. Then, when pulling the drill-bit up for the use of the slush-pump, it was discovered that the bit had become unscrewed and was now at the bottom of the hole.

To get it out Merv improvised a fishing-tool from a short length of casing and a piece of spring-steel, but soon found that the bit was leaning over towards the side of the hole and thus required a different type of tool. This meant a trip to Alice Springs, where he was fortunate enough to borrow what he wanted from Ginti Gorey and Sandy Cole, two well-known Centralian drillers.

This improvisation of fishing-tools always interested me. They ranged from wicked looking barbed spears for rescuing cables, to cunning contraptions difficult to explain. The one Merv and Len used was

Myself at the Rock at sunrise

Headwaters of the Finke River

"The Mulu with his severed nose looks with passive face"

a short length of casing cut along its length for about a foot and then bent out as a flange, the principle being for the extended part to go around the inclined bit as an arm would go around a person's waist. This would stand the bit upright so that the casing could be lowered over it.

After each job we sat down for a spell. Arthur's wife Bessie gave us a drink of tea and this we had beneath some shady mulga trees beside the bore-hole.

Our conversation during smoko varied. Len told us what sort of a place he was going to build. Arthur talked of going over to the Rock on our way back to the night camp to gather some 'ingulba' (native tobacco) for an old aboriginal woman back at Angus Downs. Bessie and her little son John were intently watching the antics of some honey-ants that were busily gathering the nectar from pink-coloured fuchsia flowers on a bush nearby. So we went each day. Morning would have us from the old camp to the bore-site. I would then go on to my duties should there be tourists about. Everything was still up in the air as regards camping sites. Water was the order of the day; till we found it we must listen to the clanging of the 'jars' above the drill-bit, as the walking-beam beat out its primitive tune—a rhythm that set me off into verse.

The bush is full of clattering noise when the walking-beams resound,
The derrick shakes as the drill-bit quakes to a crazy ragtime jog.
One hundred feet in the earth below the drill and the jars rebound
As the driller feels the slackening rope and gives her an extra cog.

Our bits are sharp and the rock is hard, down in the earth below,
With sink-bar, jars and drilling-bit, lever and walking-beam.
Covered in dust we earn our crust, for this is a job we know;
The work is ours and the water yours as soon as we tap the stream.

The engine roars a steady beat as the belt goes whirring round
The drill comes up and the slush-pump down to give us a clearer hole,
A welcome sight for the sludge runs white where water streams abound—
The stream is here but the bit goes on to reach its final goal.

The dust is over our bodies now, but water is down below,
We'll wash it off as we test the bore and hope for a mighty stream.
The driller is first to open the land, for he makes the country glow,
His song of water can ever be heard in the crash of the walking-beam.

'Water is here,' the drill-bit calls from the gurgling stream below;
'Water' the jars of steel sink-bars re-echo to us above
Who stand in the heat, where the engine-beat tells us that we must know.
Whilst walking beams clang through the land the herds shall outward move.

We drillers are now on that fringe of land untouched for a million years,
Where blackman's well and rock-hole dry beneath a scorching sun.
Our drill-rig jumps as our bits go down to the chatter of gnashing gears,
And over this land shall windmills stand for us when our race is run.

What a to-do when Merv gave out the news water had been tapped. How we waited for the cleaning out of the hole of the well sump. Then came that fateful moment as Len put up the pannikin to his lips. He lowered the mug, looked around on us and spoke, 'She's a good drop . . . she's fresh water . . . we're on the "pig's-back".'

Did we give a cheer. Merv was trying to look unassuming. Everybody was happy. Our cries brought over some hunting aborigines, and seeing them Merv held a mirror so that the reflected light from its beam lit up the water in the bore. Each one in turn peeped down. 'Kapi' they called to each other. For them the days of no water around Ayers Rock had passed; we were now entering into a different age.

We measured the supply to find out that it was only seventy gallons an hour—not much when compared with the larger bores that deliver it in thousands of gallons—but it was water and it was fresh. To go down after a bigger supply might run into salt. Len decided to make do with the water in the bore-well which would give the camp seventeen hundred gallons a day.

I am writing this five years later when the Reserve has an assured supply of water. Capable men such as Sandy Cole and Jim Yeatman have put down bores which now yield fifteen hundred gallons an hour. Their plant was one of the new type capable of going down to big depths, but each time I see the tripod over the old bore at the tourist's resort I always think of Arthur Little's bush-made plant beating the earth to give us joy beyond all understanding.

With the coming of water Len got stuck into things with a will. The merry Tuit lads Ian, Peter, and Joe came out with trucks carrying building materials, with them came the tourists, a trickle at first but enough to keep the 'Pot-boiling' while the camp was being shifted to its present site.

Now what a bustle and hustle as Mrs Tuit joined into the fray. Slowly the camp area was cleared of all grass and spinifex. The old buildings at the western camp were removed and put up on the new site. One day the tourists had breakfast in the old camp, lunch under the overhanging cliffs of Ayers Rock. By night they had dinner at the new Lodge where they slept in small beach tents overnight.

Now came my turn to select a suitable camp-site from which I could control the area in the future. As the main road into the reserve led over a sandhill about half a mile to the south of Len's Lodge, I went down that way to erect my tent under some shady mulga trees—a place which later went under the high sounding title of the Ayers Rock–Mount Olga National Park office. My term of office as Ranger was from the end of March to the end of September. Although my title was that of a 'Ranger' I was down on the wages sheet as a 'caretaker'. Since that time I have been called everything from custodian to guardian of the Rock.

Len Tuit had obligingly told me that should I want transport at any time his coaches would take me around. He also mentioned that while I was in the area I could have my meals at the lodge. I accepted his hospitality with a proviso that I would escort parties around the Rock. Len kept his word and I kept mine.

From small ideas come fruitfulness. Taking parties around the mountain I soon discovered that my knowledge of the area was nil. People came to my tent to have a drink of tea. Drinking it we would talk about the Rock. As the Ranger I was supposed to know, and I somehow felt ill at ease during the questioning. From many tourists I learnt about the trees and birds. At night I would sit beside my drum camp-fire to see the stars drop one by one over the crest of the dome. One moment they were shining, the next they were off as though a fire-fly had fluttered down the sky. Each cold night had me wandering around listening to the 'badin-badins' whistling amidst the spinifex. The aborigines said they were a sort of legless lizard; a white scientist called them 'sand-swimmers'.

Once I heard them calling quite near me but when I stole out upon them their piping ceased with an abruptness that made me think I was an intruder in some Pandean glade.

As I was half a mile from the tourist lodge my only companions were the travellers. My camp-fire was the tree of knowledge; from them I heard stories from other lands. They seemed to me in the same tradition as the gipsies and tinkers I had met overseas. They were the motley who preferred freedom to the endless round of home-life. The women seemed to be free from any inhibitions and all the time I was at the Rock I never came across a crank.

Those first years at the Rock were great days for me. Everything was 'new' as the aborigines say. Yet ever the people came and went their way. A human tide flooding and ebbing on a sea of trees and sand. Now they would dash upon the Rock, pause awhile then retreat. They went on their way but the old incredible pebble remained. As old as time, perhaps older. Watching it by night it always challenged me; the days brought wonderment at its play of colours. Sitting in my tent under the mulga trees I soon realized how ignorant I was of the country around. As a Ranger of Ayers Rock I must answer all the questions. Who shall tell me the story? Then I thought of my old aboriginal mate Kudekudeka sitting on his horse in the bed of the Finke River. Only one lot of people knew the riddle of Ayers Rock and they were the Elders of the Loritdja tribe. My mate Kudekudeka had the story and he wished to come out to the place he always called 'Uluru', after the great serpent who is the knower of all things.

Chapter Nine

Around the Rock

I HAD already written away to my friends in the right places about the geology, history, and botany of the Centre and Ayers Rock, but still the ritual story of the aborigines remained a secret to me. So after the night of decision I wrote away to the district Welfare Office in Alice Springs and as a result of our correspondence, my old aboriginal friend Kudekudeka came out my way to breathe life once again into his tribal land.

It was a cool afternoon when the tourist bus pulled up before my tent as the coach captain called out gaily that he had some of my mates aboard. Going over I was met by outstretched hands as the two elderly men got off the coach and came towards me.

Kudekudeka introduced me to his mate Imalung who had been a one-time police tracker but in his old age was pensioned off. Then we unloaded—from a rack on top of the bus—a vast array of stores, tents, beds, and other gear. As the coach went on its way to the tourist camp we began to talk.

I was real pleased to meet them for they had been born near by. How they talked away in their native tongue, sometimes lowering their voices or using the sign-talk language associated with taboos. Soon they were 'dug-in' as it were. Imalung became the cook with Kudekudeka the general factotum of the camp. Next came the setting up of the tables and a listing of the foodstuffs which went under the title of 'rations' sent out by the Welfare Branch for these peoples' need. The list was varied, and never in my life had I seen such an array. While we were checking over the supplies a bush mate of mine, who was working for Len, strolled into camp. Knowing he was one of the old timers who thought aboriginal food was the good old corned beef and damper I called out the list as we checked them off. 'Pineapple juice, butter, cheese, tinned fruit, and vegetables.' At first he thought

I was joking but when I held up each article as it was mentioned, calling out some non-existing ones such as ice-cream powder and jelly crystals —things which could not have been used as I had no refrigerator—he 'Done-his-block' to declare angrily that the 'Government was spoiling the blacks . . . a waste of good tucker'—this with all the time-honoured phrases that go with cheap labour conditions. When I replied about the money which is wasted on wars and the preparation for war he snorted, like a horse with his head in a nose-bag, declaring something about there will always be people at one another's throats.

I could have told him that the aborigines had been going many years but were not a warring people. But I knew it was useless to argue with the old chap who had fixed ideas on the matter of aborigines and their place in our society.

The two old aborigines just kept on with making their camp. They knew what the other was saying but had learned from experience that the white people wanted to be in the right, so they let him go on.

'Him just jealous that blackfellow eat good tucker,' said Imalung after my mate had departed. 'Plenty whitefellow like that . . . give we scrap from dish all-a-same dog.' Then critically he added, 'That day finished . . . gone.'

Their camp site was but a short distance away from mine. In the first few evenings, I would go over to them for a talk, but soon discovered they slept completely naked through the night with their swags rolled out on the ground and a sheet of calico as a bedspread on top as a sheet. Thus did my arrival put them ill at ease so that they would toss a blanket over their nakedness until I departed. They were too polite to tell me to go, but I took the hint and left them to their own customs.

This sleeping naked intrigued me. I knew from experience that natives never wore clothes in the bush away from the confines of our civilization, but I just could not understand why they never tossed a rug over themselves when the nights became cold. Later I learned from visiting scientists that ages of living in the nude had developed in these people a sort of metabolism that helped them in cold climates. The old saying of the bushmen that when a native sleeps he dies was correct. They did die—at times so well that the camp-fires beside their sleeping places often gave them terrible burns.

Nature builds up strange protective forces within us all in its endeavour to protect the human race. We whites have grown away from that time. So we cover ourselves with too much clothing. My aboriginal friends were close to nature. Seeing them at their camp resting contentedly on their swags with a small fire on each side so as to get their warmth from it, and not from the swag, I wondered did this metabolism arise from the weather or did this 'dead-sleep' business come from a sense of security in the fact that they did not fear invading armies that would destroy the tribe. This much I do know from experience. Tribes in secure places sleep peacefully but those who are often raided are always alert.

This deep-sleep, so I was told, came about by their sleep-consciousness keeping below the body temperature and this continued until the sleeper became dormant. I have seen drunks go through the same process as when a mate of mine toppled over on a frosty night that would have killed a sober person. In the morning he was white with frost, stiff and in pain, but as the sun rose he thawed out and got on to his feet to start back for camp—when I came upon him. Strangely enough he was little the worse for his experience and after he had a drink of tea and a good nip of rum, he was up and doing once more.

After a day of resting—and getting adjusted to their country once more—my two mates and I were around the Rock, me to listen, they to tell me the full story of its mythology. I drew a blank the first day for all they did was to just walk to 'look-look-nothing', a term which meant they were trying to get the 'feel' of the mountain.

I had learned from working with aborigines all over the Northern Territory that impatient questions would only bring on vague answers. The true tribesman has learned from experience of white people that many questioners are happy to get the answers they desire. It is not the truth that many want but an answer which will fall in with their theories. A leading question is fatal for that will give the informant what one requires, so the 'rot' begins. I have been led up this 'blind-alley' many times, and I was determined this time to let them talk freely.

To interrupt brings false knowledge. The tale must be told as it was meant to be told by the song-men over the ages—this part first and each proceeding song-cycle coming in its appointed place. One thing the aborigine has learned over the years with white people: to know one thing and answer it correctly brings on another question, and only by not understanding the primary question can they get peace from the endless questioning.

This was brought home forcibly to me when some intruder at a big ritual kept interrupting the ceremony by asking questions about sacred matters. As politeness is the order of the day with these rituals, I saw an Elder go over to the offending one to whisper something in his ear. Shortly afterwards the pair of them disappeared into the bush and as they did an anthropologist friend of mine, who was the leader of our party, gave a smile and nodded in the direction they went.

I had seen this sort of thing before and recognized it as the aboriginal's method of politely getting rid of unwanted white people. The unwitting one was about to be made a 'blood-brother'. He would be 'led up the garden path' till they were out of the sacred area. At a chosen spot he would be initiated into the so-called mysteries of the tribe. After the exchange of presents, a good one from the white fellow and some useless trinket from the black, then back they would come to the 'ring-place' just as the ceremony was over.

I know what I am talking about with this 'blood-brother-business', for I too was once led up this same 'garden path', had an Elder blow into my ears, was given a frightful lot of blows with a green bush, then brought back elated into the camp only to be disillusioned when a mate of mine explained it all to me.

With my two aboriginal friends I was fortunate in that we had plenty of time, and the fact they were working for the Welfare Branch who was paying them wages. This made everybody happy and they were only too eager to get on with the job about their 'Proper good country that was now before them'.

Our first day was, as mentioned before, just a quiet stroll around the great Rock with its circumference of five-and-a-half miles. In silence we walked, and passing by Maggie Springs I noticed that Kudekudeka and Imalung both averted their heads from the dome. Only later did I discover that this was a form of sorrow and respect for the spirits within the mountain, and a recognition to the Wanambi serpent who is said to live in the wooded valley which is a sort of tributary to the main ravine which flows into Maggie Springs below.

I soon came to realize that my two companions had been so long away from the mountain on 'white-man's-business' that they had got out of touch with tribal affairs. They were hard pressed to remember the places relating to the chant-songs of the mountain, for although they had attended the ritual relating to this Rock, in other places over the Centre, it was extremely difficult to know where the chants would begin. They were as in a dream fumbling amidst the memories of the past. They were awaiting the sign which would reveal to them, just as it was revealed to the song-men of creative times, where to begin and the sequence of the song-cycles.

This Ayers Rock, or to give it its correct title of Uluru, as it was known to the Loritdja aborigines, was the main ritual stone relating to the Loritdja creative times. Within it, resting and waiting, were those mythological heroes of old who came into this country at the dawn of time. To the ritual Elders it was a sort of memory-fix in a similar manner to those message sticks carried from friend to friend among the tribes. I myself had often carried message sticks when I was a patrol officer in the Native Affairs Branch of the Northern Territory. The procedure was for one person to give me the letter stick, explain to me each line, and on handing this over to the receiver I would put it into their hand as I repeated the message.

Thus was Ayers Rock the tribal message stick for the great ritual, which I learnt afterwards was that of the Earth-mother. Around its side were the crags, valleys, shelters, and rock-holes which symbolized the ritual. As I had been given the message stick then I was authorized to tell the story, so also was the initiate given the song-chants by a tribal Elder, giving it to him as each prominent part of the mountain was pointed out. Thus did the songs last over the ages. The tribes-people of that time passed away, others came and went their way, but the Rock remained with its story.

Oral tradition was the aboriginal's book of law in that pre-literate age, just as in ancient times our own ancestors used the same method when teaching the youth of their times. In those times, old age was respected because it meant authority and wisdom, but in this age of speed the youth have overrun us in the race called progress.

But here with my Loritdja friends I was in the past. Watching them prying and peering around my mind recalled the great song-men I had encountered over the Northern Territory. They dreamt their songs, often on the grave of a departed song-man, dreamt them just as other song-men in other lands had their songs revealed to them in dreams, and thus gave to the world some of its greatest literature. The heritage those overseas song-men gave to us is with us here with the aborigine. Anthropologists, writers, and poets have done a lot to preserve it, but much has been lost through the years. I have read that in the ancient times there were three phases in making of poetry. That of 'revelation', then 'waiting', and 'decision'. I was to discover that here at the Rock we find the same laws.

We had been tramping a lot around the Rock one cool day and had just passed around that place which is known to the whites as the Climb because it is up that spur that tourists go to reach the crest. A little farther on we entered a smoke-blackened shelter which had been made by a very large rock toppling down the mountain. On the left-hand side of the shelter as we went inside was a crude painting of an emu hunt. Here I was soon to discover was the cave of 'revelation', the Climb above it was the 'Webo', the 'tail or crouching body of the Mala' (kangaroo-men) who revealed the first song-chants.

We boiled the billy at the cave's entrance and as it boiled away my old aboriginal friends began the first of the chanting. Kudekudeka, as the senior member of the party, therefore the main Elder, opened up the chants, low at first then louder as he was joined by Imalung. The cave shelter was full of sound as they chanted. 'Revelation' had arrived. Out came my notebook and as they chanted I wrote for my life in an unknown tongue.

What a strange scene, the chanters on the job in that cave of the dreaming Malawaddi (man of the kangaroo-totem) who had received these songs from the creative spirits, with me trying to accustom my ear to the words so that I could write them down correctly.

It is difficult when one passes from the oral to the written word. Not only were my informants the tribal chanters but they must also be the translators, for I did not know the Loritdja tongue. Everything was with them, I was just the scribe. Fortunately for me their chant lines were repeated three times in a manner similar to church hymns centuries ago.

Also fortunately for me I had been to many rituals in the north of the Territory. I knew some of the tongues and was conversant with the very Ritual of the Rock. The main difficulty was that a lot of the sacred words are bound up with their symbolism. A youth of a tribe will mention a word yet he does not know its full context because he has not reached that stage of his initiation where its meaning lay.

A woman with some tribes will be called the word for a stone axe because a part of her private anatomy resembles that artifact. The word is full of ritual meaning with the Waddaman tribe. Should a man during a ritual do something wrong, or break some taboo custom, then his only way of getting 'clear' is for one of his clan to mention that word for him to be released from the curse.

The urethra beside the stone-axe is the head-man and is called the 'ear'. Thus when someone chants about the ear he forever associates that man with the origin of life. As mentioned later the 'Nginindi' is a rock-hole under Ayers Rock; it is also the name of the bean tree out of which, in the past, all the wooden water-carrying bowls were made. It is also the central object of the Mother-place. In fact it is the Earth-mother's womb. Thus does the womb of the Earth-mother become the camp (womb) of the ritual because to the desert aborigines a camp is ever associated with water.

The 'djula' (stone-knife) is made from a 'kundi', because the flints used for its manufacture came from the teeth of the Minggeri (mice-girls) who were deflowered in mythological times. As a tooth is a knife so is a woman who is oversexed called 'she who has a tooth'.

Everywhere is symbolism in words and stones, and here was I in a strange land listening to a new language and trying to fathom it all.

Did I do it well? Well, I am pretty sure by the looks on my friends' faces, as I tried to chant it back, that it was 'off the ball'. Nevertheless, not only were they good translators from Loritdja to English, but they did an excellent job of untangling my jargon. Fortunately I had been to a Kerungra before with the tribes of the north. This, with my mates' perseverance, helped me out. Yet true knowledge must not be dogmatic. Although I went around the Rock many times with other informants, to check the story, I am sure that those two old men never let me stray. They were good mates to me and if I have gone wrong in the story here and there it is my fault, not theirs.

After the opening chant, which was a sort of copyright law, and must be performed only by those who have received the chants from the correct Elder who had himself received it from others in an unbroken chain through the ages, did we proceed to the other chanting places for the rest of the story.

Days went by into weeks; they kept chanting and I wrote. We had long spells in between and during this rest period I would ask them the meaning of each word, together with the literal meaning of each sentence. What they thought of me I just don't know.

In between the chanting and questioning they would tell stories which they remembered from past days. One such tale was told by Kudekudeka as we sat in the sacred and secret shelter of Waruaki—forbidden then, as it still is today, to the Loritdja women and the uninitiated youths of the tribe. His story was how his aunt deliberately picked some ripe fruit from a fig tree that grew before the secret cave's entrance. Her crime was discovered by one of the tribal Elders who saw her tale-bearing footprint on the earth. A council was held in which some of the 'Big-women' of the tribe sat. Thus was she condemned to die. Kudekudeka told the tale simply as something that was just. The woman had broken a taboo and was destroyed just as a man would be destroyed should he attempt to pry into the secret and sacred lodges of the women. Footprints on the earth do not lie, and in a tribe that has no lawyers to pick holes in the evidence the law is swift.

So, out of the chants of my friends did I learn to respect the desert aboriginal. On the side of the roadway, along which the tourists go, they look a raggle-taggle mob, but behind that grubby exterior is a human being, as good and as bad as ourselves.

Now and then as we travelled around the Rock, a tourist would join in the chanting. What he thought of us I do not know, nor did we care. My old mates were somehow happy to tell the 'white-fellow-man' something about their 'proper-good-country'.

One such fellow took photographs of my mate chanting beside some of their cave art. Later he came to me with a 'chip on his shoulder'. It appears he gave my friends a few biscuits for posing as models and was now aggrieved because they had not given him the thanks he expected. Poor coot! I was too busy to explain to him that the tribal lore of kinship about none borrowing is constant. All must give freely. They are the gifts from the tribal spirits who are thanked each year when the tribesmen gather for their ceremonies. To the aborigines the custom of thanking people belongs to the whites.

Chapter Ten

Sun-over Side

ONLY with the help of a map can one accurately describe or understand this remarkable dome.

The mountain itself must be regarded as one complete ritual-stone because it is the abiding place of the all-knowing 'Wanambi-serpent who lives in the valley of Uluru'. He is the presiding spirit of the tribe who understands their ritual and judges their way of life. He is called the 'all-knowing one' because he knows each tribesman's secret. His footprint can always be seen in thes ky during the rain-time because it is a rainbow's arch across the heavens.

As he is the head-man, so around him at the base of the mountain are the cliffs, ravines, and rock-shelters that have become the chanting places of the tribal song-men. 'Tis they who sing the glories of the original creative heroes who came out of the darkness in the beginning, giving to the tribes that story of the Earth-mother (Kerungra) who brought life on to the earth with her sacred 'Ngaltawaddi' (digging-stick) and created the mortals in the likeness of themselves.

The mountain of Uluru was, and still is today, the Loritdja people's living symbols of those creative heroes who dwell within it in the same fashion as do the Gods and archangels in other heavens.

As the Earth-mother created the 'shades' (souls) of the spirit-children of the dawn so must the soul of the deceased person return to the mountain to be purified within, so that it can be once more reincarnated to a life upon the earth. Yet these creative-spirits demand one thing from the living. The important one that each and every one of the deceased-one's kin shall be ritually pure in all things during the Kerungra ritual. Failing this the soul of the dead must wander about the land until the next big ritual. All members of a family paint themselves with white clay at mourning rituals—to make themselves invisible so that the deceased shall not steal their soul from their body

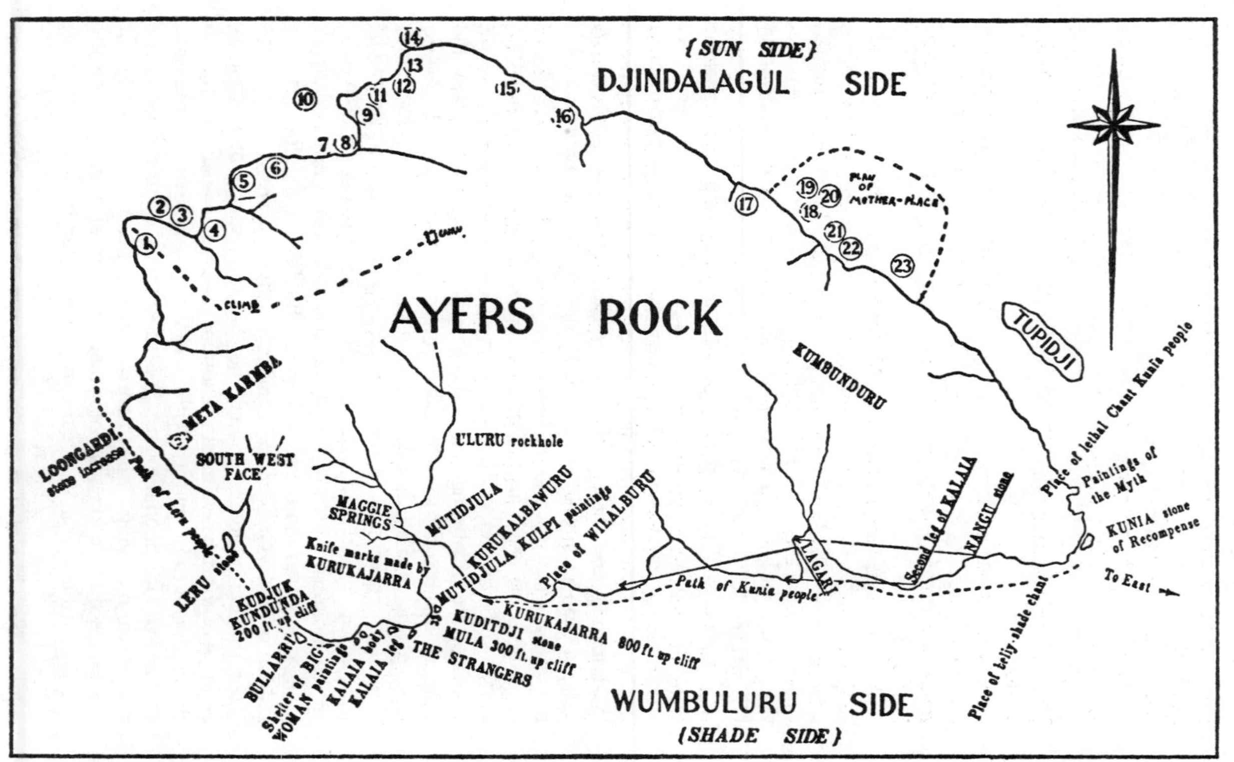
(SUN SIDE)
DJINDALAGUL SIDE
PLAN OF MOTHER-PLACE
AYERS ROCK
CLIMB
TUPIDJI
KUMBUNDURU
META KARMBA
LOONGARDI stone increase
Path of Leru people
SOUTH WEST FACE
ULURU rockhole
MAGGIE SPRINGS
MUTIDJULA
KURUKALBAWURU
MUTIDJULA KULPI paintings
Place of WILALBURU
Knife marks made by KURUKAJARRA
LERU stone
KUDJUK KUNDUNDA 200 ft. up cliff
BULLARRI
Shelter of BIG WOMAN paintings
KALAIA body
KALAIA leg
THE STRANGERS
MULA 300 ft. up cliff
KUDITDJI stone
KURUKAJARRA 800 ft. up cliff
Path of Kunia people
LAGARI
Second leg of KALAIA
NANGU stone
Place of lethal Chant Kunia people
Paintings of the Myth
KUNIA stone of Recompense
To East
Place of belly-shade chant
WUMBULURU SIDE
(SHADE SIDE)

and thus cause them to die. It is important that the chants of the rituals are correct. If not when they wash themselves at the end of the death ceremonies they will be visible for any angry wandering shade which may cause them harm.

But if everything is correct then the soul is admitted to the mountain and is cleansed. After the purification it will now await the next Kerungra ritual so that it can be 'sung' from the place of the 'putta'—that place of reincarnation which is said to be the point of the ritual Malawaddi.

Now let us see the story as recorded in the stone symbols we pass by on our journey around the mountain. Not only does the mountain reveal the ritual of the Earth-mother but it was the pattern of their kinship law.

A line drawn from the Kerungra Mother-place on the north-east side of the mountain to a ravine three hundred yards south of the Climb is a strict moiety division in the life pattern of the Loritdja aborigines. On the western side is the Djindarlagul or 'sun-over' moiety, whilst on the south-east and southern side is the moiety of the Wumbuluru or 'shade-side' of Uluru. This division is fixed by tradition in such a way that the 'shade-side' moieties hunt to the south with the 'sun-over' fraternity keeping to the westward.

As descent is in the female line, the women of the 'shade-side' naturally marry the men of the 'sun-over' and vice versa. As the patrilocal law applied to the tribe so would a mother's brother control his sister's children and not his own.

I wrote this as though it was in the present but I am sorry to record that nearly all the Loritdja have drifted into the towns, missions, government settlements, and cattle stations. A few find work around the tourist resorts, and others, as with my mates Kudekudeka and Imalung, are brought out here to show the 'white-fellow-man' the 'proper things of their country'.

An astounding thing about the moiety division is that it also divides the religious aspect of the people. The 'sun-over' side is the place of 'light and ritual'. The 'shade-side' is that which belongs to everything opposite the other.

Along the 'sun-over' side the Mala ritual men came in creative times with their cult of happiness which is symbolized by those black marks down the ravines on the cliff faces. These are recorded in the ritual as the sternal hollows of the creative men who awaited the coming of the mother in the dawn-time. As Kumbundurus they became darker in the rushing waters of the storm-time and out of this observation, black becomes the symbol of night and the beginning, with birth, as the dawn people arrive. With this sign on the mountain the tribesmen decorate themselves in the same manner to go forth as messengers of goodwill to invite the people of the tribe into the Kerungra ceremonies which are generally performed after a big rain has given an abundance of food in the prescribed area.

The mountain is but the symbol of a cult; the place where the people gather is governed by the tribal spirits who bring the rain into a chosen area.

The messengers of a Kerungra go into all the tribal land, every elder in the tribe sees the sign and decorates himself with the Kumbunduru chest mark. He has now pledged that he will be at the ritual. It is a sacred vow and should he be an absentee afterwards he must send a reasonable excuse for his non-appearance. To say one will go and not turn up is a proof of guilt that must be discussed by the Elders at the next lodge meeting.

When I saw these things and heard them explained, not only at Ayers Rock, but at the great Kerungras of the north, I could only wonder how all great lodges—whether among the aborigines in Australia, the whites in the cities here and overseas—carried within them the central core of primitive councils.

Here on the 'sun-over side of light' were also the chants of reincarnation, revelation, the sacraments, god-fathers, even the eating of the Kerungra bread as a test of faith at the Mother-place.

To get the feel of the symbols around the 'Djindarlagul' or 'sun-over side' we must imagine we are a small band of people who have got the answers right as to tribal lore and have also got that great thing which is essential to all religions—belief. Our chanters await us. As we look at the map so do they point out each place as we go our ritual round. We are a happy gang so let us talk in a friendly way.

The slanting spur on the western side of the mountain just beside the junction of the road leading westward to Mount Olga is (1) on the map. We travellers call it the 'climb' but it is chanted in as the Webo because it is recorded in Loritdja mythology as the crouching body and tail of the first Malawaddi (kangaroo-man) who was the head-man of this ritual.

Below it is the shelter (2) where the Mala man slept to dream the first songs. Along the flank of the Webo, at the base of the climb, are many other stones (3) which symbolize other creative heroes of the Mala totem awaiting the light and the coming of the Earth-mother.

Now the chanting tempo quickens (4). The Mala ritual-men stand erect with arms before them as does a kangaroo when alert. The ritual-men of today, who follow out the pattern of the creative-men, also stand erect at this period of the ritual. They have heard the voice of Kerungera whirring as a bullroarer, from the darkness. As then, so today at the rituals the whirr of the 'kulpidja' (bullroarer) is still the call of the mother who has come to create once more. It is she who steals away the youth of the tribe so that they shall be regenerated to become adults and thus enter the spiritual life of the Elders.

Now do we go on to (5). The place of the 'putta', which is a bell-shaped cavity behind a larger stone upon the ground. The cavity is the symbol of reincarnation. It was here that light came upon the earth. Before that place are a few small holes in the rock, which were the cooking fires of the creative-men as they ate their first meal of 'werin-werin' (bush tomato) and 'edonba' (wild raisin) which still remains as the first food of the ritual.

This sacred food is recorded in chants as having been grown in the first dream-time rains by the sacred 'wana' (digging-stick) of that Mother who created all life upon the earth, then, with her ritual-dancing she created the mortals out of the fruit that was thrown off her quivering body.

To symbolize that event the chanters sang about mythical trees, which were the ones the 'titjearra' (spiney-cheeked honey-eaters) rested on and chanted, 'This is the food from the great tree, let us to the fruit and eat.' This chant gave to the Loritdja people an hereditary right to that fruit.

As the 'putta' is the place of reincarnation so do all the spirit children of the Loritdja tribe come from that spot when they are called forth by the chanting of the ritual Elders.

Now come our chanters to shelter (6) which has been formed when a larger boulder slid down the face of the mountain. This is the kulpi of the 'kundji' (meeting place), a primitive form of our present-day vestry before the assembly area. This shelter has wall paintings which represent the 'Kulpidja' beside a smaller one of an initiate ready to be taken into the sacred ritual place. The 'Kulpidja'—obviously a symbol of the Earth-mother—has white radiating lines coming out of a red centre which encloses a black band running through its centre.

For a long time I sat in that shelter with my chanting mates. Much discussing went on between them and I was told that the black band symbolized happiness, the red ochre represented the ritual side of man with white as his belief in the soul and immortality.

The initiate beside the 'Kulpidja' was painted red only with a white outline. On his head was a head-dress of white cockatoo feathers which proclaimed to all that he had already chanted the traditional catechism relating to tribal behaviour and was now ready to be shown the sacred and secret places of the ritual.

From here we walk down a grove of green bloodwood trees towards a high cliff face on the mountain to pause at (7) where the pink coloured wall rises high above our heads. On our left, as we go into the place, is a pool of water during good seasons but in the dry it is but a bed of sand that carries water below should the traveller care to dig deep enough for the supply.

I notice all are silent in this awe-inspiring place as though we were near a Being greater than us all. We stand beneath the wall as puny creatures in a giant land. Somehow we seemed to be carried away into another time and place. One elderly lady once confided to me that the place was so overpowering that although she came to scoff she remained to pray. Perhaps she was nearer God than she thought, for this place received its sacred name from a fault-plane down the mountain's face which extends from a small cave at the base to the top of the cliff.

This thin crack is the 'ngaltawaddi' (ritual-staff) (8). Legend records that right on that spot did the Head-Mala of the mortals receive the sacraments from the creative-heroes after they had completed their work on earth, then returned into the mountain itself where they reside today as guardians of their people.

That 'Ngaltawaddi of the Kundju' is the symbol which records that when an initiate first looks upon it he is an 'inside' and as such is within the body of the ritual mother. There he will remain as a prisoner protected by his earthly guardian until he has passed through the ritual of the 'Mother-place' so that he can be regenerated as an 'outside' (adult) and thus wear the 'butaru' band of manhood around his head to enter a new spiritual life.

Looking at that fault in the mountain I would often speculate. Was it there when the people first arrived, or did it crack afterwards so that its noise gave them the idea of its divine origin? What must have been the feelings of that first Mala man who received that sacred 'Rod of God'? Fear must have been in his heart then as it is today with the initiates who are first shown those sacred symbols—shown them by their god-fathers who have taught them the law as a form of catechism, then led them to that place to give them words of cheer. Before that a youth is as nothing; afterwards they have responsibilities to their kin and the tribal code. To fail after they have taken the vow means oblivion.

Beyond the Kundju is a large cavity which is called the 'Kutat' (9). The word means 'bowels' and symbolizes how a left-handed man of the 'Linggi' (yellow-lizard) totem lost his 'karlee' (throwing-stick) of light at this place. The cavity was formed during his frantic digging to find the sacred object that was lost forever to the tribes. The place is the symbol of frustration, commemorated by his bowels that fell from his body as he died.

Out from this Kutat, on the other side of the road which leads around the Rock is the 'Nowamarra-stone' (10) that records how a youth of the dawn-time had his nose septum pierced at that spot. The stone was obviously put into the story as a form of imitative magic, for it has a hole in it that looks not unlike the nose septum of an aboriginal today. Old Kudekudeka and Imalung, when they chanted this story to me, proudly put a stick through their noses and during the chanting repeatedly put their arms through the hole in a fashion that suggested a fertility cult.

From that stone of the nose piercing we go to the 'Waruaki' (11) (main ritual camp), the sacred and secret place of the Loritdja tribe. Climbing over the boulders before it we passed by the fig tree which is the very one from which Kudekudeka's aunt Karardjari stole the fruit and was punished for her crime.

On the walls of the shelter one can see the stains which are said to be the blood which was first taken from the median-veins of the creative Malawaddi. The initiate is shown these stains on to which he too must let his blood flow. His guardian directs him in a sacred vow that he will evermore guard the secrets of his people.

As the aborigines of the Loritdja have departed from the Rock for a goodly number of years the place has lost a lot of its ritual significance, though it still commands respect from the youth and women of the tribe. But the phallic-stone within a circle on the floor has tumbled down and is now without meaning.

The cave art on its walls is not the abstract painting of other shelters along the face of the mountain. Here man was given the right to break away from tradition. To paint the things he saw since the last big ritual. Thus do we see strange men riding animals which look like kangaroos, and men with tails. This right to paint and record things as a sort of annual magazine is common to other tribes. When on Melville and Bathurst Island the initiates did not paint but composed a song relating to some incident over the past year. It was a sort of early eisteddfod, the main object of which was to give the words a form of symbolism.

A little farther along the same wall at a spot under a natural arch (12) was a dark stain enclosed within a white border. This was the principal Kumbunduru chant of the mountain. My chanters explained at great length that here everybody sang away the 'blues' which had been ordered by the secret and sacred objects of the ritual.

Now a little farther on at (13) are the two ravines down the mountain which symbolize how the Ningeri men of the black goanna totem came chanting the song of rain when they came down from on high. This rain was created by the tribesmen by chants which record how, 'The Ningeri, like the storm-water races down the side of the mountain.' Near this place was a one-time secret aboriginal well, but whether it has dried up or got covered with timber I do not know, for, although we searched well I was unable to discover it.

Look up at the Ningeri place of rain, you will discern that the two ravines—which are said to be the paths down which they came—have carved out a ridge between them that looks not unlike the head of a lizard. Everywhere around this place is ritual built up out of imitative-magic—the likeness of the lizard, its love of waterholes and rain.

Beyond the Ningeri place of rain at (14) is a great slab of rock lying upon the mountain side. As the Ngaltawaddi of the Kundju was the inside symbol of the cult so does this massive slab symbolize the outside part of the ritual. The well-worn boulders around and in front of it are the resting men of the myth who carried the slab to this outside place. The blue sky can be seen betwixt it and the mountain, and as one of the impressive natural features of the Rock it has been photographed thousands of times.

As all things in aboriginal mythology relate to a fixed law, this massive inclined stone becomes the profane symbol, or marker, which divides the secret things of the men from that of the women. Once we go by that spot we will be walking along the north-eastern side of the mountain and away from the secret and sacred places of the men.

Every time I walked around the Rock with tourists I explained its mythological origin. It was the sacred staff of the creative Mother, but to all the people it was 'the Kangaroo-tail' because it is mentioned so in their tourist leaflets and thus that word without meaning remains.

Our next place to visit is (15)—a large gaping cave two hundred feet up the mountain face which is called the Djugajabbi but known to all as the 'Woman's cave'.

During the tourist season the coaches always stopped near the 'Woman's cave' so that the tourists could have some fruit and a drink of water. It was a quiet spot where one could crawl away beneath some overhanging stone so as to be away from the questions which were always being asked. I discovered that the main aim of people who came to the Rock was to get to the top. As I had never been up the climb I came in for a lot of banter. They just could not understand how I, as the Ranger, had never been up there. It was useless for me to say that I didn't like heights. The fact remained that I was an earth worm and not of the gods who live on that astral plane.

One thing the women tourists listened to and that was the women's side of tribal life. To tell them that this cave shelter was theirs put them in a good mood. Over the ages they had always been told that women's place in society was on a lowly scale, yet here at the Rock was woman's symbol of power. From this shelter, above where we were resting as the others climbed into its gaping jaws, the aboriginal women sang their 'Yeripindji' songs of fertility to the 'kirakip' hawk, symbol of sex desire, as the ritual men went out with Kumbundurus, on their chests, to invite other Elders and their families to the great Kerungra festivals.

The 'big-women' of the tribe were those who had the right to protect the people, and a right to veto any man-made laws that could bring trouble to the tribe. Within their secret and sacred lodges they held rituals similar to the men. Their bodies were decorated with totemic designs and woe to the peeping-toms of the tribe who attempted to spy on the sacred proceedings.

Yet somehow everything in the woman's chant relates to sex, not the crude sex which enters as a weed into our talk, but that which relates to life and its origin. That woman's cave and its surroundings are full of eroticism. The name of the cave, the indentations on the flat surface of rock not far east of the Ngaltawaddi, all carry this form of symbolism.

Symbolism and mystery. The black marks (16) down the mountain's face to the east of the 'Woman's cave' were made when the outraged women were at their rituals and destroyed, by fire, the men of the 'Leru' (poisonous-snake) people who would seek out their secrets of love and life. Those marks are there today as a warning to the youth of the tribe what they will get should they search for those things which belong to 'woman's business'.

About half a mile farther east we come to the 'Nanguru' or Mother-place. A name known as such over a large part of the Northern Territory. Before we reached it our aboriginal chanting friends faced a niche high up on the cliff face (17). Pointing towards it they chanted the first song of the 'Lundba', she of the red-rumped king-fisher totem who, sitting on her nest-camp on high, gave a warning call to all that a ritual-dog Kurapunni was coming beneath the ground from the west to carry away the first initiates of the Kerungra ritual. The Lundba was the guardian of the tribe then, as she still is today. When she calls the people heed, remembering that she was the one who called when the twilight of the Gods departed and the day of the mortals began.

At (18) one can discern the egg-shaped boulder which symbolizes the great Kerungra herself—squatting on a ledge of rock not unlike a primitive altar with many piled up stones around her and those concentric designs on her eastern face symbolizing eternal life. She certainly looks her part, but of importance to the tribesmen and us is a thin red line shaped in the crude design of a serpent on the pedestal stone. This painting is the most important design on the mountain, for it symbolizes the Rainbow-serpent God and this was always retraced by the Elders as the ritual was being performed.

To the left as we stand before the Mother-stone is a boulder (20) which is reported to be the left-handed Mala of the creative ritual—he who speared the 'Djindra' women, of the willy-wagtail totem (21), who now lies prostrate a little to the right where she fell from her rock-hole camp in the ravine above. A small hole on her side is the central feature of her legend and it is repeatedly pierced with a spear during the ritual chanting.

Before the Mother-stone my chanting mates pointed out the sacred women of the ritual (19). Their duties were to prepare the 'wungunu' grass-seed into the 'kerungra-bread' by milling it on the platform beside the Mother, then after it was ground in the prescribed manner it

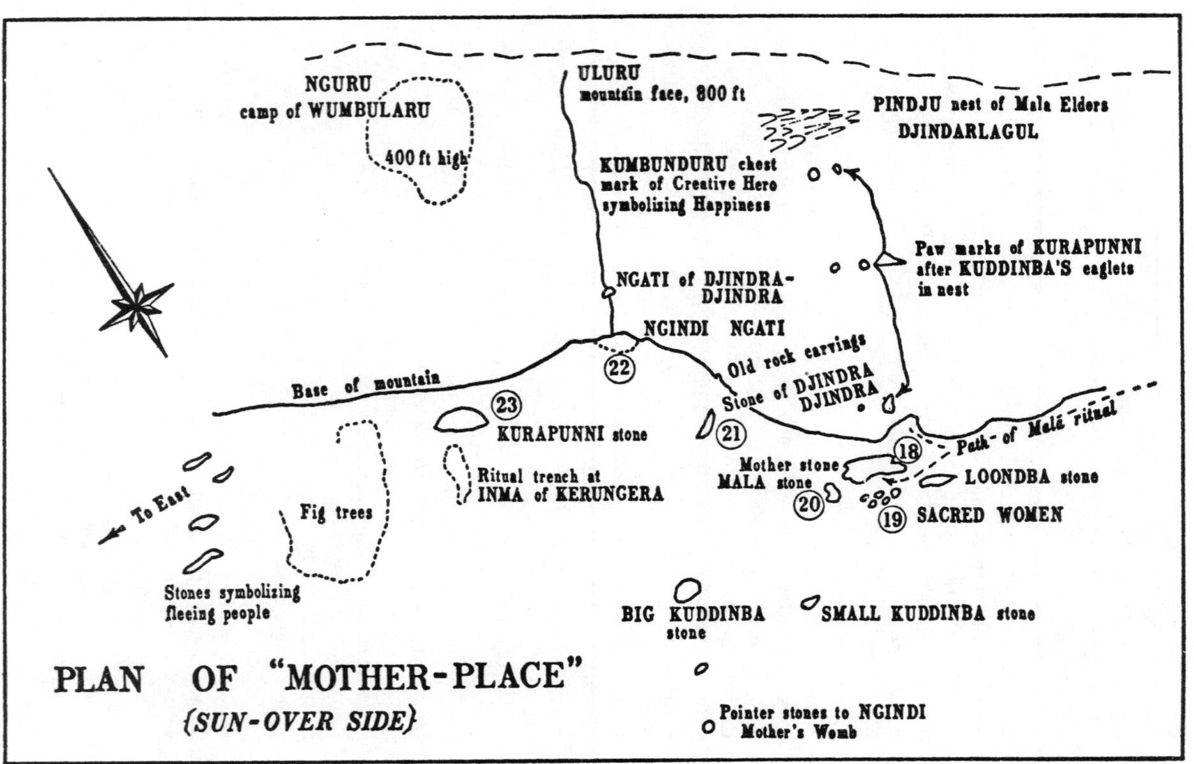
NGURU camp of WUMBULARU
400 ft high
ULURU mountain face, 800 ft
PINDJU nest of Mala Elders DJINDARLAGUL
KUMBUNDURU chest mark of Creative Hero symbolizing Happiness
Paw marks of KURAPUNNI after KUDDINBA'S eaglets in nest
NGATI of DJINDRA-DJINDRA
NGINDI NGATI
Old rock carvings
Stone of DJINDRA DJINDRA
Base of mountain
22
23
KURAPUNNI stone
21
Path of Malā ritual
18
Mother stone MALA stone
LOONDBA stone
20
19
SACRED WOMEN
Ritual trench at INMA of KERUNGERA
To East
Fig trees
Stones symbolizing fleeing people
BIG KUDDINBA stone
SMALL KUDDINBA stone
Pointer stones to NGINDI Mother's Womb
PLAN OF "MOTHER-PLACE"
{SUN-OVER SIDE}

was moistened by their breast-milk and made into cakes in readiness for the sacred feast at the closing of the ceremony.

On the right of the Mother-stone, as we face her, is the upright stone of the Lundba as she gave the final chant. But the women who were grinding the sacred bread were asleep and were only aroused when the powerful 'kurapunni' ritual-dog leapt up the cliff face after the 'kuddinba' (eaglets) who were then guarded by the ritual Elders in their 'pindju' (nest) high up the mountain's face.

Central to the ritual story is the rock-hole of 'Ngindi' (22) which is the womb of the Earth-mother herself. From her womb, leading up to the crest of the high cliff is the 'kumbunduru of the nangaru' (happiness at the Mother-place). On one side of it, four hundred feet above the base of the mountain one can see that surface which is called by tourists the 'brain'. It is known to the Loritdja as the 'ngoru' (camp) because it was the place reserved for the visiting opposite half.

So does the ritual story of Ayers Rock draw to a close. My aboriginal mates are tired, perhaps sick of me with my questioning.

Yet one thing is still to be explained; so we go over to a stone on the eastern side of the Mother-place and just on the edge of it, silent and terrible in his wrath stands that Kurapunni-stone (23) of vengeance and obedience. In front of it the ritual Elders of the Kerungra always dug a man-made trench which was the womb from which the youths of the tribe were regenerated into a new way of life.

Let an initiate be disobedient as a youth then here he will be punished by Elders, regardless of kin. That Kurapunni-stone stands just away from the side of 'light'. He lives in the side of the 'shadows', for he symbolizes death and fear just as does the stony hill of 'Tupidji' symbolize the irreligious fleeing with fear in their hearts from the wrath of that ritual monster.

Between the side of 'happiness' and the side of the 'shadows', is a dividing line formed by the two stones of the 'Kuddinbas' who were initiated in the creative ritual. They were the first mortals to be regenerated from the Mother's womb, and they are the chanting-stones on which the Elders stood to survey the ritual scene to chant the law.

And that is exactly what my two aboriginal friends, Kudekudeka and Imalung did as they gave me the end of the story of the Earth-mother cult.

Chapter Eleven

Shade-side

THE idea of 'light' being related to Creation and happiness, and 'shadow' to its opposite, weaves its way through the traditional pattern of aboriginal life. As the tribal divisions of the Loritdja have opposite shade colours so does red become the basic symbol for the side of Light with black as the colour of the other side. This peculiar custom of opposites runs through most aboriginal tribes. Should a man carry water a certain way (in his hands) then women carry it on her head; if a man walks with his toes pointing outwards then a female shall walk correctly with the toes pointing inwards; as women sit with one leg beneath them and the other extended, then her husband, brother, father, etc., will fold both legs beneath them and use the pad-side of their feet as a cushion to rest the rump on. That is the law and the greatest insult which one can give an aboriginal is to tell him that he acts like the opposite sex.

For the first few days after doing our investigation on the sun-over side of the mountain we took life easy checking the story of the chants to see that everything was correct. Then we were off once more to record the legends relating to the shade-side as revealed by the chanting.

That first morning was a cool one. The birds were chirruping away in the mulga and hakia trees whilst over the mountain were a few wisps of cloud sweeping in from the west. Every phenomenon of nature was a story for my old mates. The western wind was a sign of rain; a bird calling had them listening for the latest morning news which was generally brought to our door by the major-bell-bird who is said to be the messenger of the tribe. Kudekudeka told me how he knew the bird-language so that every time a bird called out he would knowingly impart some special item of 'news' which he must have undoubtedly heard from some other source yet kept it a secret from us.

Our morning stroll was three miles, and although I went around that mountain many times afterwards, I am positive that morning's walk with my Loritdja friends was the best of them all.

Finally we halted beneath a high cliff face with a large grey-green patch of lichen growing on its wall. Under this we stood, me to admire the scene, they to search for something in the grass and thick spinifex.

I found out from experience that it was best to leave them to whatever they were doing. Their job was to explain things tribal, mine to transcribe the story they told me. I was in the story, yet out of it in the same manner as would be a secretary at some business conference.

Suddenly I saw them pause as they peered into a thick patch of grass. Then I heard the low chanting once more as they began to tear up the grass and throw it over their shoulders. I was too busy writing to look at what they were up to, but by this time I had got used to writing as they chanted the songs.

Suddenly the chants quickened in tempo, the grass came out in handfuls and looking up I could see they were cleaning the rubbish away from a small stone which somehow resembled a dressed bird. Imagine my surprise when it was all cleared and they told me that this was the 'loongardi' (sleeping-lizard)* stone of increase, which must be kept cleared by the hunters so that a plentiful supply of these lizards would come to the hunters who rubbed it as they passed that way. The clearing away of the grass and rubbish was to prevent it being burnt by fire which would destroy its magic properties.

I could not suppress a smile when I saw the amount of grass and brush they had cleaned away. As the Ranger of the area I was ordered by the Board to prevent the destruction of native flora, yet here was I on my first round aiding and abetting the felony. On one hand the protection of flora for the National Park, on the other side a respect for the aboriginal's traditions and customs.

Looking at that increase-stone which had been well polished from countless rubbing with a stone or sand beneath the hands, I could hardly believe that this was the object of our search. Yet there it was before me. A simple stone commemorating a strange legend. As the stone looked like a dressed bird so was it an Emu which had been cooked in that exact spot by the men of the Loongardi totem.

Looking upon that stone I wondered did it commemorate some story of a ritual murder at that spot or was it the simple story as I heard it told?

That tale was one of how the Loongardi were cooking the emu at that place when they saw smoke arising to the south. Knowing that in that direction was the land of 'Jura' (poisonous flames of the Aurora-australis) they quickly cut up the cooked bird and hid it in various

* For this and other places mentioned in this chapter on the shade-side see map on page 76.

places—perhaps where the mountain now stands, because the legend relates to the origin of the mountain and its features.

Now into the scene strode the strangers of Jura. They were mighty hunters who claimed they were on the trail of a sacred emu which had come this way. In fact they knew it had been killed by the Loongardi because they had seen their footprints where they had speared and picked up the bird. 'We are hungry now and ask a feed,' they said as they placed their heavy hunting spears upon the ground in the neutral sign.

But the Loongardi were a tired people and claimed they had no food. At that insult the Jura men leapt to their feet and snatching a lighted fire-stick from the cooking fire they hurled it into the bush which soon became a blazing furnace.

As the Loongardi sleeping lizards were too tired to move many of them were burnt to death in the holocaust. Their bodies are still to be seen as large lichen-boulders beneath the place of the Loongardi-karmbi, that patch of lichen on the cliff face which is the symbol of that burning.

At that period the head-people of the Ayers Rock area were of the 'Kunia' (carpet-snake) totem, a clan whose main desire in life was to be at peace with the world. The Loongardi was one of their moieties and at this terrible insult and destruction the Head-man of the Kunia, symbolized by the extreme peak on the southern side of the mountain, decided to act.

Calling on his totem-friend the 'Pampampanella' (major-bell-bird) he ordered him to carry a message to the aggressors demanding a reason for this attack.

As in all aboriginal mythology, the peaceful people have totems belonging to the non-aggressive creatures in the land, and the belligerent totemic types are the attackers.

So was it a war of the snake totems, and as the only reptile the Loritdja fear is the 'Leru' (mulga-snake) of the sandhills, so did the Leru warriors come over the sandhills to avenge the insult regarding hospitality.

The desert-oaks of the Centralian bushmen (the casuarinas of the botanists) still grow tall and straight on the sandhills today to symbolize the attacking Leru men. From the 'Climb', when we look westward, one can see them standing as waves of attacking spearmen. Then out from the serried ranks of the spearmen sped one of the Leru. He stood at a spot south of the place of the burning then called aloud to the Kunia that his people were coming. Futile was his warning though, for as he called a shower of spears came from the attackers which, falling into the camps of the Kunia, caused those pock-marked cavities on the mountain to the right of the increase-stone.

As the protecting Leru-man called then so has that stone at the base of the mountain become the protection-stone for men as they enter that area. Should hunters go by, or trading people come in from the west, they must rub that Leru stone of protection and call on the sleeping Kunia men within the mountain that they are without evil intent. To see that they do so is the nearby messenger-stone of the major-bell-bird ready to send out a warning message should the law of neutrality be disregarded.

Now war was with the Kunia and all was confusion. My chanters told how the Leru warriors sped southward down the base of the Rock as a vanguard of the fighting. In despair the peaceful Kunia called up one of their sacred women 'Wilalburu of Bullarri', she who was head of the woman's lodges, and asked her to seek a truce. She stood upon that spot called this day 'Bullarri' (stone-place) in honour of her deed. As she stood then to protect them so is she the protectress of aboriginal women today. To leave women beside her stone is to make sure that they will not be molested. Beneath a small arch on the south side of the stone, just by a cave depicting an emu-hunt, is a small stone within the shelter which is recorded as one of her children. As she had her child there so shall the women of the tribe have protection during childbirth in that shelter. The law was laid down in the beginning so all must follow the customs of the tribe.

Resting for a drink of tea beside that shelter I asked Kudekudeka where he was born. At my question he looked surprised at my ignorance, then replied by pointing into the shelter. 'Me born here . . . plenty other Loritdja people too . . . this place lucky for woman.'

My aboriginal friend's chants told me that futile was the orders of the Bullarri. The Leru men still kept coming on, thus forcing the Kunia people to act. Kudekudeka pointed out to me the high peak on the south-western side of the mountain, just above the shelter of Bullarri, and explained that that peak symbolized the powerful Kunia head-man who knelt down from on high to cut the throats of four Leru attackers thus forming a large cavity called 'Kudjuk-kundunda' which symbolizes the 'cut-throats' of the enemy.

I look up at that large cavity he is pointing to as he tells me the finer details of the legend and seeing the place I am amazed how imitative magic has once more been used to commemorate this tale. There in that cavity one can see the vein system, even the larger arteries which run down each side of the neck. There also is the epiglottis and the epidermis; everything is in its exact spot, even the red stains caused by the iron oxide from the weathered feldspar in the mountain, mixing with the stormwater as it runs down the gaping wound.

But we must away from these observations of the present, back in the legend of the past that records how the Leru-warriors pressed on. In the van of their attack was the man who is known to the tribesmen as 'Mula—the Leru'. Should the tourist stand out from Maggie

Springs and look up at the left-hand peak guarding its entrance they will discern the mutilated face of that great warrior above them. There he stands today as he stood then to challenge the Kunia fighting men. In the fighting he had his upraised 'Kudidji' (shield) which was pierced and forced from his guard by a heavy 'Wurumbu' (javelin-spear) hurled by a mighty Kunia warrior from the east.

Below the Mula I was shown the place where the Emu-stone was hidden with, behind it, the thigh of the bird which still has the knife-cut along it as it was cut in the dream-time.

Everywhere is imitative-magic even to the two stranger-stones who still sit out from the mountain as they did in mythological times. They were the strangers then, and they remain so today as a warning to all people that none shall deny hospitality to the strangers who come into the tribal lands.

Over at the base of the rock to the left of the Peak of Mulu is a very important rock-shelter, for there under a large rock which is supported by smaller stones is the ritual home of 'Wilalburu'. It was she who tried to stop the fighting, and it was she who led the attack against the giant Mula after he had lost his shield. Wilalburu the fighter, where now are they who talk of aboriginal women being despised in the tribes. Hear then from my old Loritdja friends how she came tripping in from that lethal spot to the east of Maggie Springs. Tripped around the walls of the mountain, and forming the bay of Maggie Springs as she came, she dealt, with her 'wana' (digging- and fighting-stick), a blow at the enraged Mula to sever his nose, thus giving the name of 'mula' (nose) to that place.

Now to the west of Maggie Springs is that ritual shelter sacred to her name. As she gave battle in the valley of the shadows which is said to have come into being from the lethal-curses she hurled before her as she came, so is she the one who gives life into the tribes.

Standing in that cave of the 'Big-woman' Wilalburu, surrounded by the cave art of these Loritdja, I think of the place of the Putta on the ritual side of the mountain. On that spot the spirit-children of the tribe were reincarnated from the gods of the mountain—reincarnated to wander about the tribal lands seeking mothers so that they shall be born into the tribe as mortals. But here in this shelter of Willalburu is the 'Stone-of-conception' which the tribal women rub should they desire a child. Putting my hand on to that highly polished stone I could not believe that these people and ourselves are as one in our religious belief. Theirs the old, ours the new.

Everywhere over the broad face of this earth in all customs and beliefs have children been born unto woman through desire. As we want so do we receive. Rubbing-stones of conception and sacred groves of trees are everywhere, yet looking at this stone one thing to me is strange. The soul of an aboriginal is reincarnated from the side of happiness but it goes into the 'camp' of the mother and is born on the side of fear and the shadows. An idea as old as that belief which associates conception with a falling star sweeping across the sky.

From the place of the 'Big-woman' we go along the track which leads us to Maggie Springs. On our right, high up on the outer peak is the eye of 'Kuruka'—he who is the guardian of the tribe. 'Twas he who saw Wilalburu tripping by as she entered the fray and it was he who made Maggie Springs which is the imprint of his knee as he knelt down to stab the Mula in the side. This act, symbolized by the two ravines down the cliff face behind the Mula's nose, gave the name of 'Mutidjula' (knee-knife) to that watering place.

Such was the tale I was told by my aboriginal informants, a story which showed, by example, that hospitality must never be denied the stranger; that none must go against the order of a 'Big-woman' who has been made sacred within the fertility circle of the tribal ritual.

So has the tale been told, thanks to my two mates Kudekudeka and Imalung, and other Loritdja men who came afterwards to confirm the story.

I have left out some of the legends. Those relating to the Kunia-stone at the eastern base of the mountain will come into another chapter. But the most important one of all is about the great 'Wanambi' who lives in the valley of Uluru to look down upon the tourists as they go by.

Sometimes I think he is sad, for the cave-art of his people has been defaced in the shelter of Mutidjula by those terrible white people who like to destroy these sacred things. Once painted as designs of abstract art, they are now horrible yellow daubs without meaning.

This was before I came into the area; since the Reserve Board took over the vandals have kept away. But feet must tramp over the country as the tourists wander around. The bushes and grass must be trampled under as they go, and the poor trees that have stood up well under desert conditions have a new enemy when the travellers pluck a flower or break off a bush to whisk away the flies.

I realize that I was supposed to stop this sort of thing but what could one do against so many? Wanambi growled at me sometimes, I knew this by the way he hurled his angry breath against where I live. Then sometimes I knew that he and I are friends. To him—as with all Gods—is the power of reading people's minds. Thus does he know that I am with his people as I record his story for the white people who visit his domain.

My Loritdja friends have departed. Imalung has returned back to the government settlement he came from, Old Kudekudeka still straddles a horse to 'tail' the herds on cattle stations. I often see him as I go past Henbury, and when I do he asks after the Rock as though it was a human being.

With their departure I think a lot about what they have told me, and I see a lot of their beliefs among our own. They taught me a lot, just as the white people coming out our way gave me a great insight into human character.

Two things I remember during my stay at the Rock. One was the holy expressions in white people's eyes as they came down after going to the top of the mountain and the quiet content on Kudekudeka and Imalung's faces during our chanting stroll around the base of Ayers Rock during that year 1957.

Chapter Twelve

Dawn on the Shade-side

THE twilight is breaking over Ayers Rock. It is that strange red glow that lights up the cliff faces long before the dawn. I am watching it from the door of my straw-lined Ranger's cottage in which I live for the six months I am here to collect entry fees and keep the area in order.

My stove within is alight to give me the usual drink of tea so that I can have the morning's cup before I get to work on cooking the breakfast. As I potter about I continually peer out upon that scene which makes me think I am back in the twilight, in a part of our ancient mythology as it still is with these aborigines.

The birds of this desert land are calling aloud from the mulga trees and the desert oaks that grow over the sandhills behind my dwelling; the final hoot of the mopoke ere he goes into a hollow log to sleep the day around; the welcoming call of the bell-bird as he sends out some of the messages he has received the day before.

The pallid-cuckoo joins in the avian chorus, pausing in his notes as he hears the shrill cry of the kestrel hawk above.

Outside my door small grey birds and a group of magpies are seeking the breadcrumbs and pieces of meat I leave there for them, while over behind a broad-leafed mulga tree a wary crow peers from behind its trunk to see if the hated white fellow is away so that he too can share in the feast.

Birds seem to be everywhere in the early morn; robins with their white waist-coats, warblers flitting from tree to tree chasing the insects or peering into blooms after the nectar within. All are awake and calling in the dawn. It is the hours of peace before the winged killers from the sky come down to search for their prey.

Oftimes, on the ridges behind me I can hear the lone call of a dingo amidst the thryptamene and the flowering bushes of the sand dunes. He is calling to his mate from afar, she who is guarding their litter of pups beneath the rock ledges of the mountain.

Then suddenly, as though a blackman's fire was smothered at the approach of danger, the twilight departs and around me is that grey of dawn which stills the birds' songs as we all await the hero Linggi of the lizard totem, to hurl, with his left hand, that karlee throwing-stick into the sky from the east to bring up the sun with its welcome light.

From where I stand I can see the fires of the tourists, within the stone fire-places which the Board has built for their use. They are blazing away merrily as the people cook their morning breakfasts or have a drink of tea before they set out for the sandhills behind to get the sunrise shots on Uluru's glowing face. Soon their cameras will be clicking away to record the shots which they will later show to their friends and so revive happy memories of Central Australia.

My calendar has told me that this is August 14th. I have been awaiting that day because on that morn the sun has come so far to the south that its rays, as it rises over the sandhills, will shine on to the southern face of the mountain to show up the shade-side's places of its mythology.

Now does the clock show the time to be 7.30 a.m. and the long sought daylight is coming in upon us. I see the tourists wending their way through the spinifex up towards the red sandhills of the east. I hear their voices as they go and know from experience that they will be discussing with each other everything about time exposure, focus with all the nomenclature that goes with what aborigines call 'picture-business'.

What a business has this photography become. Everybody carries a camera slung over his shoulder. Their daily talk is films and emulsion speed. Since I have been out to the Rock, a matter of one hundred and fifty weeks from the time I came till I departed, over seventeen thousand tourists came my way. All are armed with cameras, and films. All are trigger happy, for to them the snaps they get will for ever remind them of a trip which took years of savings to pay for.

But now my thoughts must away from the clicking cameras of the tourists to watch the beauty of colour and light that comes upon the cliffs of the mountain as the sun creeps towards the crest of the eastern sandhills. First comes that rich red which is so difficult to describe. It steals over the cliff faces as though some divine painter had flicked it with a magic brush. Slowly the red deepens until it glows as the first ray of the sun strikes the tip of that peak which overshadows the Kunia's stone of recompense. Above the place of the stone is a black mark which runs down the face of the mountain to end just over a cavity above the stone. To us white people it is but a black mark on the face of the mountain, but according to my chanting friends it carries the deadly 'arangulta' (lethal-chant) that gives the power of life and death to they who own the chant-song.

Now comes the sunlight on the 'welas', the 'bellies' of the fighting Kunia men who saw Wilalburu speed into the fray. Then beyond them the light of the morn falls on to Wilalburu's peak to warn all who see it, that death is at her feet. All aborigines see and heed that warning, so well that no man or woman of the tribe will go near that black wall along her mountain-side. From this spot, legend records, the famous Amazon went forth to do battle with the deadly Wana. She was the first of the 'bone-pointers', her breath was the lethal song-chant which could destroy. As she struck at the Mulu's nose, so just beneath it is that small 'uredjumba' (tacoma tree), from which the tribesmen get the small spear to thrust into the septum of their nose as they utter the death dealing curse that can kill.

Look well on death,
Yet seek the cause in vain.
The arangulta breath
The curse of Cain.

On the eastern side of Wilolburu's home is the large cave of 'lagari' (laughter), called that because a creative hero laughed as the fight went on. The sunlight strikes it for a brief moment, but our eyes are arrested as we gaze on high, to the 'Eye of Kuruka' that watched these things go by as he stared out on all from beside the 'Kurukalabawura', or camp-fires of the watches, which is the pink wall beside Maggie Springs.

The finger of the sun's rays points out, once more to the westward, revealing to our gaze that Kunia head-man who was the first to send out the bell-bird on its message of peace. In that morning light he seems to be still on guard as he watches the lighted face of the Mulu who would bring disaster to the tribe. What a grand mythology is here before us in this morning's light which reveals the opponents in that dream-time struggle. Was it just a story to warn the tribesmen as to what would happen to those who disobey the tribal law, or was it something deeper?

The spear thrown by the Nangu could be a phallic symbol because it did pierce the shield which fell from the Mula's hand. The hole made by that spear has been well worn by the rubbing of countless hands. Even my chanters rubbed the hole as they went by, but each time I asked them about it they claimed it was not their business.

Everywhere is magic in the dawn of Uluru. A magic that disperses as the sun rises higher in the sky. Daytime is here with the tourists in their cars and coaches that roar by or stop to ask me for advice.

Sunlight brings on reality. The colours on the mountain have gone, leaving behind a brown sandstone that still changes its colour as the sun crosses the heavens. But although it has lost a lot of its glamour for us it is still brought to life in the chanting of the Loritdja

Elders. To them it is the 'Stone' just as the stone is the symbol of purity and reverence to people all over the world.

Many tourists complain about the dust and the flies, but all are interesting to listen to, for all have a tale to tell. Many complain about the entry fee. I just listen, then explain that I do not make the laws. After that we may have a session on governments and Boards and that makes us all happy. Ofttimes I would go around the mountain to tell the people its mythology as it was told to me. Some listen, but others think I am a crank to be tolerated. All take my photo and that makes me happy too, for I think it is nice to please people and terrible to offend.

But during night-time at my house I never tire of looking at the great dome of rock rising up before me. How nice to watch the stars drop down behind as though they were weary from sleep. On one such night when the very stars seemed to be just over our heads, Minyinderri of the Windralga totem told me a story about a young girl who passed into the mountain as the evening star. At that time the evening star was setting over the rock, and together he and I watched it fade out of sight in a manner that would suggest such a legend. Then after a drink of tea he departed for his camp, I to dream where . . .

I saw God sitting on the mountain's crest,
Bowed was Wanambi's head as in the gloom
He poured down water on the earth below,
Life-giving Kapi that the red earth grow
Rich fruits from old Kerungra's womb.
I heard wild laughter from Lagari's cave,
Where mirth resounded and its echoes pealed
From grim Wilalburu's peak where peered the eye
Of stern Kuruka, ready to defy
The Leru-Mulu with his kuditdj shield.
Now rise the Kunia horde beside the cleft
Where towering Nangu stood with quivering spear;
That dread Wurumbu soars and over all
Comes crashing Kuditdj as the Wela's call,
'Death to the Mulu who would rule by fear.'

'Death to the Mulu,' my aboriginal mate would tell me that such things were true. 'In my country we have plenty stories. My country got big hill . . . more better than this place.'

So Minyinderri talks as I listen. He is of the tribe that comes from sun-down-way. His people are head-men of the ritual dog Kurapunni. Thus did we plot to go out into his country. He and his kin would go there on a holiday and I would go with them. Our dreams were over the horizon where everything was as a garden which was 'full up everything and proper good country'.

Ayers Rock from the air

The rock-pool of "Nginindi", the central feature of the "Mother-place". On the top right hand can be seen the Stone of Djindra-djindra, "the Willy-wagtail woman"

Road leading in to the pool of "Mutidjula". To the right centre of the picture is the valley of "Uluru"

Tourists looking like rock-mites ascending the Climb. This part of the rock is the symbol of the crouching body and tail of the Mala ("kangaroo men")

Chapter Thirteen

Minyinderri the Windralga

My mate Minyinderri from the Windralga totem was a typical man of the desert tribes. He was always quiet, the result of coming from a race of people who belonged to a land which was difficult to live in, made so by the scarceness of water and hunting grounds which must be travelled over many miles in order to survive.

He explained that his tribal name was derived from a small variety of gravillia plant which grew on the sandhills of his country. This Minyin tree was one of their suppliers of food for it yielded to the hunters —women and men—that sweet-tasting nectar so beloved by the children. I mention it as the hunting food of both sexes because in a pattern which prescribes the food hunted by each sex, the Minyin was allowed to be gathered by all.

His totem name of Windralga came from the seed-pods of the acacia tree which provided the clans with their staple diet.

His colour was of the earth tint which us whites call 'burnt umber'. The word black which was applied to the aborigines was but a term, just as we whites are called that colour when we are of a tint known to painters as 'light-umber'. Burnt-umber . . . light-umber, just a matter of pigmentation in the skin, but what a difference does that tone make when it comes to social prestige and our way of thinking, especially if one has grown up on the lee-side of a city or town.

Minyinderri has the overhanging brow which has come about from a hunting life in sunlit places. His nose is slightly broad, due, I have been told by authorities, because his people once lived in humid places that caused the nostril to expand owing to a greater quantity of air breathed into the lungs. That part of science may be correct, but I myself have witnessed many native midwives press the nose of infants when born as is demanded by custom.

He has cuts on his body, those cicatrices made by his kin as memory-marks after he had passed through an initiation, in the same manner as a white godfather gives a gift to his godchild. Many a time have I seen aborigines stroke these marks when a person's name has been mentioned. It is their way of remembering things—a great advantage over our custom of giving presents which can become lost through the years, and with them the names of the persons attached to the gifts. He has other marks on his back and legs which are the result of ritual fighting. Every scar tells a tale relating to custom, ritual or tribal behaviour.

His wife Bulya is his counterpart in colour. She is not of the type that would win a beauty competition, but she has a kindly soul, whose main concern in life is to keep her eyes on the young black girls, who are always chanting their 'Yerapindji' songs of sex so that they can get her man in their clutches.

Minyinderri laughs loudly at her accusation, but I notice he is careful not to protest too much, because that would be proof in his wife's eyes that he is hiding something. So does he use that balanced judgement in matters of hunting and in family life which is the hall-mark of a good tribesman.

Apart from getting 'No good head' (jealous) over sex business, Bulya does not say much. She believes in the aboriginal law that the customs of the women belong to her sex, that of the men to them. Minyinderri explained the law as he cooled down one day after a general set-to with his 'better-half' (or I should write 'second-better-half' because he has an elder wife on a government settlement who came over to his camp-fire as an inheritance from his deceased brother according to the tribal code).

'You see, Bill,' he explained, 'in my tribe women hunt one way, man hunt another way . . . that right law. When woman do thing one way then it not right for man to do that thing same way. Woman-business for woman, man-business for men, we follow that law and no trouble. But white people came and give us job and black-women see whiteman do woman's work . . . wash plate and clothes, scrub floor anything, well that very good for white people but. . . .' He paused a little as though trying to get his speech in order, then continued: 'Might be that man doing woman's-work-business make trouble. White woman think-think that her man like woman so trouble start. Woman want man-man not woman-man . . . blackfellow have woman work one way, man work in another way, then no trouble. But,' he nodded his head reflectively, 'black-woman go work for white-woman and all this wrong-side business make her mad too. She think different way from tribe-business now, and make trouble for everybody.'

I nodded, to let him know that I understood the full context of his speech, then asked him as to how he came by Bulya?

Knowing that I was aware she had come over to him by stealth from a southern mission station, he jokingly replied that Bulya was 'too much clever from sweetheart-business with her "Yerapindji" songs'.

At the mention of her name Bulya had pricked up her ears so that she laughed aloud at her husband's words, replying that her man was like that mythical Pungalung of the Olgas who was always chasing the women.

His retort was a reference to the 'Willy-wagtail' woman of mythological times who was always prying into other people's affairs. So back and forth went their badinage, with a continual reference to the people of ancient times, in a similar fashion to many people who intersperse their speeches and daily talk with quotations from olden time literature, including the Bible.

My desert friend's eyes were not of the best, yet they were far superior to mine. He could somehow see distant objects, even faint tracks on the ground, but he somehow could not make head nor tail of certain photos I showed to him which pictured his friends.

I had a pair of old spectacles which I let him wear. He was full of praises at the beginning but I noticed that he soon lost them, a strange thing with a people who are such good trackers that they 'can track a flea across a clay-pan'.

My greatest enjoyment at the Rock was a walk about the bush with my aboriginal friends. With them I saw a side of bush life that was hidden to me in past years, for as we walked I observed that their hands and fingers were always moving in that strange finger-talk sign language which is a sort of reflex action from a nimble brain.

His greatest delight was when he came upon native food. How he and Bulya would examine the earth about the slit-like entrance of the honey-ant. Carefully they would look at the (to me) bare earth, then, in a manner which was not unlike a white doctor giving his verdict after a final examination of the patient, he would declare, 'Good or rubbish', as he marked the place for future examinations. Then we would go on once more.

Over countless ages of hunting and passing on their knowledge by word of mouth, they not only knew the track of each creature that will provide them with food, but the way it dug its hole during the different seasons.

To see my native friends digging out a goanna hole or rabbit warren is to see a specialist at work. No digging out tons of earth to get nowhere. They just go carefully with the job. First of all the entrance is examined to see its size. Then out of experience regarding burrows, they poke a stick into the earth at various places. Sometimes Bulya will tap the ground with her digging-stick and carefully note the sound. A flat one for dense earth, a hollow noise means a nest not too far down. No work for my hunting friends but the result they achieve is good.

'Rarbit good tucker,' proclaim my friends as they hold their catch for me to see. 'Rarbit everywhere in my country.' Suddenly he pauses as his eye sees a track upon the ground. He holds up his hand to restrain both Bulya and I who instantly freeze in our tracks. Carefully he peers into a patch of spinifex then I see him lift his kalarta-spear. Crash! The weapon transfixes a rabbit which has come out of the burrow and was crouching under the big clump of spinifex to get away from the cold wind.

Seeing the rabbit in my friend's hands reminds me of an incident when he once passed by my camp with some cooked rabbits, together with a well-cooked wild domestic cat which always live in the same burrows as the bunny.

To Minyinderri, as with all aboriginals, everything edible is food. Thus the cat was just a part of his daily diet. Imagine both his and a tourist woman's surprise when she asked him what was his catch and he nonchalantly answered 'Rarbit and pussy-cat,' with a follow up remark of, 'Good tucker'.

Next day as I was going around the Rock with her as one of the party and at a barbecue lunch I could not suppress a smile as she recounted the incident as though she had seen a cannibal devouring one of its infants. The part that amused me was the looks on her hearers' faces at such a horrible thing, yet all the while they were having a good feed of underdone lamb chops cooked to a turn.

Listening to her tale and noting the looks on the others' faces I marvelled on the perversity of the human race that abhors one food yet likes another. Perhaps it is some latent atavistic instinct resulting from tribal taboos that has built up this complex which can only be cured during times of famine.

When I first met Minyinderri he was part of a scene in the Jedda film which Charles and Elsa Chauvel produced. We were at a place called Mungrakka to the west of Haasts Bluff on one of the scenes which required tribesmen as part of the picture. So he and his kin were sent over by the Settlement people to act as 'bit-players'.

When next I encountered him he rode in on a camel from the western lands to get the job he had during my stay at the Rock.

His job at the Lodge where he works covered everything from tending the garden, helping to clean up the yard, to making boomerangs and wooden snakes for the tourist trade. Watching him at his work, hacking out the pieces of wood or burning lines upon them, I could see that the old-fashioned artifacts of the true tribesman had been swamped in the roaring tourist trade.

No more did one see the well-cut weapon with its beautiful fluted lines. Minyinderri explained to me that in the past the value of an article in the trade was fixed by ritual law. The basis of its trade worth was in the standard of its perfection. Barter was the method of trade and haggling over the price was unknown. 'When the tourist come everything go different . . . make good thing, then they sing out like crow . . . come out from coach like mob bullock from stock yard for picture-taking-business and laugh when we ask all-about for two-bob to buy kiddie some lollie and fruit from store . . . what-name they think we . . . just rubbish?'

Yet rarely did bitterness enter into his talk. Mainly it was on hunting and his country, as on that day when he and I sat upon one of the 'eaglet' stones, just out from the Mother-place, where he re-affirmed Kudekudeka's chants about the great dog Kurapunni, who came from the west to 'pull-out' the first initiate from the camps of the creative Mala people.

'Up there first Loritdja men from spirit-business been camp,' he said proudly as he pointed to the camp of the Elders high up the cliff face then rubbed the smooth grey stone that marks out the area. 'One time plenty people come to this place . . . now nothing for all my countryman went to mission and government place to send kiddie to school so that they can read from the book.' He paused then continued, 'Sometime I think blackfellow fool to leave his proper good country that knows him properly way.'

'You left country,' I rebuked him. 'Suppose that country good why you people run away. What about you?'

At my words he looked over to the west out of which he came and replied. 'My country Kikingurra, that was where I was born.' His words carried a proud note as though he was someone of high degree, then he continued. 'My father's name was Yamguninja from the "Kurakarti" (goanna totem) place, that is in the area of "Kuludunguinga" in the country of "Kikingurra" where I was made a young man. My father proper . . . he is dead now.' Then he sadly added, 'He was a good hunter and always brought in plenty tucker from the bush. He heard about the white people . . . how some good . . . some bad, so that when he get sick he come to the mission people for help and there he been die. My mother Muninga stop at that place,' he continued, 'stay there with my two brothers and three sisters.' He then named his two 'kutu' (brothers) and his four 'kungru' (sisters). As he did I could only wonder as to how those people of the desert could have so many children and everyone be alive.

His calling the names of his children brought me to attention so he continued, 'My sisters have children and they go to school that way'; here he pointed to the south in the direction of the Ernabella mission. 'That mission place teach her kiddies at school.' From him I also learnt that his own children lived at the Areyonga government place where they went to school. He then called their names, ticking each one off on his fingers as he called. 'Jarna, that my son . . . Ambindung, Kitty and June, they my daughters.' 'You proper rich man,' I remarked. 'Me proper rich man,' he replied proudly.

Knowing that the bush aborigines have no idea of their age, I asked him how old he was when that old prospector Lasseter died in his country. To my question he replied as he pointed to his chin which is the sign-talk for a 'beard': 'I was young man with this one. I been finish Kurungra and just outside with this,' he pointed to the headband around his forehead denoting he was a youthful Elder, therefore in his very late teens.

'You saw Lasseter?' I questioned him, and at my words he laughingly answered, 'Of course I saw Lasseter. We all day take him tucker but him little bit cheeky because someone been try spear him . . . him talk that way, but nobody been hurt him only try help.'

'You there when Lasseter die?' I again questioned. To this he answered that his father and he were away to the west at the time and only returned after his people had buried him.

'Blackfellow bury him?' I again asked.

'We bury him, yes must bury body from dingo that would take bone everywhere, that not right.'

After a pause he continued with his story. 'After that dead-fellow-business my father get little bit sick and we all come sunrise-way to mission place, then when my father die I go out and work for white-man with family who was proper poor bugger. That man got no meat from bullock only tucker from camel and donkey.'

'What then?' I queried.

'Well, I been just walkabout nothing . . . hard work to find tucker and can't get job, now me here and soon you and me go back to my properly good country.'

'Might be rubbish-one water?' I cut in. 'Might be you only talk-talk that way for sorry-business.'

'No sorry for country-business,' he countered. 'One day I show you.'

Thus did Minyinderri and I think of the western lands. To visit the country of Kikingurra, but first he and I must go to the top of Ayers Rock to survey the scene—I to gaze out across the country, he to tell me a little of its mythology as we viewed the profile of the land before us.

Chapter Fourteen

Profile from a Mountain

A FEW days later Minyinderri, his wife Bulya, and I went up the Ayers Rock 'Climb' to see the landscape stretching away to the west.

The first whites to do this climb was Gosse the explorer with his camelman Mahood. Behind him, as a thin trail at first, came surveyors, policemen, and 'dingo-scalpers' who sought (in this order) for pastoral land, runaway aborigines or smoke from the camp-fires of hunting tribesmen so that they could barter with them in dingo-scalps for white-man's trade.

Then came the tourists in a thin stream at first, gradually increasing in volume to a torrent that has criss-crossed the land with car tracks. Under the treading of countless feet they have formed a faint path up the Climb which we are now ascending.

As we climbed the tourists were making the pilgrimage, their rubber-soled boots shuffling out a rhythm.

> Old folk, young folk, tottery-folk, and sprightly ones,
> Climbing up the Rock towards the cairn. Wow! Wow!
> Some pulled, some pushed, creaky legs and pumping hearts,
> We're going to reach the top, we've made a vow. Wow! Wow!

What a motley with their coloured jumpers, slacks, and jeans. They swarm past us like rock-mites, some looking wise as they zig-zag back and forth across the Climb under the belief that the grade will be easier to negotiate. Others are on hands and knees, their bottoms sticking into the air, with a waving from side to side like sand-wasps during their egg-laying time.

About seven hundred feet up I begin to conk-out from the height which gives me a dizzy feeling as though I was about to fall. Reading the signal of nature I prevail on my friends to stop. Always polite, they do as I ask; so we select a suitable place to rest so as to survey the scene before us.

Looking out to the west I seemed to be in another world. A Protozoic period of time as ancient as this mountain which is said to have been laid down forty thousand times ago the period of Christianity upon this globe.

Minyinderri is looking to the west, Bulya at the elderly white women climbing up the Rock. With her is sympathy and a complete lack of understanding as to why they climb. I look over the country before me yet always listening to Minyinderri's chanting as he awakens from his subconscious mind the mythological stories of the land before us.

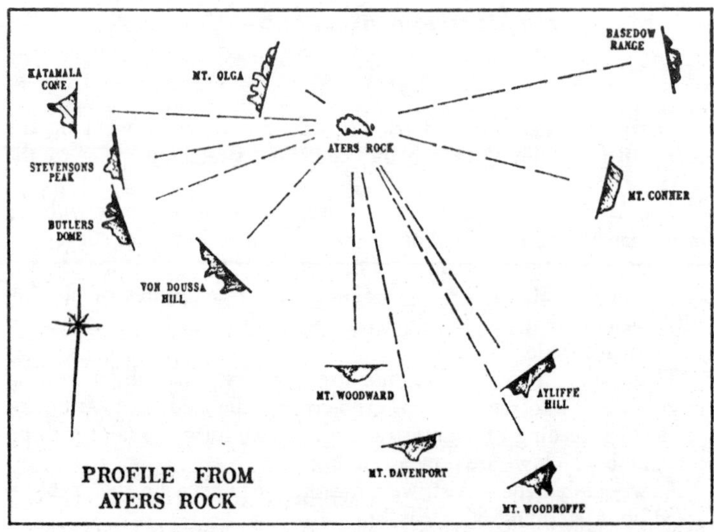

PROFILE FROM AYERS ROCK

Here is a country that has been clothed by a vegetation that has adapted itself, by natural selection over the ages, to survive in this land of low rainfall. Close to the base of the mountain I discern the 'arangulli' (sandalwood) bushes which are of small stature here because they find it difficult to survive against the bush-fires. There also is the eucalyptus called bloodwood which can only grow in a seven-inch rainfall. Therefore it must cling close to the mountain for the moisture that will keep it alive. Poor bloodwoods, how they stand like creatures in a stricken world, their mistletoe-covered withered branches lifted up to the sky as though they were pleading with some tree-god that the curse be lifted so that they might survive.

Beyond them I see the 'Jundala', 'Piljarapa', and 'Wanari' acacia trees that have adapted themselves to the dry areas because of a leaf system and a special series of lateral roots that can live off the moisture in a light rain or even dew. Further out are the graceful 'Kukkuru' casuarinas against the sky-line. The elder ones standing erect with outstretched arms, the younger ones around with foliage which reminds me of waving plumes on the hearses when I was a child.

Among them I also see the 'Windjundi' (hakia) tree with its nectar-laden blooms and its gnarled branches which remind me of aged people dreaming of their youth.

At the feet of all these trees is the brush of the desert lands. The golden 'punddi' cassis with its sulphur-yellow blooms which throw out its sweetness into the night's air. On every side I see the dark patches which tell me that there is the thryptamine with its varied coloured flowers and the rattle-pod and bottle-brush gravillia.

Red soil, green trees, and bushes. Each tree brings up memories of other days for me. The sandalwood makes me think of mustering days on the Georgina River in Western Queensland where we ate its blue-plums as we rode after the herds. It also reminds me of my sailing-ship days, when we employed the aborigines on Groote Eylandt, in the Gulf of Carpentaria, to cut and sap these trees for us so that we could send them off to the markets of China.

The bloodwood trees bring up memories of the eastern desert men tanning their water-carrying 'wanjis' with its sap, just as the casuarinas makes me think of stockyards and adzed slabs of wood for use in the building of station homesteads.

Each object brings up memories. For me it recalls the past in relation to the white people. To my aboriginal friends it is a vision of their youth and the mythology of their country.

Minyinderri somehow senses that I am waiting for him to tell me something about the country before us. So, low at first, then rising to a higher note, he chants as he points out the landmarks and peaks around our horizon. I let him go on with the chanting, for somehow it fixes the thing on his mind so that he will afterwards tell me a clearer story.

From the maps of the area I knew the English name of each feature. The blue line in the distance that was the Petermann Range discovered by Ernest Giles in 1872 and named by him after a Professor Petermann of Gotha. What a great man was Giles. His explorations were epics in this land.

With little government support he travelled 'the hard way', yet he discovered a lot. The readers of his journals and books about his journeys must feel despair when they read how he travelled far to find someone there before him. Then, reading on, they will admire his steadfastness and courage as he kept ever on into the west. We read of great navigators who discovered things because they would not turn back. Giles was such a man as they. Who can read and not feel proud of that man who just pointed his party into the west and kept on going. Westward was the course with water as his problem and his aim. Look well on that map today, with its natural features drawn for the traveller to go by, and realize that it was then a blank space on a piece of paper. Yet Giles crossed it by just riding straight on. The days of travel turned into weeks without water, for 325 miles his party steered by a compass course. Steered by that compass till a day came when the man who had it read the wrong point so that they went off course.

When Giles discovered the mistake he camped. Next morning, as one of his aborigines was out bringing in the camels, he found that water. Who can not be thrilled when they read how that black man came galloping back, shouting as he came, 'Water, water, can't finish.' By an error in travel they had found the only water in that part. To commemorate the find Giles called that place not after the black man or something to commemorate their salvation, but Queen Victoria Springs, after royalty in far away England. What a dull ending for such a dramatic discovery.

Out in that area to the westward a young lad who was with Giles went off on a horse and was never again seen alive; so Giles gave Gibson's name to the so-called desert. Thus does he live on in a history that is rarely mentioned in schools because those men traversed a land that is still unheard of.

Thinking of Giles and Gibson another name which creeps into the picture is that of Lassiter who brings up visions of lost reefs and mountains of gold.

As I dream on about the exploits of white people, Minyinderri chants about his creative heroes who fashioned the country before us, in the dawn of time. He pointed out as he explained that out there, deep into sundown way, Karndju the hunter came out of the land of Bumbwal with his pack of dingoes to follow the trail of that mythical sacred kangaroo who came from the south. The story was of death of his dingoes whose remains commemorate the peaks along their paths in the country of 'Milkajarra', and of the hunter being killed and devoured by the savage curs.

In other chants he tells me of the great Wanambi serpent that threw its coils about some women who would destroy it, and out of their struggles came into existence the rock-holes and features in the Piltardi country of the Mann Ranges.

I look into the land which Minyinderri is chanting about, and note it is the same Mann Ranges which were discovered by Gosse in 1873 and named by him after his friend Charles Mann, then my sight travels on to the Musgraves and the Davenport Range named by Stuart in 1860 after another politician in the South.

History . . . mythology. Minyinderri chants about the country as I dream. Thus do I write of the land in brief so that they who climb

Ayers Rock will know the profile before them to realize that here is a land made alive by the chants of the Loritdja tribesmen.

The foothills of Mount Olga lie due west, a distance of seventeen miles from the base of Ayers Rock. Its 'many-heads' of the same name of 'Katatjuta', as the aborigines call it, stand on a 1,900-foot plateau, rising into the sky for another 1,600 feet. In the morning's light it is a blaze of colour from the reflected light of the rising sun; in the afternoon a tone that has now become known as 'Namitjira-blue', after the famous aboriginal painter.

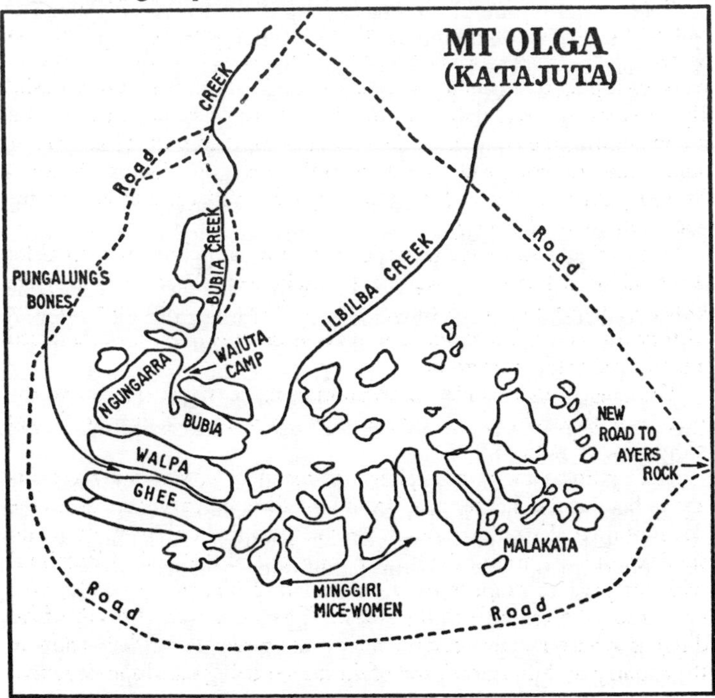

When Giles first saw it from the northern side of Lake Amadeus—which he named after the King of Spain—he called the distant mountains after Olga, the queen of that same country. Viewing it again in 1873 he wrote in his journal of how the domes had 'stood as huge memorials from the ancient times of earth, for ages, countless eons of ages since creation first had birth. Time the old, the dim magician, has effectually laboured here, although all the powers of oceans at his command: Mount Olga remained as it was born'.

Thus wrote Giles, and my aboriginal friend Minyinderri would have agreed with him, for was not part of this massive puddin-stone conglomerate made by the 'Malawaddi' ritual Elders during creative times?

That large plinth of stone which rises 1,000 feet into the sky on the eastern wall is called the 'Malakarta' because he was the head-man of that time. Around him are the Minggari (mice girls) who commemorate the ritual of how they were deflowered by the Hero Pungalung—a cult that made Mount Olga sacred and secret to the tribesmen. The bones of the great Pungalung can still be seen as fallen boulders in the western valley of his name, a deep vale lying betwixt the wind-mountain of 'Walpa' and that 'Ghee' (cyclonic) which is the peeping head of that giant Lothario, the highest peak of the Olga group.

The central feature of the Olga group is the valley of 'Bubia'. A place so sacred that only the spiritual Elders of the tribe could enter its secret precincts. The ritual chants relating to that place are lost, but similar chants are still alive in the northern parts of the Northern Territory as the Kudejingera cult of the Earth-mother Kunapippi.

The story of that area which strongly appeals to me is that of the creative Hero Yuendum of the 'Waiuta' (possum) totem.

Legend records how he became enraged because someone burnt his leg with a magic fire as he slept near the 'Kalajiri' rock-hole in the valley of Bubia. To avenge the insult he gathered up the bush foods of the area then off he went eastwards to redistribute them over the tribal lands so that the song-chants of today record where this food is found. One such spot is near 'Mungeraka'—the Mount Crawford on our maps—it is the totem-centre of the 'Yerimbi' (honey-ant). The small fossils of that area—which are shaped like an aboriginal's head-dress—are said to have been formed that way because he carried that sweet-tasting food within it.

Here mythology and reality come together. The mountain dome 'Ngunngarra'—which is the second highest in the Olga group—is also the Loritdja name for the native fuchsia with its scarlet blooms. For as 'Yuendum' the 'Waiuta' stored the honey in his head-dress to steal it away from those who had ill-treated him, so does the nectar-laden flower imitate its creator by storing at its base a supply of honey as a store for the Yerimbi honey-ants of the totem area. Thus is the deed commemorated by the Elders of the tribe who fashion their hair after that great Hero.

The story of Yuendum begins in the Mount Olga group and ends somewhere east in the Stuart-bluff ranges beyond Central Mount Wedge.

Beyond Mount Olga I discern that pointed profile which is known on our maps and the profile map in this book as Katamala Cone. To the aborigines this mountain peak is called 'Katangarra', to record in chants that story of how the Malawaddi of creative-times—while seeking for the Yerimbi (honey-ants) totem heroes who were led away by Yuendum—discovered, on their march, the fresh-water well of 'Purarra' to the north of Curtin Springs. From there they returned westward along a culture trading-path which was created by the Karlee throwing-stick, of another left-handed Linggi man who is recorded as splitting open the head of another at 'Kataangarra' or 'Head split open'.

Next in importance to the left (as we face to the west from Ayers Rock) is Stevenson's Peak, called that by Gosse in 1873 after another Honourable from the cities. To the Loritdja, however, it is 'Ultulda', a word with the same significance as that of Kumbunduru, or chants of happiness in the big rituals.

Next one to come into the profile is Butlers Dome, which is known to the Loritdja Elders as 'Mundaru-rungga' because of the red sand and ochre deposits around. It was formed, so Minyinderri informed me, because some women in ancient times attempted to dislodge the sacred serpent from his home. Just as I was about to ask my friends about that place which connects the legends of puberty with this myth we heard a great shout of victory from the returning tourists as they came down the Climb.

In a flash our chanting and dreams were gone. A loud yodelling cry came from behind us. Looking up towards the crest I saw the climbers descending. Victory was on their flushed faces as they came down in disorderly array. Women with climbing shoes, men with proud looks on their faces as befitted heroes, girls with thongs. All are sitting back in their breechings, their legs wobbling at the knees; screwing up their faces, all try to take the weight of their bodies away from toenails which are pressing into their shoes. They have seen heaven on the top of the mountain, now they are getting in touch with hell.

One elderly lady who has made the top (only because the coach-captain half carried her there and back) is boasting about her exploits. Suddenly she pauses for breath, then a spasm of exhilaration coming over her, she claps a hand over her mouth to give out a feeble yodel which is immediately taken up by her friends at the base.

I can detect that the folk at the base of the Climb are in high glee, not for her but for the discomfiture of the poor guide who looks not unlike a ewe sheep standing guard over a stricken lamb.

As they pass us the old girl mutters something about Rangers that don't do their job. I just nod in reply, so on she goes yodelling, sitting, and wobbling till they reach the bottom.

Minyinderri looks on in amazement at such stupidity. Bulya mutters something about 'Poor old woman' in such a tone that she really believes the old piece has gone off her head, and is ready to be led around on the end of a stick—the aboriginal custom for old age. To Bulya the climbing was not an achievement, but some sort of a religious rite which made the old girl go to the top of the mountain, just as people go to holy places overseas.

Perhaps it was some inner urge, for her eyes somehow looked as though she had achieved her life's ambition. She was not the frail old thing that was pampered by the children back at home, but a reborn one who had 'gone to the cairn' in the Centre of Australia.

Below me, at the base of the Climb, is a slim-looking girl in white slacks, that, from the distance, make her appear naked. She sways her body to and fro with a sensual rhythm that makes me think of that other young girl who danced before a king so that she could get the head of a saint.

From her I lift my gaze to Butler's Dome with its mythology of the two maidens who were destroyed because they defiled the sanctuary of a God. How old is that puberty maiden legend? Anthropologists have recorded that legend in the north of this land; each myth tells the same story, an unbroken tale that stretches back into the lands of Asia out from which these people came.

The religious beliefs of mankind are as old as man; each one has been evolved to suit the environment out of which it sprung. Here on this mountain is a cult so old, that deep within it are the glimmerings of newer faiths which came to life on the earth, long after these people migrated southward to establish a way of life and legends associated with the natural features of the new land around them.

With the aborigines all ritual and mythology relates to their way of life. If we cannot get to the meaning of a legend it is we who are wrong, not they. Rain-water is holy because it comes from the sky-spirits. The springs are permanent because the Rainbow-serpent of life lives deep within them and thus gives them permanency.

Sharp is the line of demarcation between woman and man. Each have their duties to perform so that the tribe shall survive. Hence both have their sacred and secret lodges which are strictly forbidden to the opposite sex.

The honking of a motor-horn at the base of the Climb has the people converging towards it. Among them our Salome lass, who has performed her pagan ritual of sex, is now seeking rewards from the males of the party. They move off in a cloud of dust, and as they depart we continue with our viewing of the places before us.

The next high peak in our circle is Van Doussa Hill, called by Minyinderri 'Kulpi Elli' (shelter of the fig tree), a place sacred in ritual because it was the path of the two 'Malawaddi' going eastward in creative-times.

Now to our left rises Mount Woodward, a name that first appeared with Mount Ayliffe on the triangulation plan by John Carruthers, a South Australian surveyor who plotted the area from 1888 to 1890. It was he who named the mountains after his friends, yet I see no name on the maps that carry his name. Thinking thus I nod my head at a mountain which is a monument to a man's achievement and his modesty.

So much for the history of Mount Woodward which was all that could be gathered from official files; now for its mythology which is not recorded on paper but in the oral songs of the Loritdja.

It is called 'Purrajungga' (itchy-place), a very sacred ritual spot where some Malawaddi Elders returned to sing a very sacred chant that enticed the Head Malawaddi into the earth. When there he returned unseen by humans to the place of 'Malakarta' (Mala-head) where he now resides forever as a large dome on the eastern side of the Mount Olga group.

The next mountain in our profile is Davenport which was named thus after the Davenport Ranges discovered by Stuart in 1860. It rises to a height of over 4,000 feet and I sincerely hope the Sir Samuel Davenport it was named after was as prominent as the mountain against the skyline.

To the aborigines this mountain was the 'Djarpeya' place of shallow water, commemorating the 'induga' (monitor-lizard) legend of how he stole the sacred 'djewa' grinding-stone by which the ritual Elders ground up the seeds to make their sacred food. The chant commemorates how they followed him; of how he swallowed the stone when he heard them coming; then denied the theft. Dissatisfied with his excuse the Elders returned to hold a council to prove that he had told a lie. The proof of his lying was in his footprints on the sand which were deeper after the theft than before the stealing. Returning once more they came upon him and in a ritual fight he was destroyed so that the sacred 'djewa' was saved as an article which can be used by the people for all time.

The legend of the 'induga' is interesting as showing us how the Loritdja had taken the characteristics of that reptile to form the story. It is common knowledge to observers of nature—I have seen it a few times too—that the monitor lizard is capable of swallowing large objects by distending its jaws, and using its body as a battering-ram literally to drive the bone down its neck into its body. The one I saw on the job was having a hard time with the battering because the object he used to ram against kept on moving. Realizing its mistake the reptile looked around, then moved over to a solid post to continue the swallowing of what I would call a forced meal.

A little east of south we see the highest mountain in South Australia rising out of the Musgrave Ranges. Named Woodroofe by Gosse after George Woodroofe Goyder it is but a few steps under 5,000 feet above sea-level and dominates all the other peaks around. Nearer to Ayers Rock and a little to the east is Mount Ayliffe, which was mentioned by Carruthers in his survey plan.

To the Loritdja it is the sacred place of 'Yerimbi', the honey-ant people of their mythology.

Our view from where we sit is now blocked out by the dome we are resting on. Those who climb the Rock will see to the eastward the flat-topped mountain of Conner which was named thus by Gosse in 1873 after M. L. Conner. Conner is the lowest of the three famous mountains in this area. All lie directly east and west out of a geological formation known to geologists as the Amadeus-Geosyncline. Conner is a 'basin fold'; Ayers Rock is in subvertical sediments as a 'rock horst'; Mount Olga is something laid down amidst roaring torrents in the valley of mighty mountains in a very early period of geological time.

Although Mount Conner is the smallest of the three domes its mythological story is full of incident. Chief of them is the legend around the 'Anneri' soak which carries a tale not unlike the Anteaus myth with its symbol of regeneration.

Last profile in our circle is the Basedow Range, which was named thus to honour the anthropologist Doctor Basedow, one who earned the honour because he travelled through that area to study its geology and its aborigines. The area has a tie-up with the Loritdja who used the red-ochre deposits of 'Eyowa' for their rituals. It carries a memory for me because of a tale which I heard as Kudekudeka, Imalung, and I sat beside Maggie Springs at Ayers Rock.

The story was of how Kudekudeka and his clan had come in from the dry lands where they had been hunting. Experience had taught them that the spring must be dry because no rain had fallen for nearly a year, but imagine their surprise when they found the spring full to overflowing.

'We been get big surprise,' recounted Kudekudeka, 'that water there not right . . . then one old man, my uncle, said, "Must be somebody make trouble for one of our people and that 'Wanambi' get sorry and pour water from wooden bowl on his head. That's why the water is here now".'

A few days later a messenger came in from the east to tell them one of the old men of the tribe had been shot by a native police tracker as he was making an arrest. It was found out later the old man was innocent, but the 'Wanambi of Uluru' knew that truth long before the white people. Thus did he grieve over an injustice done to one of his people.

Geology, history, and stories, old and new! I sit at night outside my Ranger's cottage to watch the stars sink down below the crest of the mountain. Minyinderri sits and burns patterns on to a piece of white wood which he hopes will catch the tourist's eye so as to bring him a few shillings. All the while he talks about his 'proper-number-one-country'.

'What about you and me go that way, old man?' At his words 'old-man', I wonder does it refer to my physical infirmities or is it a form of respect to aged people who are said to have much wisdom?

I doubt the second because I am not one of the tribe; as for the first I know that he has got my measure since our climb up the mountain. So I answer, 'One day we go but too much job here now.'

'When there,' continues Minyinderri, 'I will tell you plenty story. Mob story in my country . . . can't finish.'

Can't finish. Where does the story end? Everywhere over the Northern Territory I have listened to the legends of the black people. A wanderer must always wander, and so would I; to go out into Minyinderri's country where I would listen each night to his stories that 'can't finish'.

My camp will be his camp-fire where I will listen to the laughter of his children and the howling of his dogs. I will watch the native women hunting as they did long before the white people came to destroy the tribal pattern. Now it is just a dream but sometimes dreams do come true.

Chapter Fifteen

Good Seasons

My first year at Ayers Rock was one of settling in: water found and pumps erected to lift it into a storage tank; houses built with my tent well-constructed beneath the mulga trees. Thanks to my old aboriginal friends and other mates in the South I knew some of the country's history and mythology. Thus did I know a little as I walked around the mountain with the tourists. Even so the vegetation amazed me with its heavy growth under the high cliffs along the way we travelled.

Ayers Rock! Little did the spirits within it realize that a new way of life, or death, was about to come upon them. The blue-plum fruits of the sandalwood trees were plucked as curios by those who did not know they were edible, or as fruit by those who did. The aboriginal law relating to flora and fauna was but a name when it came to a pretty bloom. Here and there small paths went winding through virgin bush. Somewhere else a motor left the road. The law of the Reserve was that people must camp in fixed places, but if I happened to be away, or they went by in the night, what then? Reality was one thing, the law another.

In 1958 the Welfare Branch handed over the administration of the reserve to the Northern Territory Reserves Board. As the area went over, so did I. The only difference now was that people must pay an entry fee of ten shillings per adult, with a camp fee per head for living in the camp area.

In the past I just gave a permit of entry to each traveller, now it was the collecting of money for tickets and the paper work that goes with money transactions.

But what of these payments and the reactions on the travellers? Many paid but quite a few went 'up in the air' when they heard the good news. One tourist who went up in the air about it ended up paying for the permit. As we talked afterwards I could somehow get his side of the picture. He had brought himself and his family out to this Rock. The road was rough going yet he was pleased to be giving them this treat. The mountain of Uluru had stood for millions of years. The winds of the deserts had massaged its face to give it a wrinkled look. Hosts of aboriginals had lived around its flanks and it was they who had painted the cave art on it. Then suddenly it was 'found'. Newspapers wrote about it. Photos of it were in all the leading magazines. The bush roads into it were made by patient travellers who cut their own way, and motors coming behind them beat it into a highway. Then suddenly, out of the blue, came the edict which made the area into a National Park. With the Park came myself as Ranger to charge entry fees to bewildered weary travellers who just could not understand what it was all about.

Yet the Board was right in charging. Someone had to pay for the building of roads, the putting down of bores and the laying of pipes to carry the water to the well-built camp areas.

'Everything was too new,' as the aborigines said when they heard the travellers complaining. 'By and by they learn.' The travellers did learn, but in teaching them I came in for a lot of abuse.

The year of 1959 was the year of good rain—a good seven inches, which to the cattle-station owners meant heaven, but hell to the tourist companies and the motor travellers. At that time one had to be guarded in speech. To bless the rain to a tourist who has been hopelessly bogged for days meant a fight. To wish the rain away when a cattleman was about meant the same thing. My old mate Minyinderri refused to pass comment when someone jocularly mentioned the tribal 'rain-stones', and the only reason I was asked for an opinion, as to rain, was when a traveller wanted my verdict so that he could blame me if my predictions were haywire, thus leaving him in the lurch.

Yet who worried? Not I. For the first two years my tent kept out the rain, and many a tourist who had come in late at night during a storm slept on its floor. Then came the Ranger's cottage, but regardless of dwellings the morning would see the billy-can boiling away on the drum-fire-place; then as we sipped our morning cup we would talk about the only subject they new, which was rain. Rain on the Rock. Ah! That was a scene I was never tired of beholding, that and the smell of rain as it fell upon the warm earth, with the clouds sweeping low over the crest of the mountain.

Sun on the Rock during the rain brought out a dome of silver above the trees, with the rain water sweeping down the ravines like a river in spate. During the storms the thunder would roar and the lightning flashes streaked down the cliff faces like threads of gold weaving a pattern through a cloisonné bowl. Then everything was in the process of change. The red-coloured earth became a mass of green and yellow as the grass and spinifex was transformed. The trees, a greyish-red before with dust, were now green and upright as though reborn.

Rain in the winter months on the desert meant a profusion of wild flowers. Ayers Rock would be out in bloom but I loved most of all the Olgas with its valleys of trickling water and its wealth of flowers.

Minyinderri was with me on a trip to the 'Katatjutas', and there, in the sacred valley of Bubia, he was in high glee as he stood neck-high amidst the white flowering 'ingulba' native tobacco, to gather their fleshy leaves into sacks so that he could send some away to his kinsmen in the settlements and towns.

'Proper good one this, all-a-same white fellow tobacco, only this one more better,' he called out to me as I stood upon the green carpet of grasses and red boulders which seemed heaven after the dust and dry of the last year. How cool to sit there and hear the trickling of fresh water flowing along the ravines cutting through a carpet of lily-like blooms which the tourists call 'Harbingers of Spring'. For me the colours around were what mattered. But Minyinderri only saw plants as something which will produce things; the tobacco plant is good for 'chewing', the lily-blooms as 'good tucker for old people . . . young kiddie . . . everyone'. His talk of food caused me to look down a small ravine upon a mass of yellow-centred blooms with a white edge. They look to me likė poached eggs, and imagine my surprise when a woman tourist informed me that that is their name.

Up farther into the valley at a look-out place called the 'Valley of the Winds', Minyinderri was all agog when he saw a clump of white-flowering tacoma trees among a heap of fallen boulders. 'Urejumba', I heard him call, 'good for making "karlarta" spear.' Regardless of the law about the cutting of trees he was getting some of the long thin stems for making future spears. Minyinderri was only following the instinct of the huntsman and foodgatherer.

Everywhere around the Olgas were carpets of flowers in good seasons: the bottle-brush and rattle-pod gravillia of the sandhills near by, their yellow blooms, sweet with nectar so beloved by the aboriginal children and the adults who have passed that word 'Warma' into the wines they procure when in the towns; pussy-cat tails, showy groundsel, the convolvulus of the flats. How can I describe those flowering plants and bushes when there were so many around me? We walked around to the western side of the Olgas, and there, in that beautiful valley of Pungalung, he and I just marvelled at nature.

Here on the sandy ground were the gold-hats in abundance mixed with the flannel and the guinea-flowers. Pink bindweed trailed along the base of the cliffs, and down the watercourses were the red-centred hibiscus. But why go on to describe something that only a colour camera can record?

Flowers were in every rock-cleft and ravine. At one place we came upon some flowering fuchsias. When I explained to Minyinderri that this plant secreted a poison that killed cattle when droving, he smiled tolerantly as he picked off the blooms, and, chewing them, asked for more information on this subject. He apparently didn't believe me, for how could one of his foods be poison to anything.

On that western side of the Olga group were the three main mountains of the area. The main one, Ghee, was the aboriginal word for cyclonic because it symbolized Wanambi in his wrath. Standing beneath that tall dome we viewed it through a pink-flowering hop tree which somehow gave a rich foreground to the scene. The best time to see the Olgas is in the winter, a month or two after a good season. In the beginning and up to 1960 the road out to the Olgas was on a track which went a long way round, a distance of thirty-three miles. In that year C. P. Mountford, with his friends Ainslie Roberts and Anton Rieby, came out to study the mythology of the area and paint the landscapes of the country. I went with Monty on the first trip, which was over an old camel track used by him and the desert travellers years before. Our guides were two aborigines of the Loritdja called Lively and Captain. What a bumping we had in Monty's Land Rover, but it was well worthwhile, for I saw, for the first time, the beauty spots on the eastern side of the Olga group. Since then surveyors have come out, and behind them the graders and bull-dozers to cut a highway which is only seventeen miles from the base of Ayers Rock to the tall dome of Malakarta.

What productivity came from the earth with the first storms, when the seeds felt the moisture form the great Earth-mother and sprang into life. The plant life at Ayers Rock and the Olgas seemed to reflect the happiness that was over us all. The trees were bright and did not break to the touch as in the dry-time. The grass had lost its burnt look, and burst into a green that blended well with the red soil. Under the high cliff faces the lowly ferns from a bygone age were growing profusely once more. The very road was springy to the pounding wheels of travelling motors full of people who radiated happiness as they came out to see us.

Rain! My brightest memories of the Rock were during the rain with its lightning storms. Then I would stroll down to Maggie Springs to watch the water flow into it from the mountain above. What a howling and roaring it made as the torrent tried to overtake itself in that descent of eleven hundred feet from the crest to the rock-pool below. What a swirl of water went down the small creek, sweeping past the shelter of Mutidjula with its defaced art. Minyinderri and I loved to see the rain falling, and the hundreds of silvery waterfalls tearing down the mountain's side. With them came happiness and life as was recorded in the Loritdja chants. But greatest joy to all who understood was to pause before the 'Mother-place' on the eastern side of Ayers Rock—pause to watch the great 'Kumbunduru' of the 'Mother-place' grow dark with the falling water which started near the home of a God to finish up in her ritual womb, the ritual pool of 'Nginindi' which is the centre of creation.

Chapter Sixteen

Tourists

In camp or train,
On tramp or plane
Waste tissues show, her breeding-O.
With pose she goes and blows her nose,
And throws down those unsightly rows.
Proceeding-O, Unheeding-O.

THE year 1960 brought on the Motley in strength. I do not write the word 'motley' disparagingly. It comes to my mind when I see the coloured jumpers and slacks the women wear during the winter season; that, and their happy-go-lucky nature when on holiday, and the various places they have come from to see the Centre.

'All-a-same ant,' was Minyinderri's comment when a safari coach-load emptied itself into a camping area which I had set aside for their use. 'All-about camp anywhere in bush just like blackfellow.'

The law about litter was fixed, but because of the countless tissue-papers that blew into the bush I was forced to pen the above verse for my own protection. Strangely it had the desired effect. The people read and commented on the doggerel but from then on they put the waste papers in their handbags or pockets till they could burn or bury them.

Studying all the travellers who came to the National Park I soon realized that nearly all people from the cities are creatures of habit. On safari tours they are not unlike red meat ants that wander around all day in a sort of endless coming and going finally to hole-up around their camp-fire when darkness fell. These safari tours were nearly always composed of young folk who were associated with naturalist groups and bush-walkers from other states. Naturally they were the ones I 'froze' on to should I require information on the flora and fauna of the area. At night their camps were full of song, story, and music from instruments which were nearly always made up from tins, bottle-tops, and card-board boxes attached to wires.

The tourists were provided with everything from the day they left the cities till they returned, and this much I will say for the Ayers Rock–Mount Olga area. The conditions for the tourist's welfare were excellent. Hot and cold showers, septic systems with workers, cooks, etc., to look after them were of the very best during my stay in the area. I do not write this as a build-up for the tourist companies but in gratitude to the people who made my stay at the Rock such a pleasant one.

The tourists themselves were people from many different strata of society: elderly women who have saved a little to realize their dreams now that their children have been 'married-off'; business people who want a rest away from the worry of city life; doctors out here on a rest-cure, and young girls of various professions who have just come out into the bush to be away from those things which we are in the habit of calling 'the conventions'.

These people I would take around the Rock to explain its mythology. Everybody had questions for me to answer. How long had I been out at the Rock? Did I like being here? How deep did the Rock go under the ground? How did I live when I left here? And that never-ending one: 'Do you write your own books or do you just put them on to a tape recorder for some other good Samaritan to unravel?' Behind all their questions was a note of patronage. They had come from the city, and as the city was the hub of their universe it was only natural for them to think that those who lived farther away from that place of culture and intelligence must have a lower rating than themselves.

I tried to answer all the questions—even the one about the writing of books, which I never recorded because I always typed them.

As the Ranger, my duty was to collect the 'loading-manifests' from the permanent touring companies to send them with a report into the Alice each month, to the Secretary of the Reserves Board. The tourists who came over the road were given a permit. They would then sign their names in a Reserves Record book and the numbers each month would go in with my report. Thus do I know that from one hundred tourists in 1956 the figures rose to over 4,000 in 1961, my last year at the Rock. During those years over 17,000 people visited the area. The Rock became known as the 'money-spinner', but for me it brought in great friends to give me much happiness.

Yet there was always the ones who just could not understand how people in the bush survived. They just would not believe we liked the place. They thought we were only putting on a brave face in a manner of someone in jail who has yet a long way to go.

When I explained to one elderly lady that I was only here for six months and then went to live in the Alice or Darwin she was concerned and wanted to know what I lived on. When I told her I used up the money I received as wages on this Ranger's job, she looked surprised. Remarking that she was always under the impression we were not paid but lived on the tips we received from the tourists.

Tips from the tourists! I told her that if I had to live on what I got from the travellers I would have died ages ago. I mention this incident to show the mentality of some people who come out to visit us at the Rock. It is not their fault, for they have been encouraged to picture farmers and bushmen as strange illiterate characters not far removed from the aborigines.

Yet although the travellers had their own opinion about us 'bushies' they were full of patriotism regarding their home-places. Let something be said about where they came from and their hackles would rise up like the protective spines on an ant-eater when danger approaches.

I noticed too that their view of the purity of the water while in the area of Ayers Rock was based on their city's water supply. In this respect they were not unlike beer-drinkers whose tastes and opinions have been fixed by the local brew.

This water battle was always a source of enjoyment to me whenever we passed by Maggie Springs. Before it stood a sign which read:

> This is neither bath nor sink,
> Some who come may wish to drink.

Maggie Spring during the rain-time was always full of good fresh water. Some of the tourists would sip it carefully and naturally compare it with their home water supply, then the fun would start.

'Nearly as good as Melbourne water,' said one tourist. At her remark I would hold forth about the green slime (algae) within it being responsible for its purity and that of the pool before us. Then I would lower my voice and remark learnedly, that Maggie Springs' water was the purest in the world.

As Melbourne water is considered by Melbourne people to be the purest in the world my statement would be assailed. This would bring on a host of opponents defending their cities' water supply. At first I thought it was fun until two of the tourists nearly got to blows about the matter so I finished that line of talk. Patriotism can lead to strange things, even with people speaking the same tongue.

I enjoyed every minute of the show. Never in my life have I been the centre of so much attraction. What a posing for photographs! If I refused to pose I was considered a 'nark'. If I put on the act I was a 'vain old man'. I was as the brown bear amidst the Carpathian gipsies. Always ready to perform to the master's bidding.

How difficult it was to control the people in an area as large as the National Park. What a hopeless task to stop all the clever fellows who put their empty tins and bottles behind boulders or under the large spinifex clumps. But the greatest pest to me was those who insisted on plucking flowers which are, to me, the wonders of nature and a glory to behold. The poor flowers! What a hammering they got during the tourist season. Let a clump of dainty hairbells peep out from a larger tuft of grass that has protected it from the weather, or the pink flower of the parrakelya be showing amidst the spinifex, then down will come a human claw from on high. Out comes the flower and the plant too. Their reproductive days are over, for the seeds have perished through that inane act. Why women did it I do not know. When I rebuked them and talked about the law they looked so meekly at me and gave me the same answer that they 'loved flowers'.

What a strange answer to give for destroying things of beauty. Looking at the blooms in the culprit's hand I knew that when they faded she would cast them on to the floor of her bedroom at one of the tourist company's resorts, where they will be swept up by the cleaners.

Psychologists have written chapters in their books about these 'floral-ones'. Apparently it is a complex of old age.

Behold the Floral one who goes,
To gather blooms where'er they spread.
As youth fades out their complex grows
And treading weary years ahead,
Strike back at life where beauty glows
To leave blooms dead, where'er they tread.

This urge to destroy is one of the curses of the human race. How many people love to kill just for the sake of seeing things topple over into the dust. In every instance they justify their killing by saying the dead creature was a pest. Yet I met one person who was a member of a bird-loving society whose main object in life was to save birds and arrest the killers of them; yet he himself had gathered in the interests of science over three thousand specimens. On one hand the creatures are destroyed as pests, on the scientific side they are destroyed to advance human thought. What a strange mad world.

But for me the great days at the Rock were when my friends came out to visit me. During those times I would have the Board's 240-volt lighting plant going to light up the Ranger's cottage. What singing we had then, what tales were told! Many times my friends sent out their children to stay with me over the school holidays. What a time then as we wandered around the mountain with Penny, Peter, and Ian. Tourists and children, how much alike as they roam the bush. Each one of them seeing new things. The days of the Motley were good days for me.

Chapter Seventeen

Human Behaviour

HUMAN behaviour is alike in many places over the globe. Jove hurls his thunderbolt, yet who will burn the wood from the stricken tree? As a lad I was always warned that such wood would not burn. Heeding the story and bowing to authority I never troubled to find out if it would do so.

An elderly aborigine who was out gathering wood with me one day refused to touch the wood from such a tree because it was taboo from 'lightning-business'. He also would not pick up wood from an abandoned aboriginal camp-fire claiming that such wood may have been gathered by a person taboo to him and to use it would cause him to become sick or to die. Bushmen of old never would use an old camp fireplace, making the excuse that the place may have been fouled by the one who last used it.

Many people smile tolerantly at superstition, at the same time finding excuses to prevent us from infringing the superstition. In my war years I often wondered if the prohibition on lighting a cigarette three times related to the age-old superstition regarding three; or was it, as they claimed, a prevention against the third man getting shot by an enemy sniper who had seen the first lighting, trained his rifle on the second and pulled the trigger on the third.

The strange thing about white and black bushmen not using a strange fire was that they would use it in a place which had been set aside for cooking, as in a stove or the fireplaces set aside by the Reserves Board.

Most people live in a groove; if they see something away from the normal then questions are asked. Let a fig tree or bloodwood be growing on a rock wall on Ayers Rock and the questions would flow as to how it grew there. To my reply that it was one of nature's pot-plants in her window-ledge similar to the ones they had back home, would be met with the reply that 'this was different'. The Ranger's cottage walls were made of pressed wheat straw-board which had been pressed flat with complicated machines, and I was always asked, 'Did it keep out rain?' When I explained it was only a portable thatch which was made in the cities and sent up in a manner similar to the sending of other building material, the same answer would be given as to it being 'different'.

Apparently the word 'different' meant something outside the normal reasoning—a thing which had to be explained. My biggest problem was the mythology of the Rock.

When I went around the mountain with my aboriginal friends I soon came to realize that this story had many similarities to other religions, so I endeavoured to describe it by giving the tourists a parallel, which would give them a clearer picture.

The idea was good but I did not take into account the fixed beliefs people have about their own faiths and beliefs. Most people have been taught that the aboriginals of Australia are at a low ebb of society, and to mix the two faiths was therefore trying to belittle their doctrine. To point out that man's belief in a Creator was as old as mankind was useless. They just knew I was an atheist and not to be trusted. Although I explained at great length that the legends I was telling them were the ones I had been given by the Loritdja Elders they still scoffed in the same manner as they did when I told them I wrote my own books.

To explain to them that the fault-plane on the west side of Ayers Rock was created as a symbol of the sacraments, in the same manner as when Moses went up into the mountain of Sinai to receive the tablets from the Lord, was sacrilege. To them my tale was a complete fabrication, the black fellows a bunch of liars, with me as a pain in the neck.

To me the whole thing was interesting as giving a clue to the tenacity of men's faiths, which—in most instances—they had received from their parents. They believed and that was that, just as the aborigines reasoned that a waterhole is permanent because it is the sacred abode of the Serpent Wanambi. To explain to them that permanency in the spring or waterhole gave rise to the abode of the Wanambi would meet with such a rebuke as was given to me by my religious friends.

This strange belief I found with native healing. A doctor always arises before the illness he is supposed to cure, just as in a religion which evolves a God as a ritual way of controlling the tribe.

The spiritual side of man controls his material life, a thing brought home forcibly to me when an aboriginal from a Christian mission on Bathurst Island explained, at great length, that Darwin was not bombed during the war as part of a military plan but came about because one of his tribesmen threw some 'Devil's blood' into the sea. This sacrilege had so enraged the tribal spirits that they caused a thought-message to pass into the minds of the Japanese High Command who acted on it and so became the instruments of their wrath.

One must then ask the question, who is right or wrong? To have communion with spirits is common to all people, and leads to the question I was repeatedly asked to answer at the Rock. How intelligent are the aborigines?

To me intelligence is the ability to observe and absorb. A bush-dwelling aboriginal in a city would be just as much lost as a white city dweller in the bush. A skilled technician working on a lathe would be considered clever to the aborigine. The city man observing an aborigine tracking and hunting game would say his I.Q. was high. Each one is intelligent in his own environment.

A tourist pulled up beneath a shady mulga tree not far from my Ranger's cottage at Ayers Rock, the door opened and out jumped a small pup. It immediately ran over to the bird-bath I had beneath a water tap, where it drank some water. At the call from its owner, who never got out of the car, it returned to the running board of the vehicle where it was picked up by one of the passengers within. After a few words they went on their way and about an hour later an aboriginal hunter and his wife came by to get a drink of water at the same tap.

Within seconds they had their fingers bunched together in the sign talk for dog. Without moving they retraced the pup's movements. How it drank then went back to the car. Now came a movement of a hand reaching out and the sign of a person on a steering wheel driving the car away.

No word was spoken, yet the movements I had seen were re-enacted by sign-language which could be plainly understood. To my observing friends it was but a matter of ordinary routine which happened each minute when out hunting.

I naturally asked what their antics were about. They explained it all with a forebearance one would expect at childish questions. 'How you know they pick it up?' I queried. 'That nothing,' they replied simply. 'Suppose puppy-dog jump its leg make big mark. If lift up nothing.' As a final retort to my ignorance the woman called out 'Man-dog too', as she pointed with her digging-stick to a small depression on the earth where the little creature had relieved itself in the fashion of its kind.

Yet in spite of this ability to reason during the hunt, the aborigines are hedged in by customs as soon as the food caught in the hunt is brought into the camp. Out in the bush where the hunter must use his wits against nature is one thing, in camp another.

The animal killed must be cooked by one person, cut up by another, and each portion distributed according to the law of kinship: a certain piece to the uncle, another to the mother.

The dogs of the family will be a part of the scheme, for although they appear to be the outcasts of the tribe they too share in the laws of relationships as do the humans. Let a woman own a bitch then that creature will be recognized as her daughter. The pups from her daughter will be her grandchildren.

Aboriginal mythology teaches that the human beings were created by the Earth-mother in the beginning. To them was given the right to create the artifacts, and all those things essential to life upon the earth. As man created those things, his deed was commemorated by his transformation into an animal which became one of the tribal totems. Thus does the kangaroo become the head-man of the boomerang, the smoke-hawk the head-man of the fire with a goodly assortment of other totems in line. With this belief came that other one that the wild things of the bush are the food of man, but the creatures of the camp are of the tribe. They enter the kinship law and are protected as such. Once a person feeds or pats an animal it is a pet, and pets are one of the family.

I once employed an aboriginal woman who had a mania for pets. She was one of those eternal mother types who have every stray around them. As her pets they were also her kin who had a right to the camp in the same way as would a human. Each one was given a 'Skin'—generation-level term. In no time I was surrounded by relations from the animal world. A big fat sow was my daughter, a pup was my son. Pigs were in such profusion that I was forced to get in touch with a policeman friend who cleaned the lot up when I and my native friends went away for a week to a town. What consternation in our camp when the mother returned to find that her pets had disappeared—the pigs sold to the butcher, the dogs somewhere else. To put on a show I too had to raise my voice in wrath for a few days. Only after my friend came around to explain that he had heard the dogs were reported to be killing cattle and the pigs had some sickness which was discovered by a stock inspector, together with a small gift to the Mother, were things smoothed over so that we sailed on once more till the next clean-up.

One may well ask why people who employ aborigines tolerate these things. I can only answer that the customs of a people are a part of their lives. To live with one we must tolerate the other.

Humans claim they possess dogs when all the time the dogs possess them. A person to kick another person's dog is to start a fight, not only amidst whites but with blacks. I know of two instances when the hitting of dogs started a tribal fight that ended with one person being killed and the other in jail.

On a cattle station in the Northern Territory one of the biggest rows I knew started when an overseer foolishly killed a station pet cow because it kept getting into the garden and eating the vegetables.

The aboriginal stockmen claimed that the killing of the creature was justified because it destroyed the station property, but what they threw boomerangs over, and walked off the place for, was that the overseer had corned and cooked the meat which they ignorantly ate. The case was fought out in the Darwin Law Courts and ended with jail for some of the aboriginals—a miscarriage of justice—and the sack for the overseer, not because he was in the wrong but because no other native would work for him.

This inherent trait of aboriginal philosophy whereby they believe that the creatures of the earth were made by them in creative times, is responsible for many minor practices and superstitions today.

Let a man or woman in the Loritdja tribe be kept awake all night by the clicking of the 'merin-merin' beetle then nothing will convince them that it is the ordinary procedure of the beetle as it goes about its task of gathering food. To them the merin-merin brings messages of assignation from one sweetheart to another. The clicking noise beneath one's head, which prevents one from going to sleep, is a message from a sweetheart who has sent the beetle forth with a magic song that none can resist: 'Merin-merin, merin-merindi kowarndu wataru, bringu-bringu Kowarndu.'

A simple sing with words in it which seem not unlike English, but according to Minyinderri it is a 'Proper song full up sweetheart-business for girl.'

It is these magical chants which are really responsible for a lot of misdemeanours in the tribe. No one does things of their own volition, for all are strong determinists and fiercely resist free will. The lethal chants of the Kunia on the south-east side of Ayers Rock can kill the person who is chanted. He just dies and it is the duty of the Elders to determine, not how he died, but who chanted the magic song connected with his name.

To understand this philosophy one must realize that not only are the birds, beasts, and plants the living things of creation; but the stones, even the mountains of Ayers Rock itself carry within them the living symbols of the creative heroes. They are not dead, but asleep within the stones listening to the ritual elders who chant their songs about them. It is this belief that has given rise to the saying that 'A country does not know a person until that human can speak the language of that area.' It is the country that is a living thing, the human being is but a part of that land. He only controls the creatures around through the magical chants that can only be sung by those who understand the language and the ritual law.

Into all this hocus-pocus, superstition, and magic come those incredible white people who honestly believe they are the torchbearers of mankind. They are never 'touring' but 'working' to save souls.

To these people has come the 'light' which, in their hands, will drive away the darkness from the all-heathen minds. Fixing their belief on some passages from the Bible, they honestly believe they are right and all other people wrong. To them hospitality does not exist. They have a mission in life.

How many have sat in the Ranger's house out at the Rock to 'give me the works' I cannot recall. Each one of them has left me the literature of their denomination with an exhortation that I read it in my quieter moments.

Discussing this thing with a friend he explained he had an infallible remedy for dealing with these inerrant pedlars of religion. He cordially invited them into his house to hear his latest record of sacred music. As the record player was of the long-playing variety they certainly received a big dose of their own medicine. One side of the record generally sufficed the hardiest of the pedlars who were there to blow their own trumpet. His maxim was perfect quiet while the music was on with a short prayer as he put the record over to the other side. 'When you get the persistent ones,' he explained to me confidently, 'pray. That's the only thing I know that can stop the hardened ratbags.' I thought his cure excellent so I pass it on.

One of the highlights, during my stay at Ayers Rock, in relation to the religious ones, was one morning when I arose to behold a large covered-in van on the main road outside the house. A large sign on its side proclaimed to all that it belonged to a society that sold Bibles. At my welcoming 'Good-morning' the rear door opened and a disciple of George Burrows popped his head out into the morning air. I invited him over to have a drink of tea.

As is usual with those people he was soon on religion—he on Christianity, and the Bible which he claimed was the word of God and therefore correct in every word. I naturally asked him a question as to how I, who had grown up in the bush away from churches, would know which religion was right and which was wrong. At my question he was away to a flying start on the Bible and belief.

I quoted Saul's conversation as a sign from heaven. A sign that brought the Light to him. How then would I get such a sign?

At such blasphemy the good man looked aghast. I had dared to doubt the word of God. I quoted some of the salient facts about the Earth-mother cult but he only listened as one would tolerate a child. Useless to argue, he was right in his faith and all others were wrong, so I changed the conversation by talking about the Bibles he was selling.

He took me over to his van and showed me the interior which was stacked with religious books. Bibles from cheap editions to masterpieces of the binder's art, and showing them he gave an interesting outline of his travellings over the face of Australia. He finally asked me would I accept one of his Bibles and let him take a photo of me against

Mt. Olga facing westward, an ancient group full of aboriginal ritual and mythology

My Raggle-taggle friends

Minyinderri and myself with the camels

the Rock with him giving me the copy. I naturally accepted, so out we went to the Ranger's sign to set up the scene.

Picture me then with the presentation copy in my hand waiting as he set up his tripod. As he went through the usual routine of getting the light and time-exposure with his light meter, some tourists came up to stand idly around, and I could tell by their faces they were wondering what was afoot.

Then came the Bible-seller's hiss of attention. I held out the Bible as he had shown me, then 'click'. The camera was in motion so he sped into the scene to hold his end of the Bible. There we waited like a pair of startled crows who have suspected a trap, then faintly came the camera's clicking release. The shot was taken and the Bible was mine.

A year later at Ayers Rock a tourist claimed she recognized me from my picture receiving the Bible. It was at a local Bible-meeting in her town where they were all thrilled by the colporteur's remarks about his adventures and his conversions.

Not that I worried, for I really believe that faith is a good thing. I myself have never met an aboriginal who did not believe in a Creator.

Minyinderri came over to my place just as the Bible-man was leaving. He asked me what he was doing and, when I explained about the books he was selling, he just shrugged his shoulders muttering something about 'That him job . . . me work at wood for tourist-business . . . him work at sell book all-a-same, everybody must work.' Hearing his words I wondered did the Bible-man look upon his peddling as 'work' or was it his 'calling'?

Minyinderri's remark recalled to my mind a missionary who worked on one of the government aboriginal settlements. He was telling me about the bad drought the place was going through.

'The bores were getting low in water, so we were forced to remove all the native people out of their houses and put them on a water hole some miles away . . . it was the only way we could get enough water to keep the staff and the gardens going.'

His story was one of hardship for the white people who were administering their own homes and gardens. The aborigines did not matter, for although the place was originally built for their welfare, they apparently took a second place in the scheme of things when the question of comfort arose between white or black people.

Listening to his story I could not help wondering how one could reconcile his doctrine of spiritual equality with the existent social order. His duties were in the words of Minyinderri, 'Just job, everywhere people do work . . . some one way, some 'nother way . . . only trouble some people think their job different.'

Everybody is out to help the 'blacks', all are 'worrying for nothing', as my philosophical mate would say, 'worry, when nothing to worry about'.

Yet when I see the ragged aboriginal people living beside the road that leads out to the Rock I, too, begin to worry. Worry at the remarks of the tourists and the haggling that goes on. The Government's policy is judged by these few, yet I do know that on aboriginal settlements hundreds of native children go to school, native mothers are cared for, and the aged are secure in their declining years. The traveller only sees the ones on the roadway, for should he want to visit one of the aboriginal Reserves he has to go through a wall of red tape. Thus is the best side of aboriginal life hidden and the worst exposed to our view.

Aboriginal ritual and mission work: hymns are sung in the church yet all the while the tribal Elders visit their caves and shelters to rub the sacred boards and stones which have been handed down to them from the past. Around every mission one can see the graves of the Christian and the tribesman. Seeing them one day and knowing that in one of those plots was a native friend of mine buried as a Christian, I thought of a time when he and I had often discussed the black and white man's beliefs, now he slept there where

The night departs as day comes rolling in,
The day goes out and restful nights begin.
Shades of my fathers in their tribal land
Let they who think of me, but understand
That I am what I am, Yet first define
Whose God is right, my father's one or thine?
Our code was kinship, for we knew not Might,
Was yours the gun that made a white God, Right?
Right with that Might which bade stern killers ride
With fire and thunder through the countryside;
So sheltered we beside the White man's God,
And thus were saved from Law's grim chain and rod.
Our ritual slowly changed to Bible law
Our culture-centre was the strange church floor.
We ate the white-men's food and thus became
—Lost in your world and mine—A tribe in name.
The mission people taught us how to pray,
They came as friends, but did they know the way?
For how can mortals know what fate portends,
That secret now is mine. Pass on my friends.

Religions come and they go on their way; each gains a lot from the others. The white man's law demands a certain code of life just as the tribal Elders of the past, and in some places today, place restrictions and taboos on the youth of the tribes. Thinking thus I returned to my Ranger's house to find a lot of leaflets on the floor. They had been slid under the door by someone who was out to reform me. I looked at the titles which were something about 'Hell's flames', a good subject on that bitterly cold day.

Perhaps those who pushed them under the door had gone away happy in the knowledge that they had done their duty. I wondered if these people really thought of my soul as they 'pass on the good word', or did they do these things to save themselves?

As I cannot let such literature lie around the house for fear it might offend some opposing evangelist who comes along, I was forced to thrust the lot into the fire, which after all is the subject of its text.

PART II

THE RAGGLE-TAGGLE

Tonight I will sleep on an open field,
Along with the Raggle-taggle Gipsies, Oh!

Old Gipsy Song

Chapter Eighteen

Nomads and the Kinship Law

I HAD just returned from taking some tourists around the Rock and was taking things easy on my bunk inside the house when a great blubbering and shouting from outside had me out to see that a new lot of tourists had entered the Reserve. Some bush aboriginals had arrived.

For days past I had seen smoke rising into the sky from their hunting-fires. 'Uluru and Winmardi with family and camel come up from my-country-way,' happily said Minyinderri. 'All about been look-look for puppy-dog.'

The puppy-dog-look-lookers were certainly a grubby looking lot when they arrived, yet in spite of their rags, which they must have just put on in deference to the white people, they were a happy crowd.

Winmardi could talk fairly good English and he nattered away to Minyinderri in part English part Loritdja—the first for my benefit, the last when something was said they did not want me to hear. I had a good look over the party.

They had five camels in the string—huge beasts that stood passively still beside the women and children. What a picture they made! At the thought I was off into the house for my camera to get a few shots. As I came out, slamming the door with a bang, the camels and children peered towards me as though trying to fathom my movements. After the 'picture-taking-business' I gave out some foodstuffs and lollies to the children and watching them slowly eating, as if trying to get the full sweetness out of them, I wondered about their way of life.

Nomads and the children of nomads, how long had the forebears of these people been wandering over the face of the land? Naked hunters for ages, they had now adapted themselves to camel transport after the Afghans and Arab camel-men had been pushed off the roads by motor transport. I asked one of the men where he got the camels from.

'Some we buy from 'nother one blackfellow . . . pay with puppy-dog scalp . . . some we catch in bush where mob run wild.'

'How you catch them?' I asked him, and he replied. 'Easy catch camel with 'nother one camel . . . just follow them up all day like dingo when they follow kangaroo . . . no-more-long-time camel knock up from follow-business then we throw rope on leg and they lay down on ground just like when man put pack on their back.'

'They quiet then?' I questioned.

They laughed at my question, then Winmardi answered, 'Camel proper cheeky when caught, but we tie him down and by-and-by he savee we.'

As he was speaking some of the children were scrambling over the huge camels' backs. When there, they would give out a call so that the animal would put its head down. When this happened the kiddies were sliding down the beast's neck in a similar fashion to school-children on a slippery-slide.

The great beast seemed to enjoy the fun. Now and then it would give out a series of gurgles and when this happened the kiddies would snuggle up close to the creature to rub it between the ears.

Those great creatures fascinated me. I had been with them many years before in western Queensland. Then, as now, they seemed to be something out of another world, pausing from time to time while chewing their cud to give this strange white man a 'look-over'. I could sense they did not like my presence. Whether it was my clothes or a new smell I was not sure.

The children were in rags, but their intelligent finely cut faces looked out at me from a mop of blond hair, caused no doubt by the bleaching action of the sun in this desert land. They were not afraid, nor did they beg. When I gave them lollies they ate with the enjoyment which comes from a people who have not been pampered with abundance, and looking over the whole party I felt that I was in the presence of a people who were masters of their tribal lands.

The camels too were somehow a part of the picture. Having once opened this country they were now the chattels of a nomad race who refused to be bondsmen for white people who think they are free but are the slaves to a convention that keeps them working to survive. What mystery lies behind the story of the aborigines? What history has been made with the camels?

As I was reflecting about the people and their beasts some tourists came up with their cameras and a host of questions which I was supposed to answer. Their talking was incessant, and regardless as to whether the aborigines could speak English, they discussed the nomads with a candour one would only use at some sale-yard.

'What shapes . . . what thin legs,' said one whose waistline had been made by a foundation garment, but who had legs like hams that would win a prize at a local show. Another remark was about their cleanliness, which is what one would expect from people coming out of a dry country. The tourists ask me why the aborigines don't wash.

Naturally I wanted to get away, for I had noticed the black people were becoming fed up with the chatter. So I replied that they don't worry about B.O. because they don't read the newspaper advertisements, which put the fear of God into those who do.

So the talk goes on as the cameras click. Many of the tourists are laughing their heads off because the black people ask for a gift in return for allowing the photos of the camels and themselves. Others are trying to get an old man to pull off his shirt so as to get a shot of a primitive man. Everyone is wanting to know what the government is doing for 'these wretches'. All are interested in 'blacks'. When I ask them have they read any literature about them, they are surprised. They thought nobody wrote about them. The main concern of them all is as to why the unfortunate creatures are not left alone. When I explain that these were alone till they came up they reply testily that they were different.

As they drift away, the tourists to their camps, the camel-nomads over to Minyinderri's camp below the sandhills, I cannot help smiling as I think of the endless talk about B.O. and the incredulous look on Kudekudeka's face when he found a piece of face soap at the 'Ngi-nindi' rock-hole of the Earth-mother. From the tell-tale footprints he could see where some young girls had been in for a swim. They were the clean ones in a land where water is meant to keep life going. The old man was one of the 'grubbies' because he would never defile that pool.

Yet what is all this talk about cleanliness which we read and hear about today? In my youth it was the normal thing to have the tub once a week. When in the stock-camps we only had a swim when we camped on the big waterholes of the cattle property. The B.O. ads of the newspapers had not come into being. The 'change daily lass', with all the other fear-ads came afterwards, not because the advertisers wished for health but to sell their wares. We ride now on the waves of fear, and fortunate are those who do not read the ads that form our complexes.

The country at that time was very dry, and looking at the Raggle-taggle with their wives, children, camels, and dogs I could not but suppress a smile when a tourist woman, who was nearby at the time, remarked they were 'an awful lot'.

Perhaps she was right from her angle of society. They were certainly not of the 'change-daily-type', and instead of the little dab of scent behind the ears as is the custom of white women, they had the usual greenish ball of 'ingulba', or native-tobacco-chew in its place to add to their make-up.

The camels were certainly 'on the nose', but I knew from experience with them in the past, that their smell, like all other odours, such as leaking gas-jets of a stove and others from glue and hide tanning works in the cities, were smells soon overcome with usage and environment in our daily lives.

As for the nomads, they just did not give a damn what we strange-smelling pale creatures thought about them. All of us were humans of divers scents and different ways of thought. On they went with their beasts of burden carrying an untidy collection of swags and billy-cans that jingled with each camel's stride, a refrain that only ceased when they pitched their camp beneath some shady mulga trees at the foot of a sand-ridge heavy with the vegetation of desert-loving trees.

Not long afterwards the camels were up around the taps and tanks of the tourist's camp seeking water from the overflows. With them came the camp-dogs which were always sniffing around the camp-fires of the tourists.

The arrival of the nomad's dogs put an end to the general discussion on 'blacks'. A great emotional wave of sympathy arose over the slinking curs where the whites were divided on what should be done about them, an argument that was interrupted when a massive kangaroo appeared on a sandhill. In a flash the apparently apathetic hungry-looking mongrels of a moment before were away in full pursuit, while behind them in a straggling line followed the hunters, women, children, and tourists in that order.

Never was fox-hunt put over in such fine style. The languid dogs of the aborigines were now balls of fur and dust as they overtook the kangaroo as it topped the sandhill. Barkings and wailings from the dogs were mixed up with the shouts of the nomads as the fight went on, and amidst the uproar, as a wail of despair, came the shouts of horror from some of the tourists as they watched the kill. White mothers who thought nothing of chopping the head off a fowl were outraged at the 'callous killing'.

Not that the nomads worried about the protests and the wails. They were hunters and the kangaroo was 'good tucker'. Shouts of praise on one side with protests on the other left them cold. The carcase of the marsupial was carried away by the native who owned the dog which pulled the creature down. The kill was to the dogs but the right to the flesh was to those who owned the dog by kinship law. The nomads departed in peace according to the tribal law, leaving behind an enraged 'chook-killing-mother' outraged by the scene.

Next day I was up to visit the nomad's camp in order to discuss with them something about a trip to the westward.

How many people—who know nothing about aborigines, or very little about human nature—will tell others that the 'blacks' are stupid? My entry into the nomad's council chamber under the mulga trees was not unlike a top discussion among the 'big-shots' during world-shaking events. What a wall of blank faces I encountered when I brought up the discussion of our movements, a subject we had often talked about and a reason they had for coming into the area now. Their first reaction was one of surprise that I would ever dream of going to the West during the dry-time. 'Too dry and not much water... might-be camel die from poison-bush longa dry-time... they just came to look-look Uluru for sorry-sorry business.'

I let them talk away, then I changed the subject, and after a few stories about things away from the subject I bade them good-bye and returned back to the tourist camp.

The aborigines are people of an open mind in all things not ritual or 'woman-business'. Naturally polite with white people who are not out to deceive them, I knew they would continue their talk about the journey west.

Minyinderri was with me shortly afterwards to let words drop now and then about our trip. When he did I repeated the same excuses as the nomads had given to me, ending that 'might-be I would go out with motor that can't cry for dry road'.

As the road to Kikingurra was a long way over dry waterless country owing to the prolonged drought, I had made tentative arrangements to go with Minyinderri to the place by motor to look over the area and learn its mythology from him and his wife on the spot.

I also wished to go to another place with the camels, but, 'No matter,' I told Minyinderri, 'his friends don't want go so more better we go by motor utility.'

Utility... motor! That inanimate enemy (or should I write friend) of animal transport over the years, the four-wheeled drive that can cross deserts and go long distances without water. A soul-less mass of steel which gives exhilaration to the speedy ones, joy to the aged, and a solemn curse from the lover of nature who enjoys riding around the countryside on a quiet horse.

The mention of the motor had my nomad friends on their toes as though an unseen Kaditdja spirit-man's presence had been detected around their camp. But, strangely enough, the word brought no remorse but a shout of joy at the prospect of a ride in a motor vehicle back to their homeland.

Now the council of Elders spoke as with one voice. 'Motor-truck good for country... no more hard work... camel too slow.' When I hesitated a little, one of the Elders called Winmardi, who could see that a motor trip would not bring in the pay-off for which they had come into the area, spoke up.

'We go first time with camel into country that Bill want to write about properly way. Then when finish that trip we go into dry country with motor truck.' A pause in his oration brought a roar of approval from the others, so we settled down to the next part on our agenda. A talk about the pay and all those things which must naturally come into the discussion.

After the 'Contract longa mouth' was fixed I soon discovered a new clause in the agreement which arose out of that great bugbear of aboriginal life: a law that lays down a fixed procedure in tribal behaviour, called by the aborigines 'blackfellow-business,' but known to all who deal with the tribes as kinship law. Kinship law, how well did it bind the tribes together over past ages, yet what a stumbling block for the present-day aboriginal who wishes to break away from tradition in order to do battle with that demon called progress.

I explained how I would pay each man for his camels, 'Cash longa finger', when the job was over, but only to those who returned with me from the trip. I would provide such things as flour, tea, sugar, and jam. They in turn would hunt as they went their way so that I could get the hunting pattern around their daily life.

They understood the meaning of the word 'contract', for some of their tribe, maybe one or two of them, had worked at putting up fences and yards for the cattle-station owners. What they wanted to know they nodded agreement, what they did not want to know they just could not understand.

Thinking over that verbal agreement my mind went back to such an incident in one of the bush towns. It concerned the selling and purchase of fat bullocks. The butcher and the squatter had made the usual word of mouth agreement as to the price. On settling day the butcher refused to pay the price quoted, and when taxed about the price agreement laughingly replied that it was not in writing. 'Just gentleman's agreement and no good in law.'

The main point in my gentleman's agreement (not the butcher's one however) was that I would be as one of the nomads when we started out on our trip. Should anyone pull out on the trip then they lost their contract pay-off. During my droving days it was the general rule that should one of the drover's men pull-out then his wages would be divided equally between the rest of the men until a new man was put-on.

This procedure was useless with the nomads, for being one kin under tribal law the one who 'pulled-out' would naturally get his share from the others when we returned. So with the simple dictum of 'Pull-out then nothing', he must keep with me to get the pay as agreed upon.

With this thing settled we now turned our attention to the camels. Fortunately for me I knew the people and who owned the animals, but I had not reckoned on the kinship law.

Over past years I had taken down many lists of kinship tables, for experience with the aborigines had shown me that these things were the key to all tribal ritual, behaviour, and camp-life. In another chapter of this book I have tried to show the workings of kinship law as it affects family life. I was now to come head-on against a transport system tied up with barter and the same kinship law. Men with two camels claimed to possess only one, others half of one.

I must unravel such sentences as, 'This one only half mine, my brother own 'nother half . . . must be he get pay too?'

To this I readily agreed, with a proviso that I pay him for the full camel then he pay his brother for his half. Thus was our talk like the small print one finds in a contract. The more minute it is the more vital.

Soon our talk was a confused jumble of camel names mixed up with such kinship terms as 'little-bit-uncles, half-fathers, and grandfathers' with other complicated terms such as 'brothers-from-little-bit-long-way' in a confusion where humans were hopelessly mixed up with camels in a maze as complete as a dust storm on a dark night. Fortunate is the white man who understands a little; to the non-understanding it is one hopeless jumble of words. A mix up out of which I wriggled by reverting to the aboriginal custom of repeating a simple sentence over and over until one's opponent gave up in despair.

Minyinderri was in the fray, on his kin's side when he was talking in Loritdja which I could not comprehend, on my side when he reverted to English for my benefit. I just listened to it all, repeatedly coming into the argument with my parrot-like cry of 'One man with one camel get pay when we come back . . . one man with one camel . . . etc.'

To describe such a scene I must revert to a similar act in past days, but that time in a language I understood.

Aboriginal orator, in English. 'This Bill (points at me), him good man and he pay good money.' He nods at me for confirmation and on cue I repeat: 'One man with one, etc. . . . etc . . . etc.'

Chorus of Elders in council, with emphasis: 'Ah!'

Orator in his native tongue: 'White people have sugar-mouths (unreliable) this one is as bad as the rest.'

Chorus of Elders in council: 'Ah!'

The orator now gave an impassioned speech in his language. If I knew the tongue he changed to another, then turned to me and remarked in English: 'All about say you good man . . . but they would like little-bit money first time. . . .' Back I came with my cue: 'One man with one, etc., etc., etc.'

The curtain dropped on the scene. The nomads resumed passive faces as they stared to the westward. I bid them 'Good-bye' to return to my camp. Shortly afterwards I got a list of my friends, together with their camels. The list included all the nomads, their camels and dogs—and what an array!

The genealogical table revealed to me tnat as Minyinderri claimed me as a 'Gammon-little-bit-newphew' a sort of 'sister's son', then his

'Properly son'—and camel which came under that heading—was my 'half-wife's brother', and as such was the 'half grandfather of my wife, together with her dogs and live-stock.' All quite easy to follow when one is among the people but a hopeless mess when it is put on paper.

My coming into the kinship system was not because they wished to give me a blood-brother degree, but because as a nephew I became the hand-servant of an uncle, or mother's brother, a sort of lever to procure favours under the tribal code. I was Ego, the central unit, only because I had the key to the white fellow's food. The moment my supply cut out, I too would be out. A similar pattern such as existed among drunken white people where the one-in-the-money was the captain to be protected till he went broke. After that he was one of the gang to hold obeisance to the next captain. A sort of beggar's cycle.

I was interested to learn by the kinship law that two very old women, a young girl, two camels, and a goodly sprinkling—or should I write slinking—pack of curs were the property of my camp-fire. Those dogs were an unfriendly lot, for each time I passed them by they bared their fangs to the hated intruder—a trait, handed down from an inherited hatred of white fellows ranging from cattle-bosses and policemen whose one object was to stop them chasing cattle to keeping everybody awake around the police stations with their nightly love affairs, wailing, and fightings when the white lords and masters were resting.

Chapter Nineteen

On Walkabout

ONCE the bargaining was over an air of happiness seemed to descend upon all. It was now just a matter of waiting for a slack period in the tourist traffic to get on our way.

Even as I waited I would often be around with the nomads and their camels to try and learn a little of their hunting-pattern and the mythology of their country.

Our camel string was not such as one would expect from a well-organized trip such as went with the early explorers. Ours was a raggle-taggle array with bits of old rope and bags doing the work of the fine leather used in olden times. The water canteens, though an important item when going into dry lands, were discarded four-gallon drums with greenhide straps on to which a short link of hobble-chain was secured. The hobble chain links were there for securing the canteens on to the pack-saddles with a piece of rope. Carefully we washed them out and after re-filling we let them stand awhile to see if they leaked. If a leak was found my adaptable nomad friends would seal up the hole with the spinifex gum they always carried.

Nothing was orderly with our camel loads. Billy-cans and buckets hung in dangling array to add to the din of the Elders shouting instructions to everybody around, mainly to the children who, with a hunk of cooked kangaroo in one hand and a pup in the other, were always running among the legs of the patient creatures we were riding.

Nevertheless, with such a raggle-taggle we certainly went places in those early days at the Rock. Often our bush track led into sundown-way where, in a sense, we were following the trail of Giles the explorer. With him, the land ahead was a blank, with us an array of maps mixed up with the nomad's bushcraft which had been handed on to them by tradition.

And as we travelled I would often look over my raggle-taggle friends and wonder whether those mass migrations of past days were as disorderly as our own array. Ancient literature tells us the way those people travelled, but we get little information as to their daily habits and their hunting pattern. When I read about the vast numbers that migrated I ofttimes wonder if the scribe wrote his figures with a two-pointed quill, and I shudder to think of the unfortunate wretches who happened to live along the path of those human locusts.

One of the main trips I was for ever dreaming of came about during an extra slack period. It was to the northward towards a place called Nonin. A happy time was that, and riding along on my riding-cum-pack camel with Minyinderri sharing the front half of our beast, I soon realized that I was traversing country similar to that which I had lived in for years. The difference now was that I was not walking and sweating or riding in a roaring motor but taking life easy as one of the Gods riding above the mortals who plodded on an earthly plane. Here I could look down a little. I also discovered that when riding I could observe things more easily and, if need be, make notes on the spot without fumbling and squatting in the dirt.

How good then to look over my nomad friends and to realize that here around us was a different type of aboriginal. In the past they tracked their game on foot, now they hunted from the backs of camels, thus moving up one stage in the march of human progress.

A grizzled old veteran of many summers and thousands of tribal feasts or dinnerless dinnertimes was talking in the usual finger-sign talk to others some distance away. His conversation was sometimes directed to Minyinderri who was riding on the same camel as I. What it was about I did not know, but from the loud laughter that followed each 'speech' I somehow sensed it concerned me. Not that I worried for my time was too taken up with the country we were passing through; my new angle of approach was full of surprises.

Minyinderri was always pointing out things to me as we rode along. He had become a new man now that we were going back to his country. Each sand ridge we rode over had him pointing out to me different landmarks with an added story of some happening to him and his family in past days. An axe mark in a bloodwood tree had him talking about a time when his uncle climbed the trunk to get some sweet tasting gall-nuts from its branches. A hill in the distance had him off on a legend of how that marks the place where Mudjera, the lizard friend of Pungalung, hit the earth when he was thrown away by the great desert lover so as to outstrip the snarling mice-maidens on his heels. To add realism to his story he pointed out to me a small reddish lizard peering up at us from the sand, then explained that there cowered the transformed Mudjera of the tale.

A flowering bush gave another tale; sometimes it would be a legend, at other times a piece of advice in hunting lore. Everywhere as we travelled was story-time, the camels moving along seemed to revive memories as though a scroll was being unrolled before us.

To describe each day's travel would be but a repetition of the same scenes—the camels plodding along, the hunters seeking their daily needs, the children, with their pups, running behind wana-carrying mothers who preferred to walk with the hunting dogs that ranged from descendants of Afghan hounds to blue cattle-dogs and kelpies.

Owing to the camel loads jingling some of the hunters preferred to walk some distance away from the string of camels during the cool mornings, but as the day became warmer the pace would slacken and all would seek a shady place so that we could rest until the cool of the evening, or if needed, to make the place a night camp.

The pattern of the day's hunting remained the same. Each morning, everyone would go into the bush empty-handed but as the day went on things appeared, as though by magic, in their hands. Nothing that was edible was omitted from the daily fare: rabbits, cats, numberless small rodent mice, goannas, kangaroos, bowls of honey-ants. To my untrained eye, the apparently empty bush was crammed with food. Tucker time was any time to the hunters. Each time I saw one of the children or the women their jaws would be munching away at some morsel they had plucked from a tree or dug up from the earth. I did notice, however, that one could detect the children who had been brought up on a mission station or government settlement by the simple fact that their jaws were inactive because they were untrained for this life. Having been brought up to the white people's ways, then, they were dependent on the bounty of their hunting kin.

Thus did the nomads travel and hunt as we moved through each day. Each night would reveal the same pattern—the small camp-fires burning, the mothers busy cooking the main foodstuffs they had gathered that day; a general babble of voices that finally became stilled as the camp-fires died down and we went to rest. Yet, during the night I would awaken now and then, and peering out of my swag I would always behold one of the adults sitting up as he poked at his camp-fire. Watching him as he peered around or chanted some of his tribal chants my mind, in imagination, would go back to that time when the Elders and shepherds watched their flocks against the enemies of the night. They were guardians ready to give the call to arms should they hear something from the material or spiritual world.

Night time in the desert. Hearing the guardian of the nomads chanting I would peer up into the heavens to realize that here in this scene was the beginning of our great religions. The sleeping clan, the watchman peering around and trying to solve the riddle of it all.

Then would come the morning with its bustle as mothers tried to awaken the children while we had breakfast of a drink of tea and damper with some of the left-overs from yesterday's hunt. Everywhere around me was turmoil, dust lifting under the camel's feet as they came in behind their masters. One of my greatest memories, however, was the sight of an aboriginal woman called Katie. She had two camels and leading them in from the bush, where they were hobbled out, she always reminded me of some Biblical scene, especially when we were camped under a mountain which reflected the rays of the rising sun.

As no rain had fallen for years in the country through which we were travelling we were prepared for the worst, but I could not but help noticing that the country was becoming a lot drier. The leaves of the trees around were taking on a yellow tinge.

We had heard from other aborigines who had come in from the West, into which we were going, that heavy storms had fallen some months before over a region known to the nomads, and it was to this place we were heading as the first leg of our journey. To get there, however, we must negotiate this dry land that was in the grip of a terrible drought. The red Centre was really red here; the limbs of the trees had become brittle and the dust from our camel's feet ran as a fiery spray of red quick-lime over the parched ground. I myself would have turned back, but the proud look on my friend's faces as they faced the West and their homeland gave me heart. So on we went.

Native wells supplied the camels with water now and then, but the canteens on the backs of our camels remained our drinking supply. Then one day, just as Minyinderri had informed me that the place of the big storms was near, a haze came over us. From the north-west great clouds of dust rose into the sky and as it rose I heard a murmuring among the nomads as they held council. 'More better camp in tree shelter place to wait for dust to go,' they said.

Heeding their advice we lowered our camels in a good place to act as a break-wind, and there we awaited the attack of man's greatest enemy in the desert.

Around us was as the stillness of death. The mulga leaves hung listless as though they had given up the battle of life. The spinifex circles which always reminded me of fairy-rings were hazy and shimmering owing to the heat mirage. The only living things around us was the ants which ran around our feet and the flies that crawled over our bodies.

My aboriginal friends were looking to the westward where a great red wall of dust hung like a drape from the sky, and gazing with them I was awakened from my trance when Minyinderri's voice broke the spell. 'Big dust come up . . . proper cheeky . . . you look dog?' He pointed to the canine pack which had somehow read the thoughts of their masters and were now crouching behind bushes. 'Him savee something wrong.'

'You think something wrong?' I asked him, and at my words he laughed aloud, and replied.

'Nothing wrong, dust come from blackfellow business, soon wind come up from sundown way then we get rain.'

Reassured, I gazed upon a scene I had never witnessed before.

The wall of dust seemed to remain still when almost upon us, so that our camp-site appeared to be at the base of a high cliff. My eyes travelled up that towering wall to behold on its crest a sparkling of light with different shades of brown such as one sees on the foam of a desert river in full flood.

One of the old men began chanting a song. What it was about I never found out, but it somehow eased the tension around, not only the children who began laughing, but the dogs began roaming around, while the camels, silent before, re-commenced chewing their cuds.

Then as the old aborigine chanted the wall of dust seemed to topple over upon us. One minute we were under a fairly clear sky, the next a red darkness so gloomy that I could not see the trees a few yards away from where I was crouching behind a pack-saddle.

Yet strangely enough no wind was roaring around us as I would expect. Everything was still, a quietness as though some vast volcanic eruption had occurred outside our hearing range to roll this ball upon us.

Within that eerie gloom I thought of that Sumerian scribe who wrote of how, 'Anu the "great above" created the Bull of heaven for Ishtar, his daughter. A drought to avenge an insult inflicted upon her. . . . The Bull fell to the earth; with his first snort he slew a hundred men and again he slew two hundred, he slew three hundred. With his second snort hundreds fell dead. . . .'

My thoughts were interrupted as a grey wraith materialized from the shadows. It was one of the native women clinging to her child. I thought at first she was seeking protection, but that was dispelled when she passed some remark about approaching rain. 'You hear . . . tudundja . . . him talk.'

Faintly in the distance I heard the rumble of thunder, then a flash of lightning lit up the gloom. 'Wanungarra growl,' said the aboriginal mother. 'Him throw alkara (stone-axe) . . . big boss for rain . . . you come?' She took hold of my arm to where Minyinderri and the other members of our party were unpacking and throwing old bags and pieces of calico over our foodstuffs. My friend looked up when he saw me, then pointing to the west he remarked, 'Big wind come then rain . . . we camp here for night.'

As he spoke a strong wind came howling in from the west. A cold drop of rain struck my bare arm and as it did I heard the children cry as with one voice, 'Rain come kapi plenty . . . rain come, rain come.'

Not only did that rain come up but it just pelted down as though the rain gods of the Loritdja had tipped over a massive 'pitdi' (water-carrying bowl) on to our camping place. One minute it was warm and dry, the next a cold so intense as to make one believe that a sky-spirit warrior had riven the atmosphere around us with a 'djundba' (club of ice) that changed the gloom into a clear sky overcast with moisture-carrying storm-clouds. The sun broke through the overcast, and as it did the droplets of water on the trees were as silver orbs above the rivulets of storm waters that swept by our camp site.

One of the children, who was busy sucking at one of the tree branches for its cool water, smiled at me then remarked. 'Rain make everybody happy . . . rain good.'

She had taken off her dress at the approach of rain and, standing against a background of that bushland with its fairy-like spinifex rings, I could not but think of the fairy tales belonging to my childhood days.

Yet here life was real. The girl before me belonged to a people who accepted life as it came.

That night we camped at the place of dust and the big storm, then on the following day we packed up our loads to be on our way, and that afternoon we came into the place of storms we had heard so much about in the past days. Everywhere around us now was green. From the red to the green was but the matter of a bare mile. On one side despair, on the other a happiness that overwhelmed us as we moved through a wealth of wild flowers. The colour acted as a drug on our jaded nerves. Before our voices were hushed, now we were calling loudly to each other and our tones were happy ones. The rich vegetation with an abundance of water suggested a rest, so we lowered our camels beside a series of rock-holes within a desert mountain to take life easy for a few days.

The place was called Nonin, the traditional spot where the ritual Mala people rubbed themselves with charcoal to begin their southern march to Ayers Rock. It was not much to look at from a scenic point of view, but a haven of rest within a dry land.

Camping there, with a plentiful supply of bush food for both animals and men, I could not but help thinking that these 'storm-patches', of the cattlemen, were a form of nature's insurance over the ages in these semi-drought areas. A place where animal and plant life would be rejuvenated so that the species might carry on once more.

The creatures of the bushland would flock to these places. Kangaroos came in droves, so numerous that I myself knew one kangaroo shooter in the Kulgera cattle-station area, south of Alice Springs, who shot and skinned three thousand a month. He only stopped shooting when a heavy storm fell in another part and the drove moved on.

As I saw the wild creatures of the bush in that year of 1952 so were they around us now on our storm-patch which was but an island of green in a dry red land. I noticed, too, that in these places of abundance, taboos relating to tribal boundaries were lifted. All came, feasted, and rested, the animals on the grass and herbage, the humans on the game of the area.

Today, in many parts, borders and fences confine life within fixed areas. One day, surely, stockowners will follow the ways of bush life so that those 'in clover' will help the ones in distress by a form of mutual assurance similar to nature and the storm-patch areas.

Chapter Twenty

Bushland

THOSE nomad aborigines taught me many things outside of my own line of reasoning. They were always up at my camp to show me items of interest about their country. Chief informant, however, was Minyinderri who camped near my camp-fire and was often over to explain something about a plant he held in his hand. Sometimes it would be a special food; at other times it was a medicine to cure one of their ills.

As there was a bleak wind blowing from the south after the rain-time, it naturally came into our conversation. So he explained to me, at great length, how the 'Warri' cold weather always came from 'Jura-way' over 'Sun-woman-business'. It appears that the 'Sun-woman' doesn't like the cold and, to escape the bleak winds and frost that originate from the 'Ninya-men' who are so frozen that they have perpetual icicles hanging from their nostrils, she rolls away to the northward on a sort of annual walkabout, only returning when the tribeswomen have chanted sufficient 'Yerapinjis' to drive the poisonous-flames hunters and the Ninya-men back into their holes in the earth.

'Women very clever with Yerapindji' (sexual chants), said Minyinderri seriously. 'Not only they make Ninya-men go into ground but can make man mad for woman-business.'

'That all right for cold,' I replied. 'But what about hot weather-time when everything dry and die?'

At my questioning Minyinderri would smile as an adult would at some childish question, and then explain about rain-men and rain-chants that bring rain to make people happy.

To my native friend every phenomenon of nature can be explained by his tribal logic. If something did not come on when its time was ready then man, not nature, was to blame.

Each time he came down to my camp his searching eyes would scan the ground for 'news' as to the travellers, or to impart some latest bit of folk-lore about the weather. His sentences were brief, generally a 'Rain come up' or 'No more rain'. His generalizations always ended up with a little discourse on nature. The ants carrying eggs into higher ground as a rain sign, or a special type of cloud that denotes the dry.

Movement is observed everywhere. The dry dust sweeping over the red earth with whirlwinds sweeping through the trees to send their dust thermals swaying and tapering off into the heavens. The rock-pools' bottoms are covered with a thin layer of dried 'wananyu' (alga). How dead it looks, yet in it I know is the spawn of countless water creatures waiting the rain or a blasting wind so that they can be wind-borne into other lands to propagate their kind.

A buck-bush goes bounding by in its race to nowhere. Perhaps it will return again on the changing wind. Jump . . . jump it goes. Each leap is part of its way of life for then does it drop its seeds on to the earth so that they are spread that way. One bounds over my resting friend who sits up and then explains that it is 'Good for camel when green, but rubbish when dry and walkabout.' As he speaks a whirlwind picks up the bush to send it aloft where it is carried high into the air and as it goes its way I think of that parable about the sower who went forth to sow.

Minyinderri also watches the whirlwind and breaks the silence by again informing me, 'No more rain,' with an added rider, 'Must be somebody sing more-better rain-song 'nother way and make rain there.'

How strong for life is the things of the dry lands. What a lesson they can teach us, who despair when things are against us! Outside the Ranger's cottage at Ayers Rock a tiny geranium grew after a small shower. In a week it was in full leaf, after that it just stood still for lack of moisture. Then somehow it sensed that no more rain was coming; so out from the frail plant came a small flower.

As the plant grew near the pathway which led from the roadway to the office door it suffered many a time beneath the boots of visitors. Each evening saw the tiny bloom crushed, each morning saw a new bud. Tourists pitied it and asked why I never watered the thing, to them I replied that it was there to teach us a lesson on survival. So the battle went on, then just as I was beginning to despair I noticed a spiral-seed where the flower had been.

Thus does life go on. Each plant seems to be the servant to another life. The parakelya grows its sac-like leaves to carry the moisture which will sustain it over the dry-time, then along comes the mulga parrots, camels, and bushmen too to eat at its succulent growth. Botanists tell us that the plant carries small quantities of oxalic acid which could be a poison, but heedless of the warning the bushmen often eat the green as a vegetable to ward off those scorbutic ailments so common to hard living.

This hardy mulga tree so common to this land is at peace with this country because it has won its battle in the struggle to survive. Having a root and leaf system adapted to the dry it can, even in the dry, throw out its yellow 'inundji' blooms during the months of August–September. Only a few in the drought, but let a good season come and its seed pods will hang down like beans from its branches. Then would the tribesmen heed the sign of nature and gather to that place of the 'Windralga' for the annual festival. 'Windralga-time' was when the clans met to swop news and talk about coming ritual.

This mulga of the bushmen is the 'Aneura' of the botanists. Yet to my friend Minyinderri and his clan it is called 'Wanarri', with an added rider that it is 'Proper good for everything.'

Once as we stood in a good patch as the nomad women were hunting food I asked them to tell me about its uses and off they went to enumerate the things it could produce, marking each one off on their fingers as they went through the list which somehow sounded like a ritual chant. 'Wanarri good for karlee throwing-stick,' said Minyinderri. 'Good too for wana digging-stick too,' added Bulya. So they called the names of the 'maeru' (woomera), and the 'djunindja' (wooden club). Each weapon came from the same tree, which in some places is stunted in growth yet in other parts tall and straight.

As they called the names they also pointed out to me the foods growing upon the branches. 'Plenty tucker here,' said Minyinderri. 'This one'—he was pointing to a sticky substance which comes from a thrip insect—'this one good yirimbi honey-ant tucker all-a-same white man honey . . . we call that one kuruka all-a-same this,' he pointed to his eye, ''cause it shine like light in sun at morning-time.' He picked off a fairly large piece with his fingers and handed it to me. 'You eat it. It properly good one.' I sampled the thing he gave and noted its flavour was not unlike maple-sugar.

Noting my interest he walked over to another mulga tree and pointed to some gall-nuts hanging from the branches. 'This one we call tarrulka, it all-a-same white-fellow apple.' I had come up against this food before when we called it mulga-apple but of interest to me now was the quantity which hung down from the trees.

Now we came to the trees covered with the green beans of the 'windralga'. Proudly did Minyinderri handle the clusters on the branches, as does a gardener showing a prize exhibit. Then he gathered up some of the earth beneath the tree. Blowing on it, as a primitive sort of winnow, he soon held out to me some of the dried seeds which must have fallen from last year's crop. 'This one we gather and eat when no more tucker in country . . . more better we get black-women to get some so that you know how to get them.' So we went our way and next day I went out with the women to gather some of the 'windralga' seed.

The green ones on the trees were gathered into wooden dishes, some of these were eaten raw and although they looked like french beans the flavour was not the same. As with all seed pods in the dry lands the skin was stringy but the seeds inside of a nice flavour. Of interest to me, however, was the gathering of the dried seeds on the ground beneath the trees. These were gathered by just putting leaves, a little earth, and the seeds into a large wooden karnilba-dish which they carried for the purpose. All helped in the gathering, young and old alike, scratching and sifting to get at the seeds and all the while they chanted the songs which are said to help them with their work:

Windralga bunnu wanarri,
Turrulka . . kuruka djurata

The chant was but the names of each food the plant yielded, together with its sweetness. 'From Ilapeddi (fig tree) place in my country,' explained one of the women. 'Plenty this one tucker.'

In reply I jestingly spat on to the earth as a sign that her country might be rubbish. Seeing my action she continued, 'You wait old man, when you see my country you will talk different-way, listen!'

The women gatherers had changed their singing into one of their 'yeripinji' chants about sex. 'See,' she continued, 'when man in our country talk wrong-way about us then that song make them go mad longa head . . . you look out.'

At her warning the gatherers of 'windralga' laughed aloud, then began chanting the Pungalung song about the great desert lothario who was pursued by the mice-maidens of mythological times. Thus did the work go on in an atmosphere of mirth.

When enough of the dried seeds had been gathered the lot was separated by a method called 'kuninjed', a process known to most white bushmen as 'yandying', a method similar to the jig principles of separating particles by their specific gravity.

The 'windralga' seeds were of a brown colour and these were prepared for eating by roasting them on hot ashes in a manner not unlike that used for coffee beans. The roasted seeds were then ground into a coarse meal with a hand-stone, grinding on to a larger flat stone called a 'djewa', an article of camp life that is never carried by the aboriginals but always left at the 'windralga' food places.

When needed for food the meal was moistened with water into a paste and this was eaten in a fashion not unlike the Mongol tribes of Asia eating their millet-seed or as with our own children eating breakfast foods today.

'Sometimes bird eat this windralga seed,' said one of the women gatherers, 'but that bird not got "djewa" longa gut so can't grind, for too hard, then seed come out same way as go in . . . good thing for we just go longa those water places and gather up plenty seed.' Thinking of her words, also remembering how the aboriginal hunters of the coast lands would remove the small lily bulbs from the gullets of the magpie-geese so that the lily food could be eaten with the cooked bird, my thoughts went back to the Good Book which tells us how Elija was also fed by ravens in a desert land.

Chapter Twenty-one

Desert Wanderers

As we wandered along the bushways the observations of my aboriginal friends would revive memories of incidents over past years.

Such an incident occurred when we passed by a deserted camp beneath some bloodwood trees. With his usual habit of scanning the ground for tracks concerning the late campers, Minyinderri waved me over as he gave out the usual sign talk for a camel. I went over to where he was pointing to see a small cleared patch of earth where a camel had once rested, with, beside it, some tell-tale droppings.

'Puppanarri-man look out for dingo long time ago . . . black-fellow . . . white-fellow all-a-same . . . one time plenty whiteman with camel come into this country, travel everywhere . . . too good for bush . . . all-a-same black-fellow.'

'What Puppanarri?' I questioned.

'We call camel Puppanarri because it all time stand like puppa, our name for dingo. Dingo-man and camel-man two-fellow come same time into my country so we give the camel same name as dog.'

'Camel-man come now?' I asked, but at my words he smiled then answered, 'Nothing now, they been go away long time ago, only thing now is camel tracks and their camps in my country.'

Camel tracks and deserted camps. These and Minyinderri's memory is all that remains now of those intrepid white men who once came out with their strings of camels to gather the dingo scalps from the country. With them were the aborigines who also searched for this creature as a food and a bounty which was paid to them by the 'doggers'.

Those white Australian 'dingo-men' or 'doggers' were the prototype of the trappers and voyagers in other lands. Brumby, Quinn, Dumas, de Conlay—great bushmen who did not seek fame but were just 'out for a living'. Over sandhills and through passes in the ranges they left their tracks of their camel-strings as they moved over the western dry lands. Their job was to trap wild dingos to get the bonus which came from the dingo scalps. And should necessity arise in times of need they ate the food gathered from the country they passed through, a pattern of life similar to the aborigines who continually followed their trails. Some time later I asked one of the 'doggers' what the 'windralga' mulga seeds were like as a food, to be told brusquely that it was 'Good tucker but made yer blurt like a horse', a description which brought to my mind a similar saying about green peas during my cattle days.

Long distances were nothing to the 'doggers'. Doing things the hard way was all in the game to them. Years later, when the country was 'found' and the modern explorers went forth with the acclaim of the newspapers in their ears, they were happy in the knowledge that wherever they went their way from water to water would be marked out by the camel-pads and trading-paths of the 'doggers' and the aborigines who were there before them.

The 'doggers' were the white nomads who were following the paths of the black nomads. They and the government surveyors were the silent few who opened up the land.

'Before nothing only dingo-man, now track from motor car everywhere,' said Minyinderri as we came away from the camel-place inspection.

With the advent of Giles and Gosse the era of romance and adventure began. The chant-trails of the aborigines from water to water was soon to be covered with the tracks of camels who, with their masters, drank deep from those 'ngatti' rock-holes which are recorded in mythology as the navels that catch the rainwaters which flow down the sternum-hollows of those creative heroes which symbolize happiness to the tribespeople of a dry land.

Those 'doggers' would laugh if one called them explorers. They were just out after the government bounty of ten shillings per scalp at that time. To them it was a job, something to fill the 'tucker-bags' so that they could keep going. Yet those same 'doggers' gave to us, who came behind, a lot of knowledge. Naturally observant people they poked into the out of the way places to find waters, grasslands, aboriginal art places, minerals, plant life and a knowledge of bush creatures and aboriginal customs that seemed boundless. With the unselfishness of people who are not out to 'blow their own bags', they gave their knowledge to all with a liberal supply of 'mud-maps' on the ground to see that the seeker of knowledge, or limelight, never went astray.

From the camp of the dingo-men we travelled on to cross over the tyre tracks of a Land Rover which seemed to be heading into nowhere. We followed it for some distance to come upon a fire-place where the driver had camped for the night amidst a clump of bloodwood trees, and out of the deductions from Minyinderri's knowledge of boot tracks on the ground I discovered it was the camping place of my old friend Bill Johnson of the National Mapping Survey.

Have you ever noticed in life that the ones who are well known are those who have arisen because their findings are 'news'? The explorer whose discoveries were along a well-travelled highway is far better known that those who moved over these desert lands. In the future, perhaps, the Bill Johnsons and their like may be 'News'. Today they are unknown to the multitude because the places they travel over are unknown. It is a roadless land because he and his National Mapping Survey are just now surveying the route along which the future roads will go. Every prominent peak in this so-called western desert has been climbed by Bill. The face to be scaled is plotted by him first on to small charts so that his survey party, who follow behind, shall know where to climb as they ascend it with packs upon their backs to build cairns for a triangulation survey of the area.

Around our camp everything is as nature left it from the beginning of time. Yet somewhere out to the westward bulldozers and road-levellers are laying down roads because of this man's wanderings. He and others of the survey come and go like migratory birds. As Bill travels about he knaps off a piece of stone from a hill or out-crop, gathers a plant specimen or photographs a special bird. All these are carefully recorded and classified by geologists, botanists, or ornithologists in the South. Thus is the story of this country made known to others.

The tracks of the surveyors and their camp-fires were all that reminded me that they had passed by. But the results of their efforts had been recorded on the maps of this area I was now wandering over. My aboriginal friends knew the country out of their hunting pattern and mythological chants which gave us its original name, but without maps I did not know where I was.

To test my aboriginal friend I asked him the direction of each mountain below the horizon and never did I find him wrong when compared with the map and compass bearing. To him it was local knowledge. He knew each place because it was his homeland. He was always telling me about his country and as he did so I thought about Giles the explorer.

Giles did it the hard way when he walked 'as in a dream' back to his camp base to report that his companion Gibson had disappeared forever on a mare called the 'Fair Maid of Perth'. What courage those people had! I get a smile when I compare the way of life of those early explorers with our own. It was the same for the drovers who brought cattle into this land and the numberless people who took up the country as cattle properties together with the doggers, prospectors, and hosts of others who lived in the bushlands years ago. In those days one lived off a land in which hypochondriacs never existed because there were no doctors. The only mail, generally once a month, came by camel or horse. The nearest hospital or telegraph station was hundreds of miles away.

Now government workers in this land have four-wheel-drive motor trucks equipped with deep-freeze refrigerators stacked with the best of assorted tinned foods. They keep in touch with their base with the two-way wireless they carry and should they go 'off the air' a rescue team or a plane is over to see what is wrong.

The days of Giles drinking deeply from a 'smear of water' is a far cry from cold water in the 'fridge'. The gas cookers, tinned foods and fruits with different varieties of frozen meats are far removed from the same explorer who, being famished, 'pounced upon it'—a small two-ounce joey kangaroo abandoned by its mother—'and ate it, living, raw, dying, fur skin, bones, skull and all. The delicious flavour of that creature I shall never forget.'

I look at the map before me. Every detail in this area has been carefully copied from original aerial maps that have been photographed by trained pilots from high altitude aeroplanes. Then each photo is then made into a large mosaic for the map-maker's art.

Thousands of miles had to be travelled to make this map which I hold; men patiently at work in offices in the cities; a thousand details to complete. Everything must be correct for on one imperfection lives could be lost. When all the work is finalized it will be printed—a work of art which I can buy for a few shillings.

I turn over the map. On the back I find a blank piece of paper which could represent this land before Giles travelled over it on his first trip. He was the first to draw a line on its blank surface and from his observations the map grew to this finished job. Today my map shows every sandhill in the area for hundreds of miles around. So correct are they that I can view them under a magnifying-glass to plot out the path I shall travel without crossing over a sand ridge.

Before such evidence as this I feel truly humble.

Yet for Minyinderri and myself the job was the plotting of his tribal chant-lanes which showed his people the foods and secret waters of his land. As a true tribesman he showed me the way; but the efforts of the explorers and surveyors told me my whereabouts.

As the time of the year was July–August we saw here and there over the land the smoke of spinifex fires, which told us plainly that an aboriginal clan was on the move because it is 'puppy-dog-time'.

'Puppy-dog-time'—this is the period of the year not unlike our Christmas-time when people remember the ones of other days together with memories associated with that time. The 'dog stars' (whom we call the Seven Sisters), had already given the sign of 'puppy-dog-time' as they rose into the eastern sky in the early dawn. Not only had the tribesmen seen the sign, but the ever restless dingo had observed it long before them. Now the wild dogs were tending their pups in the sandhills or beneath the rock ledges of the ranges. So the tribesmen moved out within the hunting cycle evolved through the ages. Now distant places would be visited, old friends met and long standing grievances talked over and settled as they gathered and cooked the succulent puppy-dogs (after first removing the scalps which will later be cashed in at some white man's store).

During ancient times 'puppy-dog-time' was a gathering of the tribal clans; now the field is extended as the people come from government settlements, mission and cattle stations. To the black people it is a holiday time when they get away from the 'white fellow-man'. For the white bosses, managers, and superintendents it is a relief to be free from the 'hangers-on' who find the urge to travel greater than that of loafing around.

In the past it was just hunting the puppy-dog and a gathering of the clans; today it has added value in that the scalps are kept.

The whites, like the aborigines, are a race of dog lovers. During my visit to England I was always amused by the women discussing the merits and demerits of the various breeds—in most cases it was not on the ability of the animal as a hunter of game, but on some quality such as hair texture. Full marks went to the french poodles because their hair never came off on the clothes of women who were carrying their pets around.

Now here in this central part of Australia I was hearing dogs discussed once more, but this time it was on the price of scalps and the quality of the flesh. Science has told us that this wild dog of Australia came down from northern lands with some of the first migratory bands from overseas. Perhaps it was eaten then as now. It was a hunter of game as were its masters. This was correct until the herders of sheep and cattle came into the land. Then the dog was declared vermin, because it took away the profits from the new landlords.

Yet, to me this dingo is something we should all admire. He is with man yet apart from him, the aboriginal hunts his way, the dingo another. He is a creature which has been tamed to live in the camps of its owner, yet refuses to be petted and pampered by humans. And its scalp? This hunk of skin is something real in a land which was once without money. How many early cattle-men and mission-stations have kept going on the government bonus money they receive for this trade? 'Puppy-dog-time' was then a real event to the early battlers, on its returns would the pioneers know whether they could 'hang on' till the markets of the south improved.

Now we too were on the trail of 'puppy-dog-time'. My interests concerned the country and its stories. To my friends it was full of expectation as to who they would be meeting 'around the next bend'. Each night around our camp the dingoes called to their mates. That wail, to my aboriginal friends, brought up memories of feasting in days gone by with family reunions and 'plenty story'. To me it recalled a time when a now well-known pastoralist was too poor to pay his wedding fee, so he handed to the parson a number of dingo scalps as a payment. In those days there were more dinnertimes than dinners.

Lying on my swag and watching the stars I listened to the story-telling. Minyinderri was telling me of how this 'wild-dog proper good tucker but me can't eat because too sorry'. I asked him why? He answered that 'this dog stay in country when everybody go away'. He then told me of how he and his wife once found a nest of dingo-pups in the sandhill. 'We been dig out them little fellow puppy-dogs,' he narrated. 'Proper pretty little things with big eyes all-a-same star longa night-time . . . Bulya and me,' he continued. 'We hold them pretty things in hand then we get too sorry and put them back for we think-think that no matter we clear out from country this one mother and father stop there.' I nodded approval, for I too had seen the small fluffy creatures and could understand their feelings. Then I asked, 'What if you and Bulya hungry, you eat them then?'

Minyinderri paused a while then shook his head. 'No matter hungry I can't eat, me too sorry for country and if eat thing then might be me get bad luck and die.'

Over the years the nomads taught me something of their ways as they visited the Rock. At first I was happy with each arrival, but I soon realized that they were a greater lot of vandals than the unthinking tourists. Their uncontrolled dogs were in and out of the rock-holes, camel droppings littered the lead-ins to the drinking sites and the smell from the animals' bodies was more than all the advertisements could cope with. The dogs were always on the prowl, and so were their owners. Being food gatherers they were out gathering food wherever they could find it. The golden nectar-laden blooms of the gravillia fell the first victim to the aboriginal children who looked upon it as a sweet. Gaping holes appeared in the red earth where the women hunters had dug out a honey-ant's nest. Everywhere the acacia trees were pressed down, or hacked at, for the tasty witchetty grubs at their root and branches.

The trees provided the nomads' only means of getting a little money to purchase foodstuffs from the store at Curtin Springs. They hacked them down to make boomerangs and wooden dishes. I had already explained to Minyinderri that nothing must be cut down close to the Rock. Should they require timber for their curios then they must get it from some distance away.

He in turn explained my desires to the nomads who seemed eager to fall into line with my wishes. Forewarned is forearmed is an ancient dictum. Everywhere around me I saw a hive of industry as the crafts-

Djuwerri beside the djuta marks on the river gums of his land

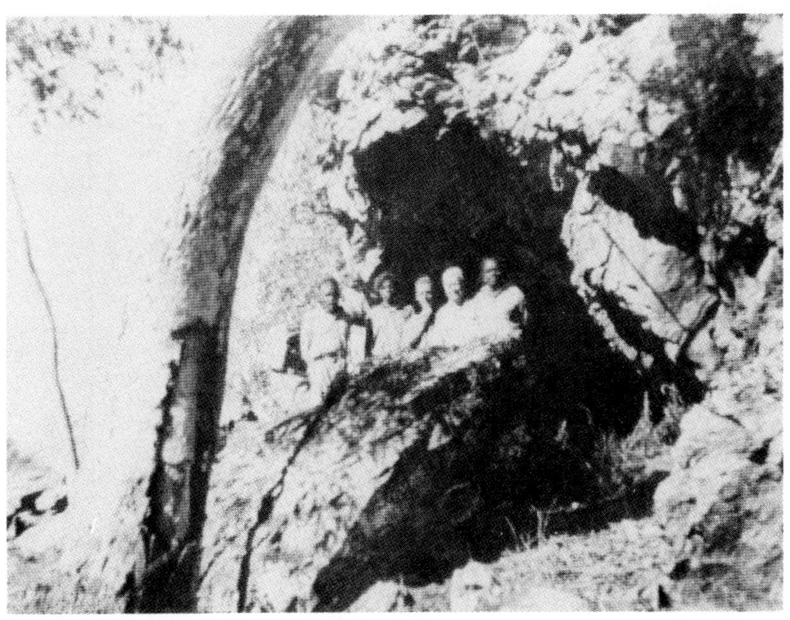

"Peter Severin took our photograph as we stood in Lassiter's Cave"

"Djuwerri rubbed and chanted the 'kura-kardi-stone' before Kikingurra"

"Djuwerri outside the sacred Kulpidja place"

men plied their curio trade. No trees were cut facing my way. Only when I went for a walk on the opposite side of the aborigines' camp did I see the damage they had done.

The aborigine is an expert on not using up his energy. He has learnt from experience when working with stone-tools that in the cutting of trees for his weapons it must be done in such a way that the tree can still grow. So he puts a small cut on the top and bottom side of the wood he requires, he then cuts it out in the shape he wants then splits the lot off with a wooden lever. This is exactly what the nomads had done. All trees were hacked at close to their camp, but on that side away from my sight.

When I showed Minyinderri the damage they had done he looked surprised and talked loudly in his tongue. I let him talk on for I could see that grumbling would get nowhere. By the old look on some of the axe gashes I could see that he was one of the culprits.

The kangaroos and emus received special attention from the huntsmen's spears, but they were careful to cook their kill out in the bush and carry it secretly into their camps. The ancient law of the hunter was to use bush fires to trap game, but the Reserve Board forbade the lighting of fires. When the nomads were around smoke signals were everywhere. Two laws were in action, the old and the new. One day, perhaps, the wandering nomad will join his fellow tribesmen at a settlement or mission. When that happens the old days will be gone forever.

Chapter Twenty-two

Westward to Kikingurra

It had always been my desire, since I had been in the area of Ayers Rock, to go out into the Petermann Ranges with some of the Loritdja aborigines so that I could hear from them some of its mythology. Though my last season as Ranger was 1960 I returned to Ayers Rock for the first part of 1962 to help the tourists as a guide until my nomad friends could come together for that great day.

How I watched the smoke signals rise from the hunting fires of the nomads. At one time they would be from the south where some good storms had fallen, at other times to the eastward. Minyinderri himself was with his children at Areyonga Government Reserve, but one of the Loritdja natives who worked around the Rock came along now and then to give me the latest 'news'.

Strangely enough his news item was nearly always correct, whether he got it by the traditional 'major-bell-bird' messenger, word of mouth from some passing hunter whom I never saw (which was doubtful) or a sort of mental telepathy I could never determine.

I myself did not worry over a thing I could not control. The drought of the previous year just would not break. Clouds came into the western sky—a good sign of rain—but went away giving the cattle people around another dose of worry as to the movement of their famished herds.

As a precaution should the country be too dry for the nomad's arrival on time I had contacted my good friend Peter Severin of Curtin Springs regarding the use of his Land Rover for a trip to the Petermanns. As he had never been that way himself he was only too willing to oblige, stating also that he knew of a good Loritdja man who would bring out some of his clan to show us what he called 'his properly good country'.

Thus did I guide tourists around the Rock till Peter Severin arrived

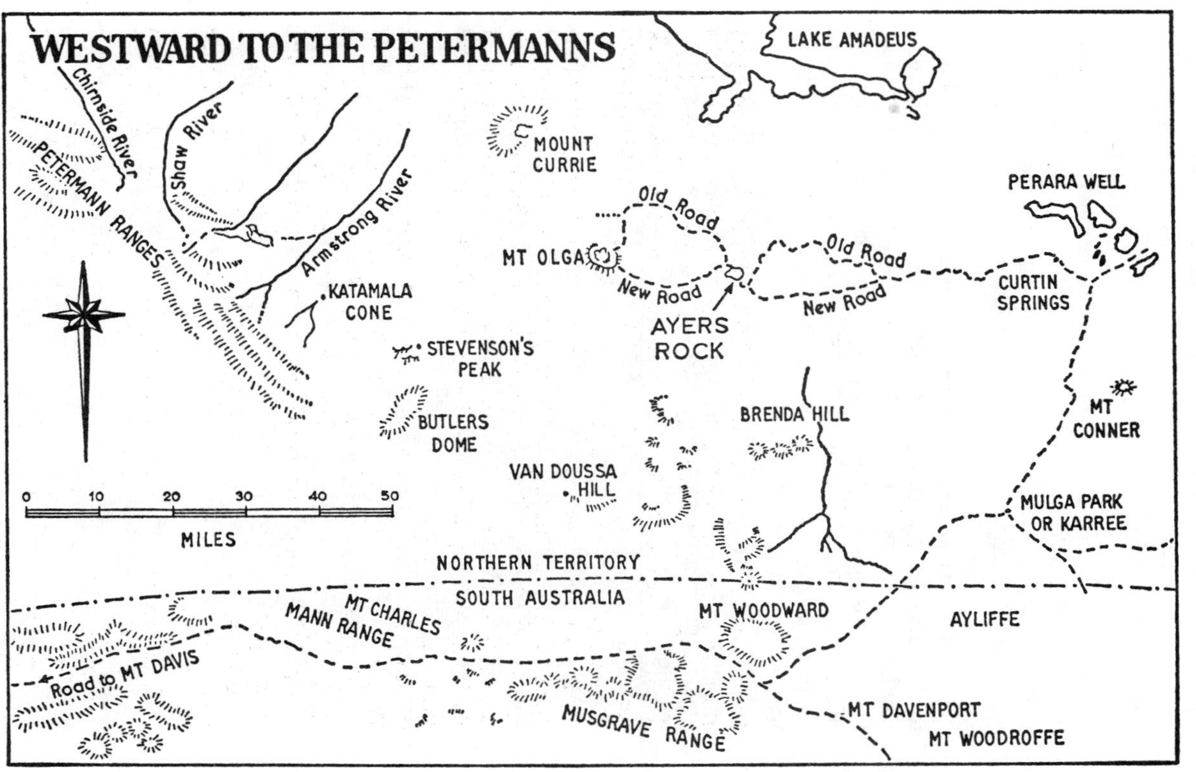
WESTWARD TO THE PETERMANNS
LAKE AMADEUS
Chirnside River
Shaw River
Armstrong River
PETERMANN RANGES
MOUNT CURRIE
Old Road
Old Road
MT OLGA
New Road
New Road
AYERS ROCK
PERARA WELL
CURTIN SPRINGS
KATAMALA CONE
STEVENSON'S PEAK
BUTLERS DOME
BRENDA HILL
MT CONNER
VAN DOUSSA HILL
0 10 20 30 40 50
MILES
MULGA PARK OR KARREE
NORTHERN TERRITORY
SOUTH AUSTRALIA
MT CHARLES
MANN RANGE
MT WOODWARD
AYLIFFE
Road to MT DAVIS
MUSGRAVE RANGE
MT DAVENPORT
MT WOODROFFE

with his utility and supplies for our trip to the west. As an extra precaution Peter brought out his head stockman Ray MacDonald who drove a Land Rover.

I had already been to Angus Downs to pick up some Loritdja men who knew the Petermann country well and understood its mythology. Two were old timers with visages of tribal Elders who had passed through many secret and sacred Inma ceremonies. The other was a youth called Wulmunjungu who went under the English name of Lindsay.

One of the old men called Djuwerri of the Windralga totem explained to me that he and his tribal father Maggi of the Leru totem wished to take Lindsay, whom they called their tribal son and sister's son respectively, into the home of their clan so as to show him the sacred Bubias of the area and explain to him their secrets. Thus was Lindsay one of the party, a lucky break for me because his English and understanding was excellent as an interpreter.

I had gathered a little of the country's mythology from the nomads over the years, but I soon found out that unless one 'puts his foot' upon the places to be chanted and talked about, the area around regarding the stories is a blank.

With Peter and Ray's arrival we were soon packed up and on our way. Ahead of us was country new to me from a mythological point of view. The road itself had been used by both heavy and light motors over the years; along it had gone survey parties and many travellers who just love to poke into these out-of-the-way places.

This road we were travelling along, though rarely used owing to the fact that it was a long dry stage, was nevertheless crammed with stories. There was the tale of a family who came from Perth and broke down forty miles from Ayers Rock. As the Ranger at Ayers Rock I met the man who told me he had walked in that distance for assistance. His wife and family were on that lonely road, a waterless bush track of nearly three hundred miles from the last settlement of Giles in Western Australia. Waterless, except for the tribesmen who know the rock-holes and soaks in that lonely land.

Yet where roads go, so do the adventurous ones. A woman friend of mine called Francis Kay drove blithely along it without a companion. Her starting point for the desert journey was 800 miles westward from Ayers Rock. It was about Christmas-time when she arrived at the Rock to astound the caretaker when she told him she had come from the west and could she get a bath.

Wonders never cease, for only a week before Peter and I with the Loritdja went west, a black heavy sedan with a trailer carrying an upturned dinghy came over the desert road. From the sea shores near Perth they had come, a man and his wife, their destination Borroloola on the Macarthur River which flows into the Gulf of Carpentaria—a run of about 2,500 miles across Australia on a fishing holiday. Not since Sturt's day has a craft been transported over such waterless land.

Such then was our westward run, a bush track somewhere in the direction of the doggers and camel trails in years gone by.

Travelling along the path of the doggers I thought of the early thirties of this century when dingo scalps were worth only ten shillings each in the Northern Territory but over three times that amount in Western Australia. Perhaps in that rate of exchange lies the secret of that westward movement of the camel strings through the Petermanns and the ranges to the west. Or an excuse, maybe, for those who were continually seeking Lasseter's gold reef, a gold, not found in the hills, but in the hoarded dingo scalps which had been gathered by the hard-pressed settlers of the Centre.

I now see that western scene in a new perspective. The doggers are transformed to traders out to drive the hardest bargain with their border raids. Thus was 'puppy-dog-time', a period when the tribes wandered and the police camel patrols roamed the country. One to prevent, the other to evade. With the law rode black trackers who looked upon his job as 'just tucker'. With the experienced doggers were aborigines with a knowledge of the desert—big men in ritual and taboo law. Thus did the doggers evade the ones who sought them. I have heard many tales from the doggers of that time who told me stories of how their aboriginal companions somehow sense in which direction the law travelled. Was it telepathy or a message from the black trackers with the camel patrol, or was it the morning call of the major-bell-bird or red-rumped-kingfisher which are said to be the messengers and warning birds of the Loritdja people?

What stories of adventure will one day be written about these western lands! Stories of this one-time deep 'Outback' that is slowly becoming 'Inside'.

My reveries of the area were rudely awakened by the chanting of my Loritdja friends. I turned to see them pointing towards the low gidyea-covered ridges of Kilinya, the 'hot hills' of quartzite about fifteen miles from Ayers Rock. That was the place to which the seekers of Lasseter's reef camped for months to scratch around that hungry country awaiting the time when their funds ran out so that they could return to the southern cities once more.

At that place in the 'hot hills', not far away from one of the old camp-sites of the bogus gold-seeker's digging spots, we camped the night to boil the billy-can for a drink of tea and a feed of rib-bones grilled on the hot coals of our camp-fire. That first night was a try-out for me with my swag rolled out on hard red earth. To make matters more trying I spread out my bed upon a patch of burrs which kept me scratching far into the night.

Next morning we were on our way with the red glow of the rising sun gleaming from the eastern walls of Katatjuta which lay to the south of our road. About twenty miles out from the Rock our westward road branched to the right and we were off on our journey towards the Petermann Ranges.

Our road passed through the usual desert vegetation; mulga scrubs so dense that our bush road twisted and turned as though the ritual Wanambi serpent had made it as he crawled over the country in the dawn of time. Passing through the mulga we would come out on to sandy plains studded with acacia nablus interspersed among the stately desert oaks. As become the cattle-men with me Peter and Ray were talking about the cattle pasture along our way. The abundance of brown mulga so beloved by the cattle-man as a stock food, and the open grasslands along our way had both Peter and Ray amazed. To them the area was valued for its stock-carrying capacity, but to the aborigines with us, it was of interest only because of the legend and mythology within the creeks and ranges around.

Eighty miles out our road passed by a small outcrop of rock with a dry rock-hole that went under the name of Katatngarra. At this place we paused a while and as we did Djuwerri told me that it was sacred in Loritdja mythology as marking the path taken by the women of the 'Kurakardi' (monitor-lizard) totem who made the country and formed the small rock-hole as a place from which spirit children came in the dream-time.

Onward we travel to cross the sandy creek of 'Moanyu' (a lizard not unlike the 'kurakardi') and, fourteen miles farther on, the Armstrong or 'Puta-puta' river of the Petermann aborigines.

We pulled up for lunch on the opposite bank of that dry sandy river and as the billy-can boiled I strolled around with my aboriginal friends to hear their story of this place near the foot-hills of the Petermann Ranges.

This 'Puta-puta' river, they explained to me, was created by the women of the 'Kurakardi' totem when they came from Kunpingin to chant the road and country northward towards the Wanambi place of Piltardi.

As they told me the story of that place I was amazed at the wealth of mythology in this country. What I was getting was along the line of our travel, yet each and every mountain and river around was a place belonging to the country's ritual story.

Our road from the path of the sacred women was, for a time, over a sandy plain. Then we came up to the Petermanns proper where the high red quartzite bluffs gave rise to a mythology relating to another Katingarra which was fashioned when the left-handed Linggi of the Ayers Rock legend once more threw his throwing-stick of light from the east to create the ritual story of the Earth-mother in this land.

Farther on we came upon one of those desert storm-patches as in my former camel walkabout, and all of us were overjoyed at the wealth of green vegetation around that spot. Green 'pussy-cat-tails' covered the earth in profusion, a mantle so thick as to obscure the road we were travelling along. To Peter and Ray this was a food much enjoyed by cattle; to me those wild flowers in that red land were something to remember; but to our aboriginal friends that wealth of green and violet blooms were just rubbish, 'alpuraddi'; nothing to rave about because it could not be eaten as tucker. Everything in that land was according to our needs.

We naturally pulled up in that Garden of Eden to feast our eyes on its beauty; while doing so our natural hunters of food scattered around searching the grounds for the tracks of game. What a twiddling of fingers and sign-talk there was as they moved along. Each track seen was recorded in the finger-talk to his mate, and great was the hand movement when Djuwerri signalled an emu's nest was around. I naturally enquired as to how they knew, to be told briefly that the emu footprints proclaimed it so, and that was my answer. Yet all the time we were in that area I noticed the mouths of the aborigines were in constant action as they chewed away at the succulent parrakelya and berries of the storm-patch.

At Peter's call we were once more on our way and after a mile or so we passed from the green to the dry red land as though the rain-spirit had seen fit to bless one area and scorn another.

A few miles farther on we came to the Shaw River at a place known to the aborigines as 'djundi' (the thigh) and made famous in literature as containing a smoke-blackened cave in which Lasseter rested a while on his search for gold.

Gold in them hills! All I could see was hungry looking strata overlying an older land. Djuwerri and the others soon found a patch of yalka root-plants growing on a flat near by, so grasping a stone in their hands they were soon gouging the earth after the small yams. Food everywhere around, yet Lasseter starved here because he distrusted the very people who could have kept him alive.

I noticed that many of the river-gums of that area had pieces of bark cut out of them in the form of a circle and on inquiring of Djuwerri he explained they were called *Juta*, a sort of wheel to roll along the ground for children to throw small spears at.

A toot from Peter's motor cut off further information and once more we were moving on our way to cross the Shaw many times before we came out on to a sandy plain studded with stately desert oaks which gave the landscape a park-like scene.

All the while as a background towered the blood-red walls of the Petermann Ranges, with ahead of us a tall peaked mountain, blue in that evening light. We paused to view that remarkable scene and going behind the motors I was amazed to hear loud sobbing coming from my old aboriginal friends. 'Kikingurra,' sobbingly said Djuwerri as he looked unashamedly at us whites with tears streaming down his dusty face, 'my country proper good one . . . my country'. I looked towards Magin who was crouched on the floor of the utility and sobbing bitterly.

We rested as they wept, for to move then would be as one laughing in the presence of a deceased loved one. I myself somehow knew how they felt for I too had re-visited the places of my childhood and felt the heart pangs as I remembered the many kind friends of that time. Memories flowing in with the setting sun. Kikingurra . . . Minyinderri's country, the country of the Windralga which I had heard so much about. Now it was here before me and the sobbing of my Loritdja friends told me how great it really was to the tribesmen.

Our road led out to a small plain and pausing on it Djuwerri proudly informed us all that this open space was the plain of 'Pupialla', the head song-place of the country and the sacred and secret resting abode of the ritual dog 'Kuapunni'. This dog is not as a dingo, but is black and tall, its ears long and standing above fiery eyes that gleam in the night. When it opens its mouth to wail the doomed one notes that its tongue is red between large fangs. Such is the description of the ritual dog that carried the 'Kuddinbas' (eaglets of the initiation) away from the Mother-place at Ayers Rock, as it was told to me at Kikingurra. I had heard the canine demon described in the ritual myths of many northern tribes where he was recorded as speeding along with the dreaded Wolgaru who is the guardian of the deceased ones awaiting to be re-born. It is he who also travels underground to the magic song of death and destroys the unbelievers of the tribe.

Now here in the Petermanns I had planted my foot upon the place of the demon. Djuwerri's voice aroused me from my reveries, 'Kikingurra big place'. Thus into the 'shadows' of the mountain we drove our motors. We proceeded to a clump of mulga trees where we made a night camp amidst the sacred emblems of an ancient people.

Chapter Twenty-three

The Petermanns

AT long last I was in the country of the Petermann Ranges. From where I stood I could see around me a country which is a part of the South-western Aboriginal Reserve. A strange title and a name only because it is devoid of the Loritdja tribespeople who once hunted in it. Very little apart from scientific papers has been written about the area.

Of the earlier discoverers, men such as Carruthers, who surveyed the area during the years of 1888–90, nothing remains but his survey reports in the archives of South Australia, with a mountain in the Bloods Range, to the north of where I was to commemorate his name. He and his party came, surveyed, and departed to be remembered only when someone is inquiring about a mountain's name in the area he plotted over seventy years ago.

Few people today, and only those who are scientists or seekers of rare editions, remember the Horn expedition who explored this western land in the latter part of the last century. Their books are real spell-binders for anyone seeking information regarding the flora and fauna of this country, made more so because one of the party was Baldwin Spencer. He was a zoologist who later became famous with his friend Gillen—the postmaster at the Alice Springs telegraph station—for their studies of the Arunta (their original spelling) which put us on the right road to a correct scientific understanding of the Australian aborigines.

During that time a party under Larry Wells travelled over much of this area on a general survey. A bush mate of mine, Jack Carriage, often told me about their exploits, but the one thing that always stuck in my youthful mind was his story of how they tethered their camels in a ring around the night-camp when they got into 'bad nigger country', knowing full well that those nervous ruminants were the best guardians against Loritdja attacks.

Geologists tell us that the Petermanns belong to the Middle Protozoic epoch above the Lower Archaeozoic Musgrave Block, a land so old that they talk in years by the hundreds of millions, ages of building up and eroding away. Only the fossil life overlying the land in other areas tells us a little of the story. This was an unknown land until wandering man came upon the scene to people its ancient peaks with the story of his Gods. Now man too has moved on to the east taking with him his traditions and his rituals. A few of the old die-hards remain in the land, a footprint here and there on the sandy flats. For those like myself who try to pick up a remnant of the mythology must depend on men such as Djuwerri and Magin.

To the south of us was the ancient land of Yalgarnia and thinking of that place I was reminded of how in 1939 grim death struck at a pioneer family who had taken up virgin country and called the place Shirley Well. The settler was one Harold Brown, his wife not in her thirties, their child but a few years old. They had improvised a crude homestead dug-out in the side of a hill with a cover of logs and spinifex—a cool place during the heat of summer but one that proved to be a death-trap when a storm cloud burst upon them one night as they slept.

Next morning a young aboriginal woman called Minnie 'Pooni-pooni' came upon the collapsed roof with the child sobbing in the wreckage. Few people today remember how those aboriginal people cared for the child while 'Pooni-pooni' ran thirty miles to the mission station of Ernabella to get assistance.

How full of surprises are the Petermann Ranges; a heap of stones tell a story, a peak records a sacred myth, even those 'juta' cuts on the river-gums at the place of Lasseter's cave has me thinking of how this now desolate land was the scene of children's games. Children's games in this strange land—the thing somehow does not seem correct to me. As my friend explained how he and the other children lined up for an adult to throw the 'juta', he remarked laughingly how 'We been have good game and proper laugh when one spear hit wheel and stand up as Juta fall down.'

I had seen the same game played by aboriginal children when I was a lad at Mount Molloy in North Queensland. It was one of those games that teach children of the tribe the way to future hunting, just as were the games made by fingers and hands on the earth and feats of memory and eye which are performed by aborigines while they are resting during the heat of the day.

Yet somehow I just could not reconcile those Juta marks on the river-gums with this locality. My reasoning was undoubtedly obscured because I had always thought of this place as being something away in the distance—in the never-never. To me it was nowhere, for I was 500 miles from the nearest town. But to Djuwerri, and his people, this place was their homeland, the centre of their culture, and their little world. To me . . . well I just could not believe that children once shouted and played here in this now apparently desolate land. Played, hunted, loved, and reared families from time immemorial back to a remote age when these waning creeks and river systems were watering the hunting areas for the Loritdja tribes, or perhaps an even more ancient tribe that was overthrown by these migrating, ruthless invaders.

The only voices I heard there were the muffled tones from those who had come with me into this country, yet up to fifty years before this area was controlled by a compact tribe governed by its kinship and ritual law that had served it so well over the years.*

Then came the inroads of our civilization, and the clans departed for the missions, cattle stations, towns, and government settlements. A sad thought for those who think of the aborigines as museum pieces, yet a welcome change for the Loritdja who were hard pressed in that slowly drying, dying land. The drought during the late twenties was the final blow. Slowly they watched their waters dry away. Eastward was permanent water but they were controlled by the white people. They could have gone that way, but many aboriginal people perished because they feared a punitive expedition where police and white men rode with guns to avenge the killing of a white man.

A few years later a prospector called Lasseter came seeking a hill of gold. Books have written of how he searched and then died in the Petermanns. His death during those years of the dole gave many a new vision. So the search was on. With such ingredients as an inaccessible country, a fabulous reef of gold and wild blacks, there was no better locality for the company promoters of the cities.

As a result of his dream and his death the western lands became connected with Lasseter's name. From Alice Springs to the Petermann Ranges the camp-sites of the gold seekers were dotted like the droppings of the camels some of them rode. Those who had money gleaned from shareholders came, dug holes anywhere, then returned with tales of bigger and better things on the next prospecting trip. Everywhere there were people who knew where the gold reef was. Many used other peoples' money, while some came under their own steam to follow their dream.

Each time I see one of the dried salt-water lakes in this western country I think of Kurt Johansenn—one of the ablest and most versatile men in the Centre—flying a prospector called Jimmy Prince out to seek the golden lode. Jimmy claimed he knew the exact location of the place, but Kurt's aeroplane met with a mishap while flying along one of the puntus and, forced to land, he was unlucky enough to break the tip off his propeller. Undaunted, the redoubtable Kurt soon trimmed and balanced the blades with the only cutting tool he had, a sharp toma-

* A well-known bushman, Allan Brumby, told me he saw 500 aborigines in this area in 1927.

hawk, then discovered he could not take off with the full load. Once again the bushman Kurt overcame the difficulty by fashioning a crude distilling plant from a water-can and some copper piping. This, with a fire from the local mulga, and salt water from a soak on the edge of the salt-lake had Jimmy fitted up in a good camp, and away went Kurt in a mad race over the tree-tops finally to reach Alice Springs. A neat landing and soon a party was on its way to rescue Jimmy Prince. Everybody was happy except Kurt who got into trouble with the Civil Aviation powers-that-be who only thought in terms of regulations instead of decorations for Kurt for such a remarkable achievement.

From Lasseter's gold, attention was once turned to the prospector's bones. In 1958 a film unit, composed of heavy land vehicles, went out into the area on a publicity advertising stunt. How the motors roared in the sand, a gimmick easily achieved by putting heavy chocks under the wheels away from the cameras. Their destination was Lasseter's grave. The end of their trek came when they returned to Alice Springs police station. There, with cameras at the ready, the star of the show walked into the scene with a bag in his hand and dramatically announced to the constable in charge that he had brought Lasseter's remains with him. As it was after hours, and the officer in charge at the time had recognized all this as a film stunt, he told them to come back in the morning.

No cameras whirled that afternoon, but next day, when it did come off, great was the uproar. The film people got their 'shot'. A good scene for them but not a good idea for Jeff Millgate, the constable, who was ordered to proceed immediately to the up-rooted grave-site to investigate the matter.

A modern detective story where the 'private-eye' has a swig of grog then darts down the street or goes for a ride in an aeroplane or train is one thing; to Jeff it was five hundred miles of bush road in the heat of summer, the last two hundred miles over spinifex with a curse for the film crowd with each jolt.

Jeff Millgate took with him as a guide Merv Andrews—the driller of our boring days at Ayers Rock—and after much travelling they finally arrived at the deserted film camp in the sandy bed of a creek. The site was littered with film packs and empty tin cans. But of Lasseter's last resting-place nothing remained but the newly turned up earth surrounded by footprints and empty cigarette packets. The slab of Petermann stone which had been originally placed as a mark of respect at the head of the dead prospector's grave was not to be seen.

Jeff told me of how, when he and Merv were standing near the grave, they heard the news over the wireless that Lasseter has been given a Christian burial in consecrated ground at Alice Springs. With that news came another item that the boss of the film unit had been issued with a summons over the removal of a body from a grave without official consent. The story was a good headline for the southern

Yet each time I think of the Petermann Ranges I see Lasseter's dug-up grave surrounded by empty cigarette packets. That old prospector may be buried in Alice Springs but I like to think of his restless soul wandering around the place of his dreams. Roaming thus, I am sure he must hold communion with those countless shades connected with aboriginal mythology, those spirits who live in the blow-holes from which the ritual dog Kurapunni emerges growling before setting off underground, to seek out the uninitiated and evil-doers of the tribes.

When Minyinderri told me at Ayers Rock about the original burial of Lasseter, he was emphatic that his people 'been bury that dead white-fellow proper Loritdja way.' This was confirmed thirty years later when the film company exhumed the body. During the digging they discovered that the dead man had been buried in the bent-sitting-up position which is closely related to re-birth and re-incarnation. Only a Loritdja tribesman would have buried the body in that way which conformed to tribal custom. That he was buried not long after he passed away is evident by the fact that the body had not been discovered by the numerous wild dingoes of that area. Minyinderri, in explaining about the prospector's death, remarked to me that, 'All-about been proper cry for that dead one.'

Sitting in the Petermanns I could visualize that burial scene—the tribesman digging the hole as the women around wailed loudly so that the dead one's soul would find eternal rest.

To me that grave scene would be a fitting tribute for that seeker of dreams, and who knows but that his wandering shade may be as one of those spirits that hold council each night at the 'Wanambi' ghost-camp of Wolonga seven miles from the 'Eyowa' red-ochre quarry north-east of Angus Downs. This is a spot so taboo that no tribesmen will camp near enough to hear the wild laughter that seems to come out from the darkness around. It is a sort of tribal Valhalla for those who have died in battle.

The Petermann Ranges is in a fenceless area, yet it has a boundary fence as formidable as that made of posts and fencing wire. To reach here one must apply for a permit from the Welfare Branch in the Northern Territory. That application must have affixed to it suitable references regarding one's character; only then when the permit has been given can one enter this uninhabited area.

Should I wish to go south of this Reserve into the South-Australian Aboriginal Reserve then I must apply to the Aboriginal Board in Adelaide. With my application must go the character references and a medical certificate. If my application is approved then I must enter after I have signed a paper explaining in detail that I must not sleep with an aboriginal woman or keep her as a mistress. My original intention was to go south but as I had to go into Alice Springs three hundred miles away for the doctor I gave the idea up. The strange part of the medical procedure was that only I must be medically examined, not my nomad friends who have been in contact with tourists for years. They may go in and out as they desire.

I was going to go westward but soon discovered that in that direction was the Rocket Range Reserve—an area crammed with regulations and security prohibitions, more difficult to enter than a sinner trying to crash the gates of heaven. Medical certificates, references, permits. What a strange free world. The ranges of the Petermann were around me, yet over to the West we saw a strange yellow light. 'White fellow make trouble,' muttered my friend. 'Proper devil business.' In peace we prepare for war.

Yet at the Petermanns, as we boiled the billy-can for breakfast, it was good to watch the dawn-light spreading over the hills around our camp. It was a time of day when one felt close to a divine power that somehow controlled all.

I have heard it said that dawn has always been a special hour of worship for most of the human race. This may be so for many religions, but I do know that with the aborigines dawn is that moment when light floods the earth around to drive away the shadows of night and fear. At that instant the shades of the dead return to their resting-places, there to remain during the day. As the sun goes down they return once more to their wanderings. Thus at sundown and sunrise do the tribes-people remember the departed ones. In the country of their forebears I watched the actions of my Loritdja friends. What thoughts were in their minds was not for mortals such as I. Though silent, I thought I saw their lips move as is the custom of the tribes when they breathe the names of their deceased kin to recall the many kind acts they had received from them during their lifetimes. Sundown was the time of remembrance. A sort of Angelus bell silently tolled by primitive man.

Chapter Twenty-four

Kikingurra Country

How strong now does the memory of Kikingurra flow upon me as I write this story of that strange place which is so sacred to the Windralga aborigines of the Petermann Ranges. To portray the emotional upsurge of those Elders who were with us as we passed under the shadow of that great mountain is beyond my power; all I can ever hope to do is record the events which happened to us all.

What proud looks were on those old men's faces as they solemnly told us that the plain of Pulpialla which we had just passed over was so sacred that should an uninitiated one, or any woman, put her foot on it they would most assuredly die.

As our utilities pulled up beside some mulga trees they were out and beckoning us to follow them. So great was their haste that we all realized that they were intent on showing us some sacred spot before the sun went down. Old Magin, so silent on the way out, was now full of talk and chanting. Djuwerri and Wulmungungu came to a stop before a circle of upright stones. Then, with much talking and pointing, they moved rapidly from one to the other as though bursting with some inner knowledge they wished to explain. All the talk was Loritdja and fortunately for Peter and me the head stockman Ray knew the tongue well so that after the jumble of talk died down he explained that this circle of stones was the lead-in to the holy of holies in the deep ravine before us.

At that place of the stone circle the 'lorka' or chants began and out of them came the story told to us onlookers. The first upright stone, and that farthest away from the ritual mountain, was the 'Boonyin', or the one who was about to be made an 'inside-one' as was the 'Kudindbas' at Ayers Rock. The central upright stone was the 'Kuda Bulka', or 'big brother', with over to our left as we faced the ravine, the 'Malumpa djugga-djugga' symbolized by two upright stones representing the 'little brothers' of the ritual. All were of the Windralga totem, and as guardians of the mountain they also explained to the ritual men how they too must stand before that sacred spot. From that place the old men led us onwards to another upright stone symbolizing the 'Djimiar' ('Grandfather') not only of the Windralga, but of old Magin who was also the brother of Minyinderri my friend of Ayers Rock.

The western sun was now casting a strong light on to the high red cliff walls beyond the ravine. Loudly the old men chanted as we walked along, explaining now and then, as they pointed out a white upright stone at the base of a red cliff wall high up on the mountain face. 'Paradjuka,' proudly said Djuwerri. 'Him Big-man for Windralga and boss for everybody.' I had heard of 'Paradjuka' during my many talks with Minyinderri. The great 'Paradjuka' watched from that high place to punish those who disobeyed the laws of the tribe. To his place on the mountain only the wise in tribal and spiritual lore went to reside and sleep within a small shelter near by. Owing to its sacredness and maybe its height, I never attempted the climb, but I would have liked to go up there to sit among the shades of those tribal Elders from days gone by. Perhaps they would have revealed to me some of their spiritual life, just as they were said to transmit it to those who dwelt among them.

Magin had been there, Djuwerri never. 'I been go away from my country long time ago . . . white fellow been take me, but,' adding proudly, 'this time I go there to see all-about.'

To us whites at the base of the mountain the cliff wall towering above was but a sort of jasper-like strata of stone, but to these old Windralga men it symbolized the shades of their tribal ancestors awaiting the arrival of new Elders.

So we travelled up that ravine in a glow of twilight. On our left was Kikingurra, the mighty one pointing towards the heavens. Before us was the wall of the Elders with Paradjuka painted white as the symbol of death. Everything was eerie in that place of the shadows, above us the wind whistled, a sound only broken as the old men pointed to a small cave on our left hand and explained to us all that there was the shelter of 'Kurupuka' where a sacred fire was lit by a magic song that drove the first Windralga men from the mountain in those creative times.

Thus did they sing as we advanced into that place of gloom finally to come to rest before a long, flat, reddish increase-stone that strangely resembled a goanna's head. From its polished top one realized it was connected with the tribal way of life, a stone of warmth that decoyed fat lizards from the cold earth. But I and the others with me were astounded when we were solemnly told that this 'Kurakardi' was also the stone of vengeance on which women were killed should they dare to put their foot on the sacred plain of Pulpialla near by. When I doubted the old men's word a little later they demonstrated to us how it was done, Djuwerri beating with a stone as Magin chanted and nodded assent. I still somehow doubt that such a thing was actually done, though there was the stone before us. This was the first time I had ever seen a sacrificial stone used to placate the wrath of spiritual Elders and their tribal deities. Yet it must be remembered that on top of this same Kikingurra is said to be that talus of stones where the tribal Elders of old stoned two old wanderers to death because they refused to obey a warning given to them by the sacred Kudong-women of old.

This country is sacred to both the Windralga and Kurakardi and everywhere there are legends of the two 'Kudongs', dream-time women who carried children on their backs—a symbol of the Earth-mother. All mortals were made by her from the fruits of the earth which sprang from her whirling body as she danced the first ritual of fertility.

Djuwerri explained the story to us that night as Peter cooked a damper in the ashes of the mulga camp-fire and boiled a bucket-full of corned beef in readiness for tomorrow's meals.

'My country proper good one,' said Djuwerri. 'That's why Magin and me been bring Wulmungungu here to show him country properly way.'

After his little speech the old aborigines spread out their swags on the ground as did Peter, Ray, and I. Then to the sighing of the winds in the peaks above we were soon asleep.

But although I slept for the first few hours I was soon awake and tossing about with aching hips against the hard earth. The years creeping on had softened me up since the early days when I could sleep on a wire fence. Usage then had given me a fondness for flat hard beds; now the old bones rested more easily on a soft mattress.

How easy, when one is sleeping on a soft bed, to talk about the softness of today's youth and boast about oneself. Now was the time of testing for me and I was found wanting. Aching bones in the cold swag had me watching the stars overhead and listening to the night-winds sighing in the mountains. What messages had they to give to my sleeping aboriginal friends—perhaps tales of by-gone days before the coming of the white man when these Windralga people were strong in law and ritual.

Suddenly I was alert, for plainly I could hear a ghostly crying as of a woman on the Kurakardi stone. Then came a sound of ghostly feet that swished and soughed down the ravine before the red wall of Paradjuka. On it raced by our camp, a sound not unlike an army of demons sweeping westward through the gloom of those sacred mountain valleys.

After this I slept on fitfully to awaken when I heard old Djuwerri breaking wood to light our camp-fire. I peered out upon the scene to behold the old man naked to the waist in that cold morning air. Tough and hardy men are the desert people. How they have helped us in the past, yet too often have we given them hate instead of the kindness they so richly deserve.

After our morning meal of damper with fat corned meat grilled on the coals of the mulga fire, Peter informed us that we would use this place as a base camp and go on with the Land Rover to survey the country beyond. Thus onward we journeyed to the west to reach a sacred place which was to be the end of our road into the Petermann country.

Our track now was between parallel ranges along a valley studded with countless 'pilpirra' ghost-gums that were said to represent groups of virgins who came with the people of creation in the dawn of time. Looking at those ghost-gums in that morning light I could well believe the story, for each one with its snow-white trunk and green leaves could easily have given rise to something fresh and virginal from another age.

Djuwerri pointed out to us a high red wall on our left, and explained that those places were made by these virgins as they danced across the land. Then suddenly all thoughts about mythology were dispelled. Calling on us to stop the aborigines leaped out of the utility and began scanning the earth. 'Tracks . . . human footprints,' said Ray. 'They say women were here but a few hours ago digging out yalka food on the banks of the river nearby.'

I myself got out to look at the tracks that were plain upon the red earth. Humans! If someone had told me I was looking at the prints of some prehistoric monster I doubt whether I would have been so surprised. Yet not only were the footprints there, but my aboriginal friends could tell me who they were, where they were going, and all about them. The apparently empty land had become alive. Somewhere along our road we had passed through the border of 'Outback' and were now 'Inside' once more.

This sandy river we were now following was the one mentioned by Djuwerri last night as the place of the 'Kudong' women making the pass through the mountains, so we followed their trail along a river flat where we pulled up before a low hill of jumbled stones.

Here we were ordered to stop, then with much hush-hush and signals we walked up into the hill. 'Kulpidja place,' whispered Djuwerri as he scrambled up over the rocks with us behind. A few small paintings were on the roof of a smoke-blackened cave. From a crevice of the rock, Djuwerri pulled out the sacred boards of his Windralga people. I noticed they were of wood, well cut and finely grooved. The centre piece was the Windralga totem, those on each end the djewa grinding-stones to prepare the seed for eating. Two further long boards were in the crevice. These were the sacred boards of the Mother, and associated with them was a small bullroarer or Bubia with a hole at its end denoting that it was ready to receive the next initiate to be made an 'Inside' at the Mother-place of the next 'Kerungra'.

Then as we took photos, the old men held the objects in their hands, and looking towards the mountain of Kikingurra in the distance chanted the story connected with them. What a proud day was that for those two old men and the youthful Wulmungungu—five hundred miles west of Alice Springs they were now back once more to the land of their ancestors.

The chanting finished, they put the boards back once more into the crevice on that hill and Djuwerri informed me that he was not returning with us, but would remain in this his Kikingurra country. At first I demurred, for it did not somehow seem right that we should leave him behind. But he was adamant, and it was all his proper country.

I learnt afterwards from Wulmungungu that all this business had started the year before, when I had my talks with Minyinderri about going into the Petermann Ranges. The trip had then been organized by the Loritdja tribesmen months before. Djuwerrri, Magin, and Wulmungungu were to go out as messengers into the Petermanns. People from other parts had been informed about this movement, though the dry-time had held up things a little. I had already told them that I was going out by motor, so the plan was laid. Those footprints at the gorge of the 'Kudongs' told the messengers the people from 'Warrakuni' to the west had arrived for the ritual.

Ray, Peter, and I just looked at each other in amazement as we heard the full story. All the time I was under the belief that it was I who had laid the plan. When I went to Angus Downs to pick up Djuwerri and his friends, who were coming out with me, I was informed that Minyinderri was on his way from Areyonga with camels and donkeys, and with him was the rest of his Windralga clan.

Minyinderri had told me last year that this year they were going out to Kikingurra. The dry-time had held them up so they had used me to carry the 'messengers of the Kumbunduru' into the Petermanns. Behind us would come Minyinderri with his people along the trail of 'puppy-dog-time'. The old, old saying was true, that those who take the aborigines for fools are bigger fools themselves.

Well, I did not mind being taken for a ride. I had picked up the story I required and learnt something more about the aborigines. So we returned to camp and as we boiled the billy for our midday meal, Peter got his portable wireless out and was talking to his Curtin Springs station over two hundred miles away.

Listening to him calling, 'Nine Double Roger portable to Nine Double Roger', and hearing the answering reply as though it was someone talking on the other side of the camp, I thought of Giles the explorer who came this way nearly a hundred years ago and had done things the hard way.

So after our midday meal we packed up for the return journey. As the story of Ayers Rock was revealed to me by Kudakudeka and Imalung so was my trip to Kikingurra the final part of that long research into that Mother ritual.

As Djuwerri wished to remain I paid him his money in that storeless land. We gave him abundance of foodstuffs and asking him what he was going to do with his supplies I smiled at his reply of, 'Just put it up tree and go look for the people who are camped at the Wangurri rock-hole place.'

So we said our farewells to that grand old Loritdja man but I somehow could not help feeling sorry for him, though I am pretty sure that he pitied us who were returning to a land of much worry and trouble. Ray and Peter started the engines and the last glimpse I had of the old fellow was of him putting his foodstuffs on to an improvised platform in the branches of a mulga tree. His clothes were partly off as one who wished to be at ease with his naked friends.

Gazing at him thus I realized that in that Australoid man before us still embodied the spirit of the people who came into this country ages ago. That ancient man stood, maybe, on a mountain such as Kikingurra to survey a land he knew nothing about at the time. Yet with him and his kin was a faith which gave him the will to live. Out of his chants to people, rivers, and mountains grew the ritual and rich mythology that exists today. Everywhere in those mountains of the Petermanns was mythology. Each mountain carried its legend. Only the Djuwerris and his kind keep them alive.

Yet overshadowing them in our own literature is the story of Lasseter who searched in this country for a fabulous reef of gold. But the treasure had already been discovered by old Djuwerri who remained behind in a valley of contentment at the foot of Kikingurra.

Chapter Twenty-five

Lasseter's Gold

So we left Djuwerri behind and, travelling through those ranges named by Giles after Professor Petermann of Gotha, my mind was a long way from the legends of the Rhineland. Rather did I think of that incredible man Lasseter who himself began a legend.

Was his tale of a mountain of gold founded on fact, or was it just a dream that arose out of the geological reports about worthwhile gold-bearing country which might lie in the large fault planes and dykes north-east from the Kalgoolie goldfield?

So much for the reports of one lot of geologists. Now read the report of Joklik, a geologist with one of the well-equipped parties that went out to seek the reef of gold. He wrote in his report: 'The Ayers Rock–Mount Olga–Mount Currie line of residuals is close to the southern limit of the Palaeozoic outcrops. . . . The rock is a coarse Arkose which shows no secondary directional structures. In thin sections Ayers Rock contains fairly rounded grains of quartz and plagioclase, cemented by a soft matrix. Various ages have been assigned to this line. . . . The whole of the area is non-auriferous.'

All geologists agree that the red earth of this western area was once the sea-bed of an ancient ocean. The hills and mountains around are older rock strata that appear as witnesses attesting to the extreme age of this country.

The red overburden of earth has to date revealed no gold. The only ones who have discovered it are the company promoters and drillers who have tapped the waters of the desert so that life can flourish on the surface above.

But Lasseter—one of the dozens who had been that way to seek and return—was his story a dream or was it fact?

In every land we have stories of lost goldfields: tales that begin with prospectors on the drunk and are after a few shillings for a booze;

others that begin in novels such as Sayces' *Golden Buckle* which was published ten years before Lasseter told a similar story to the union men of Sydney.

Golden Buckle is a fair novel written by a man who knew or had heard a lot about this area. His 'Toolooru' is the 'Uluru' of Ayers Rock. Shaw creek in Sayces' tale is the Shaw Range of Lasseter's story, and Office creek fits the Colonel River in both stories. Both tales tell of a lost reef, the prospector dying of thirst and being revived at the last moment. Sayces' book was fiction. Lasseter claimed his story was true.

How often have I heard the same kind of story from gold prospectors when I was a child on the goldfields of Charters Towers and elsewhere. Everywhere the old miners talked of lost leaders, faults, dips, and underlies, interspersing their yarns with mud maps or on scraps of paper which in time became clues that would lead other dreamers on the trail. Not only did lost reefs come into the legends but also misers who distrusted banks and buried their gold in tins around their old shacks.

I scratched about a lot with my dad in those days of dreams, but the only eldorado I found was when we lads scratched under the floor of an old demolished hotel to reap a harvest from the coins that had fallen from the drunks' hands through chinks in the wooden floor.

Every land is rich in poor 'lost-leads'. The first time I heard of the Macdonnell Ranges around Alice Springs was in a yarn from an old prospector from Ultunga way. He talked in true Sinbad the Sailor fashion of the Macdonnell Range rubies that were so plentiful that they were classed as garnets by the jewel merchants so that they could sell their own rubies from overseas.

I myself heard from Billy Liddle of Angus Downs about a nomad aboriginal from the western lands of the desert over which we were now travelling, who had a piece of precious opal as a cutting flake on the end of his maeru throwing-stick. He saw the stone and procured it from the black man. Examination by an expert proved it to be a gem of first quality.

Knowing that the material used for the flint flakes of the western Loritdja came from an opalized stone, I was on my toes when Minyinderri brought me in some small flakes of opal which he had found in an old aboriginal camp near Maggie Springs at Ayers Rock.

Thinking of Billy Liddle's story and knowing that the hunters always dressed their core-stones near a suitable camp-site, I went down that way with my old mate to discover it was the one-time camp of an opal-miner from Coober Pedy who had dressed a stone in that area on one of the Loritdja Djewa grinding-stones. Nevertheless the opal cutting-flake on the old aboriginal's throwing-stick was the real thing. It may have come from Coober Pedy years before, then again it may have come from . . . where?

To the tourists with whom I went round the Rock the name of Lasseter was synonymous with gold. Gold! I wonder would the questions have come in so quick if Lasseter had been searching for a baser mineral. To me Lasseter's search was not for gold but it was the symbol of man's eternal quest for the elusive.

A deserted camp, half way between Ayers Rock and Mount Olga, was the subject for much talking when the tourists heard it was a campsite of a party searching for Lasseter's reef of gold. It was just a mass of old packing cases around some upright poles beneath a clump of gidgea trees. Of the gold, there was nothing except some pot-holes in a barren buck-reef of a quartzite range.

The story of that camp is the same as that of the other prospecting parties who went that way: the old torn map, a new clue to the lost reef; the same lot of promoters under another name or a fresh lot with a different prospectus; the money comes in, an endless round with the same ending. The prospecting expedition breaks down or there is a disagreement among the leaders. The days drag into weeks and months with the wireless breaking down as the shareholders in the south hold meetings, demanding a report on the expedition. Then the final round, when the one who owns the maps and knows all suddenly refuses to reveal the secret place of the gold. He has overheard talk about a secret code that will go out by a hidden wireless and with the claim pegged out and registered he will be chiselled out of his share. So does the tale of the lost reef go out because people believe that it may be there. And strangely enough, they might be right.

The mere fact that the reef of gold has never been discovered is proof to many that it is still there. The question is . . . is it? Geologists range from sure to doubtful. A heavy mantle of earth covers this land we are now travelling over and who can tell what lies beneath, or at what period some strong wind might sweep the surface to reveal the cap of some ancient reef formation carrying gold?

Poor Lasseter His Golden Buckle had come home to roost. His was not an isolated case, for how many prospectors have gone out after such dreams in this old world? They were the people who opened up wide vistas from the days of Jason to those Spanish soldiers who sought elusive eldorados, yet discovered violent death, sickness, empires, and sometimes gold as their reward.

Even Minyinderri seems to have the prospecting bug. He somehow cannot get away from the idea that I too am seeking gold or some other mineral. He—as with many tourists who visit the Olgas—see copper or uranium in every green or yellow stone. As the Olgas is a mountain made up of rounded boulders ranging from quartz, olivine, hornblende, and other rock in every range and colour, the area naturally comes in for much secret napping of stones.

Minyinderri has bits of stones in his pockets and these he quietly drops into my hand, scrutinizing my face for some expression of surprise that will let him know its true value. To date he has found nothing, only pieces of ironstone and bits of polished quartz. Even barren Ayers Rock comes in for its share of hope for hidden wealth, for in every sheltered place and cave around its base one can see small mounds of a black pitch-like substance that has the seekers after oil on their toes. Every time I went around the base with tourists one of them would pry into the numerous crevices, then as we had the usual rest he would sidle up to me with the usual look of one who has discovered something all others have overlooked.

The standard pattern of the scene never altered: the 'dry-nose' look, an aboriginal expression which means 'one who knows something overlooked by others'; the clenched fist and the remark that 'one day oil will be discovered in the area'. Now comes the curtain-raising scene as the hand is opened to reveal a piece of the black pitch-like substance of the caves.

'Bitumen,' he exclaims to us all, 'a sign of oil-bearing sands!'

'Bat dung,' I inform him. 'Good as a fertilizer, but not enough around.'

The oil-seeker drops the specimen from his hand, and we all laugh, the seeker as well, for all are on holiday and are happy.

Yet the real wealth in this land is water, the good old liquid that lies cool and fresh in many places beneath the surface of this red earth. Water, a treasure greater than gold for the cattleman. Could Lasseter or any other person get such a kick out of life as did Peter Severin when—during a period of drought—he found that fresh water in the drylands of Curtin Springs?

Imagine, if we can, the dust and the dry. The struggle and hardship of getting a boring-plant over the sandhills to the selected bore-site. Trucks and tractors on the pulling job, then finally the bore-rig is up, the engine started, and the drill is on its way. Everywhere around is saline ground. A few miles away they have already put a bore down containing salty water. They know if water can be found here the country around will support a herd of cattle till the rains come.

The drill clatters away till it reaches twelve feet, then comes the sound that it is in water. The drill is brought to the surface, the hole is cleaned out, and then, with the aid of a mirror, the reflected sunlight lights up the hole to show Peter the water running in. He had tapped a reservoir of water beneath the ground and it was fresh.

Can we of the wetlands and the places where water is 'laid on' visualize such a moment as when Peter tasted that water and found it fresh? If we can feel as Peter did then we too will have a vision of greatness and shall explore the places beyond our horizon in our different fields of endeavour.

Dreaming thus about the land I look over into the west. 'Tis morning and the eastern walls of the mountains gleam as a ball of gold with the rising sun. In a flash the scene changes to the blood-red of rubies then through a range of shades which remind me of some giant pedlar of gems who is displaying his wares upon a platter grey-green tree shades.

Lasseter's gold. Perhaps that poor deserted man was too hungry to enjoy such a scene.

With that canny something which the aborigines possess Minyinderri replies to my thoughts. 'Him proper sick man, we been try help him but him get cranky and shoot rifle so we all run away.'

The same old story as with many people who have lost their lives in early days here. The aboriginals would help but were chased away. The ones who were distrusted by Burke on Cooper's creek when he was leader of that expedition were of the same tribe as those who felt a 'great compassion for King', the sole surviving member of the party, and maintained him till he was found by Howitt's second in command of the relief party sent out to find them. Lasseter's drama was such a story with the aborigines. He searched in a hard land and perished where other humans had lived for ages. What then was the secret?

On one hand a person in a hurry, on the other a people who took everything as it came. The heat and the flies were a part of the tribesmen's existence. The cold of winter was overcome by the warmth of a camp-fire and failing that they simply went to sleep and slept 'as one dead' till the warm rays of the sun roused them from their slumbers. The aborigines were super-optimists in that they did not worry about the things they could not avoid. They lived, hunted, created life and ritual; then when the time came they passed away in peace because they had a strong belief that their ritual was the only way of life.

Many white bushmen, myself included, just cannot understand that type of literature which continually prates of the endless hardship in the bush. Each one of us sees the beauty of their environment and the misery of the others.

Every tourist who comes to the Centre will find gold in the hills if they are not disgruntled with life and care to get up each morning to see the golden glow upon the mountains around.

Lasseter's story of gold began in Sydney where he was an expert among men who were not too sure what he was talking about and most certainly did not understand the locality he was going to.

During my stay at Ayers Rock four private prospecting parties went to the westward. They never told me their business, and I never asked. They returned a few weeks later but no story of discovered gold was in the Press. With Lasseter it was a different story. He sought and died in the search after a mountain of gold. So he hit the headlines and the plot thickened as the legend grew. The tourists still look westward to dream of gold. Minyinderri fumbles in his pocket as he reveals to me another one of his 'finds'. This time he knows he has it. I look at the specimen he holds out. It is mundic or new-chum's gold. I hand it back to him with a smile but from his face I see he does not believe my judgement. I am, to him, like the men who decried the Macdonnell Range rubies because they would have flooded the world's markets.

I go down to a rock-pool nearby, as I wander along the acacia and cassia blooms sprinkle golden showers upon me. I hold some of the scented flowers in my hand for they are, to me, the gold of this country—they and the cool clear waters in the rock-hole I will shortly be drinking.

Chapter Twenty-six

Return

WE have now turned our backs to the west with its mythological land of shadows, our faces are 'sun-rise-way' into that ritual country of light and happiness.

Yet is the land ahead a place of light for my aboriginal friends? Behind is the tradition of a nomad people, ahead are the 'Experts' who tell all what others should do to these people.

Over thousands of years the aborigines have fought the good fight within this semi-arid environment. Anthropologists have gathered much material about them, yet our knowledge regarding their actual place of origin is unknown. Those tribal historians, the song-men, only passed on to the future the details which would keep the tribes functioning. A deeply rooted aversion for personal tales gave us no measure of time in their mythological chants as one finds amidst the Maori of New Zealand and other races of mankind. Everything to the aborigine was ritual or the present. To them, the night does not arrive but rather the day departs. Individual worship was not for them. All gathered in worship at the appointed time each year. Then all became 'clear', a form of collective confession by faith where each received the 'will to live'. Thus priests and prayer were unknown, for to offer up prayer after ritual would bring the wrath of the 'unknown one' upon the culprit.

Prior to us whites coming into their land their knowledge of conception was as vague as the stories I was told, as a child, of how the spirits of babies came from the fruits and vegetables in the garden. The aboriginal mothers still tell their children the same tale, though instead of a garden it is the bushland. With them it is a truth, with us a form of evasion using an ancient myth.

In the tribal pattern they only collected what nature gave to them; yet in this gathering they observed a fixed procedure well attested by my own observation. Often have I seen them leave a portion of a wild potato or some turtle eggs in the jungle lands and sand beaches of the north so that the food-spirits of the land could cause more foods to grow. The ancient idea of leaving the first fruits of the tree to the Gods was strong in these people. I have also discovered that the desert man loves green around him. Although Minyinderri came from a non-agricultural race his was the only garden I saw during my early years at the Rock. He knew nothing about soils or what to plant in season, yet he was proud of his garden but hated to eat its products, a trait arising from their belief that pets cannot be destroyed and eaten.

I look at my nomad friends grubbing out their daily food from the earth we are travelling over, or stalking with spear or throwing-stick the creatures of this bushland. Gazing thus I marvel at their dexterity and lack of the complexes that disturb most of the human race. Here around me is the tribal pattern; ahead is that turmoil called civilization where people are waiting with their calendars and clocks to measure out their days and their time. Radios keep those people abreast of the times with 'news' and numerous advertisements which contradict each other. On government settlements and missions they await Minyinderri and his people to teach them a new way of life. The missionary will explain a religion to a people who have gained much spiritual understanding over the ages. The school teacher will be there with his book of learning to put them on the right road. Where? Well I just cannot foretell the future. The road is tough both for those who teach and those who learn. Everywhere one will find critics, but not in the battle-line.

As I worry about their future my raggle-taggle mates are always talking about their wonderful country behind, but I notice that all are looking eagerly ahead to a land of stores and picture shows.

Now and then one of them tells an olden time story using such perfect mimicry that I, who do not understand the language well, can follow the tale. At one camp an old woman was describing a tribal brawl. All laughed as did I when she cursed and swished the air with her digging-fighting stick at an imaginary enemy. Watching her I thought of Wilalburu's lethal chant-curses as she advanced at the head of the Kunia warriors at Ayers Rock. Gazing thus I also thought of Saint Brigid throwing out curses as she too routed the pagan enemies who marched against the Irish King of Leinster.

Remnants old as time are around us here with the Australian aborigines. Myths that were ancient when the scribes of old engraved the epic of Gilgamesh on baked clay tablets that recorded flood legends known also to our aborigines as well as to other peoples.

Everywhere one discerns parallels with other religions: Moses and the Mala, both leaders of race migration and givers of the sacred laws; Cybele and Kerungra, both Goddesses of fertility; one with her symbols at the base of Uluru in the Centre of Australia, the other in her Egyptian temple at the base of Mount Sinai, and each in their turn a symbol of man's belief in the immortality of the soul and a life hereafter. They gave life to all on earth. The Gods of Man dwell high on the crests of the mountains to see that man's way of life is upheld. We believe or we do not believe, that is the basis of all faiths. Only life is real.

As this Australia was once a blank piece of paper for the original map-makers, so it is now becoming a blank for anyone who would study the tribes *in situ.* Only a few nomads remain, clinging desperately to a tribal life in some out-of-the-way spot in the desert land. In a few more years they too will be gone. When they have been absorbed into our culture then nothing will remain of a tribal way of life that gave us a glimpse of ourselves as we were thousands of years ago. Only the books written by anthropologists and others, together with ancient camp-sites, will remind us that they existed.

Their cave art must surely fade beneath the wind's erosive power. Only the coloured photos will remain. To-day we have it in our power to save them, but I am afraid the workings of man is slow, the eroding dust fast and terrible.

Around me is the talk and laughter of my nomad friends. They were of the past but now move on into the future.

So we returned by motor from the Petermanns, though I thought of the camels that were used by my nomad friends to come this way. They are not unlike their aboriginal masters, for both have obscure origins. Thinking of them I recalled how the camels first came into history when they carried the warriors of Shepherd Kings against Egypt ages before the birth of Rome.

Since then they have been recorded in literature along the silk roads of China, or as racing demons carrying the zealots of a great religion. Our cattle stations were supplied by them till they became outmoded by the motor so that they are now beasts of burden for the hunting aborigines of the desert.

As the camel ritual men came into the West so we in the motor went eastward. So after many miles we saw Uluru in the distance, a deep brown in the midday sun. The chants of Kikingurra and the Windralga had been replaced by other thoughts. Peter and Ray thought about the cattle on their drought-stricken land. The aborigines, Magin and his son Wulmungungu, were composing the message they would be giving to Minyinderri and the ritual men. I myself thought about the chapters I would have to write to complete this book. Everywhere was worry. Only out in the Petermanns did we forget. Ahead was turmoil, yet behind us 'sundown-way' my mind returned, and somehow heard my grubby looking friends chanting a ritual song about the Mother of us all. Each man believed, be he black or white. It was the essence of our life regardless of established religions.

'Kapi agalyu Wanambi' (strength in the waters of our Creator).

Epilogue

ON June 28th 1962 I left Ayers Rock on one of the tourist coaches.

What a party my friends gave me on the night before I departed. It was a complete surprise so far as I was concerned for I was invited over to the Alice Springs Chalet for an evening meal and returned to find the Pioneer Lodge in complete darkness. Only as I entered did the lights go on to reveal my friends all gathered together.

Even now as I write these lines my heart swells with gladness as I think of the welcome they gave to me. Helen, Barbara, and Joan all decked out in oversized desert boots and old felt hats, and saucepan timbrels in their hands which they clanged as I entered. Bill Mac was there twanging away on a base fiddle made up of an old broomstick, string, and an old tea-chest. Peter of Curtin Springs. Ian—my mate of early Rock days, together with Jack the new Ranger. The Cawoods of Alice Springs Tours were there in strength with Dot who had made a lovely cake with 'Farewell Bill' iced upon it.

As I saw that scene then so do I recall it now. Each face in that room brought up memories of our days together, and, standing darkly against the skyline through a picture window was the giant of them all. The great dome of Uluru that had been named by the Loritdja after a tribal God.

Looking at the Rock my thoughts were on my nomad friends who had passed that way on foot and camels. With them were their children from the government schools and missions who now sang hymns and cowboy songs.

But in that happiness and good-will my thoughts were of old Djuwerri and his final return from Kikingurra.

What a pleasant surprise he gave me when—three weeks after our return from the Petermanns—he appeared as by magic before my door at the Lodge. That old Loritdja man was as lively as a cricket as he told me of how he had recognized his sister's footprints among those we saw at the gorge of the Kudongs in the Petermanns. Twenty years had gone by since he last saw her, but he knew her footprints together with other tracks beside her which he knew were her children. Tribal law must prevail so he decided to follow their trail, for under kinship law he was their tribal guardian.

'I saw my sister's girls,' he told me proudly. 'They were proper nice children . . . that's why I been stop . . . I like to ride back in truck but man must follow Loritdja law . . . when tribal business finished then I walk back here . . . proper long way.'

'How many days?' I questioned, and he answered simply as he held up three fingers. 'Three day . . . no water for long way so must come quickly.'

I looked at him in amazement. He had travelled on foot from Wangurra, west of Kikingurra, 160 miles by road, 120 miles in a straight line. Covered that long distance in three days.

To that old man of seventy years it was no feat of endurance, but something normal to a tribesman on tribal business.

I got him some food from the kitchen and he ate this as he sat on the red earth. He ate slowly and as he did I thought of all the white people he and his kind have helped over the years. To me he epitomized the Australian aborigine. People who helped us freely in the past, yet because of their colour and nomadic way of life, were on the scrapheap in our social structure.

Yet Welfare is moving on. Obstacles are overcome slowly. The pressure is on from both sides. When the day comes that we understand them as they understand us I hope they will have it in their hearts to forgive us our trespasses against them.

Bill Harney was born at Charters Towers, North Queensland in 1895 and died at Mooloolaba on the Queensland coast on December 31, 1962.

His personal life knew great tragedy. His part-Aboriginal wife, Linda, died at the age of twenty-one from tuberculosis, leaving him with a son, Billy, and a daughter Beattie. Beattie died in early childhood, also of tuberculosis, and Billy was drowned at Alice Springs, aged fifteen.

Although Bill Harney had only three years formal schooling, he broadened his education during his many years in the bush, and achieved an intimate knowledge of literature, geology (in which he took a diploma by correspondence) and anthropology. He had an ability to communicate easily with the Aborigines and gained a remarkable knowledge of the languages and customs. This first-hand appreciation was often sought-after by eminent persons from all over the world.